AJWD. 2000

LONGLEAT

*The Story of an English
Country House*

LONGLEAT

The Story of an English Country House

———◆———

DAVID BURNETT

With a Foreword by
the 6th Marquess of Bath

COLLINS
St James's Place, London
1978

William Collins Sons & Co Ltd
London · Glasgow · Sydney · Auckland
Toronto · Johannesburg

First published 1978
© David Burnett 1978

ISBN 0 00 211470 4

Set in Bembo
Made and Printed in Great Britain by
William Collins Sons & Co Ltd Glasgow

CONTENTS

ILLUSTRATIONS

THE FAMILY TREE OF THE THYNNES

Christian, dr. of Sir Richard Gresham, Kt, Lord Mayor of London
1st wife
= † Sir John Thynne, Kt B.1515, D.1580
Builder of Longleat
= Dorothy, dr. of Sir William Wroughton, Kt
2nd wife

† Sir John Thynne, Kt D.1604 = Joan, dr. of Sir Roland Hayward, Kt, Lord Mayor of London

Mary, dr. of Lord Audley
1st wife
= † Sir Tomas Thynne, Kt D.1640 = Catherine, dr. of Charles Lyte-Howard
2nd wife

Thomas Thynne

Stuarta, dr. of Walter Balquanquill = Sir Henry Frederick Thynne, 1st Bart. D.1680 = Mary, dr. of Lord Coventry

† Sir James Thynne, Kt D.1670 = Isabella, dr. of the Earl of Holland

† Thomas Thynne ('Tom o' Ten Thousand') Assassinated 1682 = Elizabeth, dr. of the Earl of Northumberland

† Thomas (Thynne), 1st Viscount Weymouth D.1714 = Frances, dr. of 2nd Earl of Winchelsea (Finch)

Henry Frederick Thynne D.1703 = Dorothy, dr. of Francis Phillips

Thomas Thynne D.1710 = Mary, dr. of the Earl of Jersey

Henry Thynne D.1708 = Grace, dr. of Sir George Strode
without male issue

Elizabeth, dr. of the Earl of Dorset
1st wife
= † Thomas (Thynne) 2nd Viscount Weymouth Born (posthumously) 1710, D.1751 = Louisa, dr. of the Earl of Granville
2nd wife

† Thomas (Thynne) 1st Marquess of Bath, KG. D.1796 = Elizabeth, dr. of the Duke of Portland

† Thomas (Thynne) 2nd Marquess of Bath, K.G. D. March 1837 = Isabella, dr. of Viscount Torrington

Harriet Robbins = Thomas (Thynne) Viscount Weymouth D. January 1837

† Henry Frederick (Thynne) 3rd Marquess of Bath D. June 1837 = Harriet, dr. of Lord Ashburton

† John Alexander (Thynne) 4th Marquess of Bath D.1896 = Frnaces, dr. of the Viscount de Vesci

Daphne, dr. of Lord Vivian
1st wife
= John Alexander (Thynne) Viscount Weymouth. Killed in action 1916. = Anna Gael Gyarmathy

† Thomas Henry (Thynne) 5th Marquess of Bath, K.G. D.1946 = Violet, dr. of Lady Harriet Mordaunt

† Henry Frederick (Thynne) B.1905 = Virginia Penelope, dr. of Allan Parsons Married 1953
2nd wife

Alexander George Thynne, Viscount Weymouth B.1932

Lenka B.1969

Ceawlin B.1972

(the descent of Longleat is shown by a dagger)

FOREWORD

by the 6th Marquess of Bath.

My ancestor, John Thynne, bought the priory of Longleat for £53 in 1540. Ever since then it has remained in our possession. I was actually born and brought up in the house, but now my son lives there with his two children. Since 1949 it has been kept open for the public to visit and enjoy. No one can deny the beauty of Longleat or its setting and, although the paintings in the house are not very impressive, the books, furniture and interiors make it one of the most rewarding country houses in England. I hope everybody who reads and enjoys this book will learn something of the contribution that houses like Longleat have made to our national heritage. The farms, gardens, life below stairs, have all played their part in its history and ever since my father handed me the estate in 1929 I have done all I can to maintain Longleat and keep it in the family. But I am not optimistic about the future and I can only hope that this absorbing and satisfying book about Longleat and its past will make more people realize that the English country house is worth preserving.

Upstairs at Longleat in the Old Library is the Muniment Room – rarely visited, even by me! – and it was here that David Burnett went when he set out to write this story of Longleat and the Thynnes. I had no idea what he would find out about my ancestors. None of them have been generals or major statesmen, and I had always thought of them as dull and uninteresting. After reading this book I am not so sure. Longleat's builder, John Thynne, was undoubtedly a remarkable man. As another of my ancestors kept leopards and wolves and the 1st Marquess of Bath employed a hermit, I am beginning to realize that many of them were a lot more eccentric than I thought. If only they hadn't been quite so extravagant!

9

ACKNOWLEDGEMENTS

The possibility of attempting this portrait of English country-house life was first suggested whilst on a visit to Longleat in 1974. Walking around the house I became curious about the lives of those who had lived in it, the how and why of its construction and survival, and the part the surrounding countryside had played in its history. The country house and its landed estates were once an essential feature of the English landscape; their wealth, power and influence were immense. Today only a handful remain intact, but I hope that in piecing together Longleat's past I have captured something of the vanished way of life it so superbly evokes. When I first began the research I had no idea where curiosity would lead me, or how absorbing the journey might become. Longleat's history spans four centuries and its Muniment Room contains a unique record of those years. Amongst the papers to have been preserved are the sixteenth-century records of the building of the house; four centuries' worth of family correspondence, diaries, inventories, servants' wage books, bills and receipts; as well as the kitchen, farm and forestry accounts. There are poems, wills, letters from seven English monarchs – including both Elizabeth I and Elizabeth II, game books, menus, garden plans and a correspondence that includes letters from many of Longleat's stewards, bailiffs and agents, as well as people like Sir Christopher Wren, 'Capability' Brown and Disraeli. By preserving virtually every scrap of paper that has found its way into Longleat the Thynnes have left behind a seam of social history of such richness and variety that it embraces every aspect of country-house life. To the present custodian of Longleat and its past I owe a debt of gratitude that this story of his family and home can only partially repay. The Marquess of Bath's generosity in providing a foreword and allowing me access to the Longleat Muniment Room, his willingness to provide information and answer questions, his constant encouragement over two and a half years, are merely an indication of the kindness he has shown to me.

Miss Betty Austin, Lord Bath's librarian, has guided me through the great mass of papers stored in the Muniment Room. She has read and corrected the entire manuscript, made innumerable suggestions and fetched and carried every document I have consulted. I am also grateful for the loan of her notes on the formation of the library and for her patience with an author whose lack of experience must, on occasions, have been exasperating. Without her support this book could never have been written.

I am also indebted to Lady Kathleen Stanley. A morning in her company is as entertaining as it is illuminating. Without her co-operation I could never have attempted a portrait of life at Longleat in the early twentieth century. The friendship of Alexander Weymouth, Longleat's heir, was a great help when it came to writing the final chapter of the book. Without his frankness and good-humour the chapter would not exist in its present form. I am also grateful to the staff at Longleat for all their kindness throughout the years I have spent working in their midst.

The critical advice of my editor, Richard Ollard, has been invaluable. His scholarship, devotion to historical accuracy and vast experience – both as author and editor – have helped shape my attitude to thinking and writing about Longleat. I still marvel at his patience with an author who had to write one chapter five times in order to get it right. I am also grateful to Kyle Cathie and Michael Russell, both of whom have sacrificed a great deal of their time to reading and correcting the manuscript.

My final debt is to Canon J. E. Jackson, antiquarian, historian and West Country clergyman. Canon Jackson has been dead for nearly a century, but his memory lives on in the Muniment Room he created at Longleat in the mid-nineteenth century. It was he who first collated and catalogued its contents and in a sense I am reaping the harvest that he sowed. Without the benefit of his knowledge and labours this story of Longleat and the Thynnes would be sadly impoverished.

The main bulk of the documentary sources that I have consulted and used when writing this book are stored in the Muniment Room at Longleat. Their quantity is prodigious. Those covering the years 1540–1760 extend to 190 books of mixed accounts and 100 volumes of letters and other family papers. Virtually all the correspondence, accounts and papers preserved since 1760 are kept in parcels on open racks. Dispensary books, servants' wage books, game books, allotment records and a further collection of estate papers are stored in the same way. The 3 volumes of 'The Records of the Building of Longleat' compiled by Canon Jackson are kept in the Red Library, as is 'The Big Accounts Book' containing the building accounts covering 1567 and 1568. The Wiltshire County Records Office are in the process of returning to Longleat the 116 boxes of papers and large number of miscellaneous documents relating to the house, estate and family which until recently have been kept in their charge. It would be foolish of me to attempt a complete list of the manuscript sources, both at Longleat and in the Records Office, that I have consulted. So much of the material has been absorbed into the background, some has proved irrelevant, but where I have quoted from any of these sources it has been acknowledged in the footnotes.

I have followed the same guidelines when preparing the bibliography of printed sources. Many of the titles mentioned in the footnotes and a large proportion of the books I have read whilst writing about Longleat contain only a brief reference to either the house or the Thynnes. It seemed unnecessary to include every title, whatever its relevance or value, in the bibliography; but the list on page 201 should be consulted by anyone interested in the evolution of Longleat and the country house, the history of the Thynnes, and the social, cultural and historical climate through which they have lived.

I would like to thank the following for permission to quote excerpts from the sources indicated: Eyre & Spottiswoode Ltd (*Mercury Presides* by Daphne Fielding); Hodder & Stoughton Ltd (*The Royal School for Officers of the Army* by Honor Osborne and Peggy Manisty); The Hogarth Press Ltd (*Virginia Woolf* by Quentin Bell); William Collins Sons & Co Ltd (*The Education of a Gardener* by Russell Page); Chapman and Hall Ltd (*Vile Bodies* by Evelyn Waugh); The Longleat Estate Company (*Before the Sunset Fades* by the Marchioness of Bath); Viscount Weymouth (*Lord Weymouth's Murals* by Alexander Thynne); The Longleat Press (*The Carry-Cot* by Alexander Thynne).

I

JOHN THYNNE — BUILDER

*'I want only a reasonable and competent kind of life on
this earth.'*

John Thynne, on his release from the Tower of
London, June 1552.[1]

John Thynne was born in 1515. The son of a Shropshire farmer whose
ancestors had crossed over from France in the thirteenth century,
he survived imprisonment, envy and the defects in his own character
to become one of the wealthiest and most successful men of his era.
Towards the end of his life he remarked that if he had been afraid
of every 'injury offered me by my betters, I should have left more
quarrels than I trust I shall leave whensoever God shall call me.'[2]
It was a philosophy that had served him well. He died, leaving
behind not 'quarrels', but Longleat, the massive stone house which
today, over four hundred years later, remains the finest memorial
of his achievements and is, perhaps, the most perfect expression of
High Elizabethan architecture still standing.

In the spring of 1540, when John Thynne was twenty-five, he
paid £53 for sixty acres of land, a rabbit warren, orchard, water
mill and tumble-down Wiltshire priory called 'Longlete'[3]. It was a
purchase that was to lay the foundations for his own career and the
future of the Thynnes. The estate now extends to nearly 11,000
acres. Time has destroyed all trace of the rabbit warren and orchard;
only a chain of man-made lakes remain to indicate where the mill-
wheel might once have turned. The woodland surrounding Longleat
was then rough moorland and the park, landscaped by 'Capability'
Brown in the eighteenth century, and now a refuge for deer, lion,
giraffe and elephant, was originally a marsh. Even the stream or
'lete' which gave Longleat its name was probably choked with weed.
The priory itself lay empty, a victim of the dissolution of the

monasteries. But it was on the site of the priory, after it had been devastated by fire in 1567, that John Thynne began building Longleat House.

Longleat's south front faces the chalk ramparts of the Wiltshire Downs and to its east lies Salisbury Plain. The house can be approached either by cutting straight across the park along a tulip-tree-lined drive, or by winding through shrub-filled woodland which gradually unfolds to reveal the distant Mendips and the far side of a broad valley. Far below, and nearly a mile from the edge of the woods, stands Longleat. This first view of the house is breathtaking. Three lines of mullioned windows rise vertically from the valley floor, and on a still day the outline of the east wing can be seen mirrored in the waters of a lake. Today, nearly 300,000 visitors a year pass through Longleat's doors, but the unspoilt English country-side, the sense of space and timelessness, lend its setting a beauty that four centuries have not dimmed.

Inside the house the portraits of the thirteen generations of Thynnes who have lived and died beneath its roof stare down at you from the walls. Some have been eccentrics and others dull, but they all owe their descent to a man whose success was achieved through greed, cunning and complete ruthlessness. It is ironic that so fine an example of human creativity as Longleat should have been designed and built by a man such as John Thynne.

With receding hair, a close-cropped beard and square jaw, Thynne was ambitious and brash. The only painting of him to survive hangs in the house and hints at his energy and single-mindedness. Largely self-educated, he was enterprising and aggressive. Instinct for survival made his intelligence intuitive and he belonged to a group of civil servants who used their undoubted talents to acquire wealth and benefit for themselves.

John Thynne left his Midlands home at an early age and with the assistance of his uncle, William Thynne, who was Henry VIII's Chief Clerk to the Royal Kitchens, found employment as a £4-a-year kitchen clerk. Little is known about his early life, but he was determined to make his own way in the world and by the date of Longleat's purchase he had become an important member of the Earl of Hertford's household. Hertford was Henry VIII's brother-in-law and as the king grew older and his health worse, muc h of the business of running the country was placed in his hands: in particular the profitable task of selling and dispersing the lands confiscated from the monasteries. The patronage of his uncle and then Hertford had far-reaching results for Thynne. From his uncle he learnt much about the hazards of serving the crown. Hertford enabled him to buy Longleat and gave him his first glimpse of a larger horizon; of a world in which ingenuity and ability, mixed when necessary with a little subterfuge, would reap their own reward.

Thynne was acquisitive by instinct, and the speed with which he made his fortune proves that he rarely missed any opportunities to add to it. For seven years, from 1540, he followed faithfully in Hertford's footsteps. As his steward, Thynne's natural flair for administrative work, for weighing up information and reaching quick decisions, made him indispensable. It would seem that he had little sympathy with those who stood in his way. Casualties, to anyone with John Thynne's arrogance, were inevitable.

Thynne's creed was accumulation. Woods, farmland, orchards, park stocked with deer and game, pigeon-houses, mills and fishing rights all added to his wealth and made possible further acquisition. Noting down each purchase in a large brown ledger, he bought manors and church livings, monastic land scattered throughout the West Country, meadows and coppices in Gloucestershire and Oxfordshire, as well as land in Dorset, Shropshire and Herefordshire.[4]

Later in life Thynne was to be accused of counterfeiting the coinage and mining an undeclared vein of silver.[5] We know that he once assisted his brother-in-law to smuggle bullion out of Flanders in bales of silk, and he seems to have been prepared to ride rough-shod over the law whenever it suited his own interests. Other appointments, more honestly acquired, came his way during the years he served Hertford. Amongst them was the Packership of London, from which he received a small fee for all wools, skins, leather and pewter packed and exported from the city.

The date of Thynne's introduction to building and architecture remains unknown. But as Hertford's steward he was responsible for supervising a building programme that was later to include Somerset House, his employer's mansion on the banks of the Thames. The sheer joy of seeing scaffolding and then masonry rise, of watching master craftsmen at work, of stone heaped upon stone, must have touched some dormant ambition. Nothing was ever again to affect him so profoundly. Involvement with Hertford's houses fired his imagination, and in the spring of 1546 he appointed a steward of his own and gave orders for the priory at Longleat to be rebuilt.

Thynne's steward, John Dodd, was faced with a thankless task. For the next two decades he was to be a slave to Longleat and his master's capriciousness. Rarely rewarded, but frequently accused of selling off lead and timber to line his own purse, he was often bombarded with a daily barrage of instructional letters, many of them insisting on 'Haste, haste, haste'. Thynne's intentions were plain from the start. He wanted, in his own words, 'a pennyworth for a ha'penny';[6] and Dodd must have realized from one of Thynne's first surviving letters to him that any delay in the acquisition of men or materials would not be excused. 'I require you to look substantially to all my business and see that my money is not wastefully spent nor lashed out, but all things to be considered and used to my most profit. So that you shall see that my workmen do not loiter for lack of stuff but diligently apply themselves to the work. For you know I have no cause to spend my money in waste.'[7]

During its declining years the priory had been occupied by only a handful of monks leading a simple life. The orchard provided fruit, the stream gave them fish and the rabbit warren ensured a plentiful supply of fresh meat. The priory itself probably consisted of little more than a central courtyard surrounded by cloisters, a chapel, and the monks' living quarters. Under Dodd's direction workmen concentrated on making it habitable again. The roof and chimneys were repaired. Three bedrooms were built in the squat tower guarding the entrance to the courtyard, and on its guttering the Thynne crest was placed.

In January 1547 Henry VIII died. The new king, Edward VI, was only nine and his succession to the throne had been guaranteed by his uncle's influence. In return for his support Hertford was created Duke of Somerset, appointed the young king's guardian and Protector of the Realm. For the next two and a half years the most important man in the land, he ruled England in all but name. Necessity made him increasingly reliant on his steward, and Somerset's sudden rise to power marks a major turning point in John Thynne's career.

In May Thynne accompanied his employer on a military expedi-

tion to France. But Longleat was not forgotten and he sent Dodd
detailed instructions for cutting and seasoning the timber needed for
new doors, 'for if I shall find any fault with the workmanship or
seasoning of the stuff it shall be made again.'[8] On his return to England
he ordered Dodd to employ additional masons and carpenters so that
he could take up residence as soon as possible. Speed, as always with
Thynne, was vital. The labourers' working day began at five o'clock
in the morning and finished at seven at night, but Thynne insisted
they reduce the length of their meal breaks. Fine weather in July
prompted him to borrow additional waggons from Somerset and
'others of my friends' so as to cart stone from local quarries to
Longleat.[9] He ignored the traditional custom of stopping outdoor
work in late autumn and the masons spent the winter months
squaring and dressing stone. The priory's potential provided a sense
of direction and gave purpose to Thynne's ambition. Even Dodd
found it hard to resist his employer's sudden enthusiasm for bricks
and mortar and he told Thynne that by the time Longleat was
finished it would be the 'first and fairest within the company of the
four shires, and so doth all the country report, some grieved, some
pleased.'[10]

Thynne's interest in his Wiltshire property did little to endear him
to his landowning neighbours. Their roots were embedded in the
area. Many of them had lived and worked there since time im-
memorial, and a boisterous ex-caterer buying large estates and with a
cupidity to match posed a threat to their independence. But for the
moment John Thynne's wishes were simple enough. Longleat was
his and he was determined to make it his home. The inside of the
priory was gutted, and its rooms replaced by a lofty hall complete
with minstrels' gallery. The kitchens and pantry were paved.
Nails, plaster, sinks and hinges were sent down from London by
ox-cart, and two tons of lead acquired from a local abbey to reline
the roof. He ordered Dodd to lay in ale, air the blankets, and hire
a woman capable of running a dairy and dressing meat for the
growing household.

Reading through Thynne's early letters to his steward one is
struck time and again by his commitment to Longleat's future. As
well as closely involving himself with the priory's renovation he took
an absorbing interest in the most trivial of details, even turning his
attention to the scrub and moorland that surrounded the house.[11]

Four Dutchmen were sent for from Glastonbury to dig the ground for a hop garden. All trees near Longleat that impeded the visitor's first view of the house were felled and removed. Stands of oak and ash were planted, and an approach road repaired. This characteristic meticulousness does much to explain his success. When it became necessary to employ someone to run the farm, Thynne, snappish as ever, wrote to Dodd. 'Let him be both handsome and skilful, for I will sow all my ground myself. Let me not be served in deeds as I have hereforeto, but let the doings appear.'[12] A farm bailiff was taken on the pay-roll, and immediately besieged with directions about the harvest, the sale of corn and the need to build haystacks where they would be sheltered from gales.

Thynne was obsessed with money. He begrudged the expenditure of every penny, and at the first sign of waste or extravagance would launch an attack on his long-suffering steward. When torrential rain turned a lane leading to the unfinished stables into a quagmire, Thynne would stand for no delay. Only when Dodd informed him that the waggoners refused to bring in any further slate and timber unless they were paid double the wage was the work brought to a halt.[13] It seems that other than the unpredictable nature of the English climate little was allowed to interfere with Thynne's plans. His arrogance strengthened his self-confidence, and in combination they performed like a battering-ram whenever he was confronted by any obstacle to progress. For years his ambitions had been checked by a shortage of capital, but now he was in a position to consolidate his estates. Dodd was constantly criticized for hiring incompetents and knaves, men whose sole purpose was to cheat their master at every turn. But gradually woodmen, ploughmen, housemaids, a warrener, and even a poultry girl, were added to the numbers already dependent on Thynne for their livelihood. Throughout the summer of 1547 his bulldog persistence and cunning helped spin the web by which he was to become owner of land, houses, mills and farms, fill them with his own tenants, and make himself independent, self-sufficient lord of the manor of some 6000 acres round Longleat.

In August 1547 the Protector Somerset, determined to bring about a union between England and Scotland by arranging a marriage treaty between Edward VI and the four-year-old Queen of the Scots, Mary Stuart, decided to invade Scotland. Thynne went with him, as he had done three years earlier when he had returned with a copy of *The Chronicles of Scotland* inscribed as having been 'found' at the 'winning and burning' of Edinburgh. On 10 September Somerset's army attacked and routed the kilted Scots on the banks of the Esk at the Battle of Pinkie. For Thynne Pinkie was a triumph. On the battlefield and still bleeding from his wounds he was knighted by Somerset.[14] So long as he remained in favour and Somerset in power he was certain of acquiring the wealth needed to create the Longleat of his dreams. Many years later he was accused of being a coward, a 'durtie squire', of spending Pinkie hidden in a carriage.[15] But of Thynne's courage there can be no doubt. If any man's character was suited to the blood and thunder pugnacity of sixteenth-century warfare, it was his.

The knighthood appears to have provided him with little cause for celebration. Within three weeks he was back in London, and in reply to a letter of congratulation from Dodd he made no mention of the battle, merely ordering his steward to build pigsties in a local wood. From pigs Sir John Thynne turned his attention to the gardens. Beehives were to be installed, and ditching, grubbing and planting finished before winter set in. He employed a destitute monk to supervise the work, leaving him with instructions to break up the orchard ground with his bare hands before planting out peach trees.[16] Strawberries, apricots, walnuts and plums were also planted. But, by the date of Sir John's next visit to Longleat, the plum trees had mysteriously disappeared. Quince and cherry trees were dispatched in their wake. In the accompanying letter Thynne attacked Dodd for the loss of the plums. 'I keep you there to look to all my things, and it doth appear you look to nothing.'[17] He next demanded that a pot-holed lane leading to the house be regravelled so that the wag-goners could not charge for injury to their vehicles. Sheep were driven overland from Norfolk, a distance of 150 miles, and pens built so that they could be kept throughout the winter without having to be slaughtered or sold. By the end of lambing in the following year Longleat's flock totalled over a thousand.

And so it went on. Letter after letter charts Longleat's transition from dilapidated priory to productive estate. But there is something rather relentless about Thynne's improvements at Longleat. Moti-vated almost entirely by the desire for profit and prestige, he seems to have been incapable of enjoying any of the pleasures that living in the country could then provide. In all of his letters to Dodd there seems to be not one word of gratitude or praise. It would be wrong to suggest that he was totally insensitive. Longleat itself is proof of his imagination and vision. But the gradual climb from kitchens to knighthood had toughened him, made him dispassionate and restless.

Thynne's shrewdness had so far won him both property and cash, but he still lacked a wife. In March 1548 he married. Characteristically he chose a bride who brought with her a substantial dowry of both money and lands. She was Christian Gresham, the twenty-four-year-old daughter of Sir Richard Gresham, London's Lord Mayor, and one of England's wealthiest new rich. They were married in the gallery of Gresham's Milk Street mansion.

The Greshams originally hailed from Norfolk, their fortune from sheep and the wool trade. Christian's half-brother, Thomas, was to become one of Queen Elizabeth's most influential advisers. As Crown Agent in Antwerp, then Europe's financial centre, he controlled the raising and borrowing of funds for the monarchy. Dealing unscrupulously and brilliantly in the art of exchanging gold at differing rates of interest, he kept the queen's coffers full, founded the Royal Exchange, and turned London into a major money market. Broker, banker, and financier, he was just the sort of man Sir John liked to number amongst his friends. In 1567, lame and gouty, owner of five houses and yet desperately unhappy, Sir Thomas Gresham died of apoplexy.

Of Christian herself, we know very little. No portrait of her survives, but her few letters suggest that she was eminently qualified to be Thynne's wife. Unsentimental, forceful and loyal, she was quite capable of running Longleat and, whenever her husband was away, she took as much interest in the woods and farms as she did in motherhood.

Sir John seems to have wasted no time in using Christian's dowry to acquire additional land round Longleat. He bought the manor of Horningsham, the village nearest to the house, as well as woodland near Warminster and a mill in Frome, thus extending his interests to include the two local market towns on which he relied for much of his labour force.

Thynne's marriage to Christian provided further proof of his status. But in the following year his career suffered a setback that was to have a major influence on his future. Not yet thirty-four and already the Protector's right-hand man, his duplicity and cunning had made him many enemies; and his management of Somerset's affairs was the cause of widespread envy and suspicion. Will Darell, an eccentric Wiltshire landowner and one of Sir John's most constant opponents, would later state that he had thrust himself into Somerset's service by 'sleight and flattery', 'creeping and trudging here and there apace.'[18] A close friend of Somerset's had already written to warn him of Thynne's 'covetous disposition', informing the Protector that there was 'no one thing his Grace hath need to take such heed of as that man's proceedings.'[19] None of this appears to have mattered much to Thynne. He viewed attack and praise with equal indifference. Truculent as ever, seemingly immune to insult, he was busy with plans for completing Longleat. But then disaster struck. In October 1549 Somerset was arrested, and John Thynne thrown into the Tower of London.

Somerset's Protectorship had foundered. Surrounded by men as dishonest as his steward, men more concerned with lining their own pockets than serving their employer, such an event was almost inevitable. The exchequer was empty and the nation under martial law. Earlier in the year rebellions had broken out in Norfolk and the West Country. The Norfolk uprising had been brutally crushed by the Earl of Warwick, and confrontation between Warwick and Somerset, both of them avid for absolute power, became unavoidable.

In the Tower Thynne was closely questioned about Somerset's affairs. Resourceful as ever, he evaded the questions. Making light of his own involvement with Somerset whilst assessing the risks to his own head, he steered a predictably subtle course between loyalty to his master and the danger of offending the ambitious Warwick. Although during the rebellion he had been given the right to grant the King's Free Pardon, it was hinted that secretly he had aided the revolt to further his own ends. But nothing could be proved and early in 1550 both Somerset and Sir John were released.[20]

John Thynne returned quietly to Longleat, leaving Somerset to be fined and stripped of his powers. Thynne had learnt a grim lesson: the nearer one stood to the source of power, the farther the possible fall. Thereafter he did all he could to avoid the undercurrent of plot and counterplot that marks this phase of English history. And he at once wrote to Sir William Cecil – a close friend who had joined Somerset's household at much the same time – asking to be relieved of his post as Somerset's steward.

As far as we know Sir John spent the next eighteen months peacefully at Longleat with his young wife. But rural tranquillity was to be short-lived, and by the autumn of 1551, Warwick, now Duke of Northumberland and the most powerful man in the land, was ready to overthrow his rival. In October, almost two years to the day since he had first been imprisoned, Somerset was returned to the Tower on a trumped-up charge of treason and conspiracy, and his supporters rounded up. John Thynne was arrested at Longleat and placed in the Tower.

For Somerset there was no hope. Shortly after dawn on a chill winter's day he walked on to the scaffold at Tower Hill, adjusted his doublet, knelt in the straw, and died beneath the executioner's axe.

John Thynne was alone. His uncle and Somerset were both dead and, for the first time in his career, there was no one but Christian he could turn to for support. Condemned by his past, mistrusted and disliked by many of those who were now to judge him, it was vital that he beg forgiveness if he was to avoid sharing the Protector's fate. Called before the Council early in the New Year he asked them to take into account 'the poor estate and condition that I stand in, having lived the life of an honest poor man.'[21] The Council was unimpressed by Thynne's plea of poverty, and reminded him that his 'living and substance' were common knowledge.[22] In reply Thynne catalogued his assets, juggling the figures with such slyness that on paper it appeared that his debts exceeded his income. The Council hesitated, but before reaching a verdict criticized his stubbornness, took away his servant, and placed him in solitary confinement.

Christian, obviously determined to support her husband, but still recovering from the tragic death of their first child, travelled up to London and pleaded his case before the entire Council. We have no record of what she said, but courage and her Gresham name won the day; Thynne's life was to be spared. He was fined £2000 and the Packership of London was confiscated. On learning the news Sir John's instinct for thrift reasserted itself. The knowledge that he might have to part with much of his hard-won capital was more than he could stomach. And in a letter to the Council he begged them to reduce the fine and let him retain the Packership, stating that he could not decide whether death, imprisonment or the loss of £2000 was the lesser evil. Even in the Tower he was incapable of accepting his fate, and shortly afterwards he wrote the Council a second letter. After reminding them of his 'long and painful service', of his father-in-law's intention to leave Christian well-provided for, he ended up by insisting that life had brought little else but misery, and that he and Christian would spend 'all the days of our life both beggars.'[23] The Council ignored Thynne's self-pity, and it quickly became obvious, even to him, that the full fine would have to be paid.

The most important person to be placated was Northumberland, and over his letter to the duke – drafts of which still exist – Thynne struggled laboriously; scratching out phrases, amending others, until the final result was as polished and polite as his obstinacy would allow. 'As for stubbornness,' he wrote, 'good my Lord do not think it in me. There is no man more ready, humbly and obediently to receive your orders, and to submit myself most lowly to your clemencies.'[24]

Before leaving the Tower, perhaps as a sop to his wounded vanity, Thynne called in a tailor and shoemaker to re-equip his wardrobe. In the process he ran up bills of nearly £300, and they make a mockery of his assertion that the future promised nothing but poverty. Amongst Longleat's accounts there is a note, in Thynne's handwriting, stating that he had to pay £50 to 'Mr. Lieutenant of the Tower for my charge during imprisonment.'[25] But such sums were a small enough price for his liberty, and in June 1552, after eight months' imprisonment, Sir John Thynne was released and ordered to remain on his estates until further notice.

At thirty-seven Sir John Thynne was in his prime. He had survived what was to be the only major crisis in his career. For the next fifteen years he was content to spend much of his time at Longleat, collecting his rents, indulging his passion for building, and enjoying the accumulated fruits harvested as Somerset's steward. During those years Christian was to give birth to ten more children, of whom only five were destined to reach maturity. At the fourth attempt she produced the son and heir needed if the Thynnes were to found a dynasty.

The interruptions to family life at Longleat were rare. When Queen Mary succeeded to the throne in 1553 she granted Thynne a pardon, before attacking him for his 'intolerable disobedience and negligence' in not paying rents due to the Crown.[26] In the following year he was appointed Comptroller to Princess Elizabeth's household, a post he must have regarded with unease, it being fraught with the pitfalls surrounding the succession. Amongst Thynne's papers in the Muniment Room at Longleat is a letter from the princess, dated February 1555, and addressed to 'our assured Loving Friend', which hints at the complexity of her predicament.[27] We do not know how much of Thynne's time was taken up with the appointment, but Somerset's fate had been a chastening experience, and it is probable that he studiously avoided all threats to his own reputation. Thynne, for all his arrogance, was a realist. The past two years had taught him that only by attracting the minimum of attention could he hope to preserve Longleat's independence.

The period following Sir John's release from the Tower witnessed the first flowering of Longleat into something other than a renovated priory. In 1552 the house contained only a hall, parlour, great chamber, bedrooms for the family, servants' quarters, and a series of rooms dedicated to the manufacture and storage of food. It was a country house rather than a 'stately home'; functional, uncomplicated, and a far cry from the ornate classical perfection that awaits today's visitor. It had no pretensions to architectural splendour, but over the next four years a wing of six rooms was added. Amongst them was a new parlour, complete with shove-ha'penny table, to which the family could escape from the labourers who then populated the house. A three-storey tower was built over the hall door, a new porch was built and the hall remodelled. It seems that the work was supervised by a Mr Throckmorton, to whom Thynne was always in debt, and to work under Throckmorton Dodd was asked to hire a band of skilled craftsmen.

Painful experience had taught Sir John much about the character of his potential labour force. A few years earlier a gang of Frenchmen sent to Somerset's West Country steward by Thynne were 'the worst conditioned people that I ever saw, and the drunkest. For they will drink more in a day than three days wages will come to and then lie like beasts on the floor not able to stand.'[28] But the habits of the English stonemason were no different from his French counterpart, and ample liquid refreshment had to be guaranteed before the contracts could be signed. In 1559, when Thynne appointed William Spicer, who had first come to Longleat four years earlier, as his master-mason, his men had to be provided with a place to sleep and as much beer as they wanted, 'at the rate of five bushels of barley malt to the hogshead.'[29]

William Spicer's promotion led to an acceleration of the building programme. In October 1559 Thynne appointed him bailiff of a Somerset manor (an unusual post for a mason) and an agreement was drawn up for the construction of two more wings at Longleat. The work was to cost £300 and to take three years. Sir John agreed to provide scaffolding and timber, as well as the teams of oxen needed to haul stone from local quarries. The contract is of great importance to Longleat's evolution, for it marks the moment at which the house began to differ from the majority of Tudor buildings. We do not know which of the two men was responsible for the change in emphasis. But Thynne, egoistic as ever, had a great deal to do with the drawing up of the plans and was undoubtedly eager that Longleat should reflect his own sense of achievement and self-assurance. Although the new wings retained the steep gables and battlemented towers of traditional English design, the accounts mention payment to Spicer for 'pulling down and altering all that part that is to be changed to make it (Longleat) uniform.' Thus, for the first time, Longleat acquired the symmetry and proportion that characterizes Renaissance architecture.[30]

The collaboration between Spicer and Thynne soon ended. Spicer had contracted to build twelve chimney-pieces for Longleat but by October 1562, when the new wings should have been completed, only one chimney-piece had been finished and the building programme was well behind schedule. Spicer was not entirely to blame, for Thynne's correspondence mentions the inefficiency of the carpenters and the refusal of his tenants to provide carriage for stone until after they had sown their crops. But Sir John was not interested in excuses and he transferred the mason to the less glamorous task of building forty windows for another of his houses at Corsley. The work on the windows was done so shoddily that Thynne refused to pay Spicer's bill and he soon left, taking with him £34 collected in rent but not yet handed over. Thynne was enraged; but there was nothing he could do about it, for Spicer had found shelter with the queen's favourite, the Earl of Leicester, and in 1595 he was appointed to the Surveyorship of the Queen's Works. Spicer's abrupt departure was typical of Thynne's relationship with the craftsmen who worked for him; time and again the brief honeymoon ended in mutual dislike and recrimination. To finish the chimney-pieces a new mason was employed, Thynne perhaps taking some comfort from the letter of introduction in which the mason stated that not only was he qualified to cut stone and carve chimney crests, but that he was proficient in the art of laying 'sinks to convey ordure to the brook.'

Middle-age failed to have any effect on Sir John's temper. If anything it grew steadily worse, and the brunt of it was borne by his steward, John Dodd. 'Thynne commands what he likes, and Dodd executes what he likes', wrote Thynne on more than one occasion.[31] When Dodd inadvertently allowed chimney shafts to be built in brick rather than stone, he was forced to pay for their alteration out of his own pocket. Thynne never hesitated to interfere. Again and again he made last-minute changes in the design of the two new wings. Dressed in doublet, leather girdle, and fur-lined coat, perhaps followed by his spaniels *Quail* and *Ludlow*, he rampaged about the house, checking the work and insulting the labourers.

Sir John seems to have genuinely believed that only ruthlessness produced results. Throughout his entire correspondence only two letters survive which suggest the slightest spark of kindness or interest in anyone other than himself. The first of these concerns a grass bank near the house which he wanted levelled in case 'a man should come down that way on a dark night and take hurt by falling there.'[32] The second was written to Christian shortly after the birth of their eldest son, and in it he asked her to make certain that his heir did not catch a cold.[33] In her reply Christian mentioned that whilst out with the woodmen felling a tree of the perfect length for Longleat's floorboards they had been disturbed by the Queen's Foresters. His son's welfare apparently forgotten, Thynne ordered his wife to acquire the timber at all costs; adding as an afterthought complete instructions for cutting it into planks and then removing them without being hindered.

The farmland surrounding Longleat was as important to Thynne's plans as the house itself, and his attitude to its improvement was simple, effective, and characteristic. When he wanted the servants to spend part of each day pulling out brambles in the park, those that refused to help with the work were forbidden to eat meat at supper. Roses were planted in the borders round the orchard, and a programme of grafting fruit trees on to quince stock started. The stream was dammed and a small lake made, and Thynne even paid to have eight dozen gulls brought to Longleat from their nesting-grounds on the Bristol Channel. The sale of timber and wool provided the estate with much of its income and with the money the bailiff bought new teams of oxen, fodder for the livestock, as well as ploughs and oxen and equipment for the dairy.

There were always petty problems to be attended to. Sheep were harassed by wild dogs. Twice a year the stock on Warminster Common had to be claimed, and those that remained were impounded by Sir John and their owners fined for trespass. Arguments with tenants about rent and sporting rights had to be resolved. In a severe winter the poultry girl lost all but one of the cock pheasants kept for breeding, and once the Privy Council had to be placated when a group of Thynne's men killed a buck out hunting. Sir John became involved with the Bishop of Salisbury in dispensing justice following a case of bigamy; and then, when a jail to house local criminals was built within sight of the good bishop's palace, he poured oil on troubled waters by ordering the work to be halted and a new site found.[34] These irritations were essentially trivial, and although they indicate the scope of Sir John Thynne's influence he still had time to ride out over the moorland with his hawks in search of partridge and rabbit.

By 1562 Longleat's household had swollen to fifty-six. Thynne employed huntsmen, a falconer, cook and gardener, as well as maids and grooms. A maid earned a pound a year, and most of the servants slept on fowl-feather truckle beds in the attic. Conditions were hard and Sir John's domineering manner must have made them worse. The house was damp and its chimneys smoked, water had to be fetched from the stream, the sanitary arrangements were primitive, and there were few of the comforts normally associated with life in a country house. The household led an exacting and monotonous existence, but they appear to have eaten well, and some

of the cook's recipes from the period are still at Longleat: amongst
them partridge in almonds, trout baked in a herb sauce, and wild-
fowl, mutton or veal boiled with capers.[35] Butter was melted down
and preserved in wooden tubs, and the kitchen maids were kept
busy salting down fresh meat and fish, especially herring and sprats,
into barrels. Although much of the food came from the Longleat
estate, Sir John owned land in other parts of the country and the
diet was given variety by the lease of parkland and fishing rights.
Typical of these was the grant of fishing on the Wye at £24 a year,
the tenant undertaking to supply pike, trout and 'four good sweet
salmon of the best and largest sort, ready baked and seasoned.'[36]
The main meal of the day was eaten at mid-afternoon in the hall
and the household was sometimes entertained afterwards by
jugglers or travelling players. Ironically, Robin Hood's wholesale
robbery of the rich was amongst the plays performed before Sir
John, and the payment to the players was noted down in the Longleat accounts.

In the same year the submissive, and probably worn-out, John
Dodd either died or retired, and he was replaced as steward by
George Walker. But a change of face had no effect on Sir John,
and before long Walker was treated in the same way as his pre-
decessor. On taking office he was faced with a severe food shortage
in the house and at once wrote to his new employer saying, 'I
must now spend cheese for my fish is all done and your household
was never so great. I wish to God you were at home to see what it is
to serve in so many places.'[37] A familiar plea, but one that always
fell on deaf ears. In reply Thynne ordered his steward to finish the
chimneys and hurry along the masons, carpenters and plasterers
at work in Longleat, ending his letter, 'I pray God confound all my
enemies.'[38]

Thynne's obvious wealth and Longleat's growing splendour
made resentment inevitable. When a local earl, jealous of Thynne's
success, complained to the Privy Council accusing Thynne of gaining his fortune illegally, Thynne was called before the Council
to explain the source of his prosperity. As most of the Council's
members owed their position to much the same tactics as Sir John,
he spoke calmly of his marriage, his hard work and frugal character,
ending his statement, 'for the rest you have a good mistress our
gracious Queen, and I had a good master, the Duke of Somerset.'

With that Thynne left the room and the case was dismissed.[39]

Queen Elizabeth had succeeded to the throne in 1558, and by early in her reign Sir John Thynne had matured into a prominent West Country landowner. In 1562 he was ordered to attend the queen with horses and servants at her abortive meeting with Mary Queen of Scots at Nottingham.[40] He had become Member of Parliament for Wiltshire, High Sheriff, and High Captain of the County Levy, but none of these appointments prevented local squabbles, and there can be no doubt that many of them were caused by Sir John's sudden affluence. Poachers were the prime offenders. One year a pitched battle took place between eight of Longleat's gamekeepers and a Warminster poaching gang; one of the keepers was killed, 'but in time the fellows were so galled with arrows that they fled.' Two of the attackers were wounded, captured, and placed in Crockerton stocks, and 'by report are like to die rather than recover.'[41] Such events were frequent in the rough and ready shires of Elizabethan England. No one lifted a finger to help the unfortunate poachers, and within two days both were dead.

Death itself was an all too familiar feature of sixteenth-century life, and in 1565 one of Sir John's sons, the five-year-old Henry fell ill and died. Henry was Christian's favourite child and she had once told her husband that if he died she would outlive him by less than a month.[42] Three weeks later she followed him into the grave and Thynne, after noting down the double tragedy in the fly-leaf of the family bible, added 'and so it came to pass.' The loyal Christian had given her husband eleven children. For eighteen years she had lived with his ambition and arrogance and when in the Tower she had saved his life. She was buried in Horningsham churchyard by the man who married them and for a short while the house went into mourning.

But Sir John seems to have taken Christian's death in his stride. It meant that once again he was free to choose a bride, and in the following year he married the heiress Dorothy Wroughton, another Lord Mayor's daughter. Dorothy was splendidly severe and nearly as cunning as her husband, and she was to bear him a further eight children, seven of them sons. By now many of his daughters by Christian had reached maturity and the task of marrying them off to suitable families was taken in hand. One kept on rejecting her proposed suitors and, to help overcome her apparent unwillingness to marry, Thynne promised her £500 when eventually she took a husband. Three years later she married a local squire, but by then her father was so deep in debt to Longleat's workmen that he could only produce two gowns and a length of silk on her wedding day. The £500 followed by instalments.

Marriage was one of the most important ways in which Sir John could extend his influence and, although minor squires made adequate husbands, he was obviously eager to acquire rich, well-connected noblemen as his sons-in-law. In this he was often thwarted, and a plan to marry off another daughter, Elizabeth, to a cousin of the Earl of Hertford, the Protector's son, ended in failure. Hertford had been befriended by Thynne after his father's execution, but it did not prevent him from hindering the match. No portrait of Elizabeth survives to dispute his reasoning, but his interference infuriated Thynne who wrote him a scathing letter which ended with the words, 'If you treat your friends as you have me, you will lack for them when you most need them.'[43] Snubbed he may have been, but this letter suggests that Thynne at last realized the value of qualities other than avarice and self-interest. Perhaps, as he grew older, he found the contentment that Longleat and his family offered.

In 1563 two Frenchmen, Allen Maynard the sculptor, and Adrian Gaunt the joiner, were hired to work at Longleat. The three surviving carved Elizabethan fireplaces - in the Great Hall, State Drawing Room and Servants' Hall - are almost certainly the work of Maynard. Under Gaunt's guidance the porch was decorated, the gallery panelled, and work begun on building bookcases for the library. Sir John Thynne's library was small but select, and many of the books - all of them remarkably valuable - still remain in the house. It was formed round a collection left him by his uncle, amongst them the first book to be printed in the English language - *The History of Troy*, but it also included early Caxtons, Chaucer's works, books on herbs, horsemanship and the West Indies, and a cookery book whose pages contain a recipe for roast porpoise.[44] The importance of the library and the wide range of its contents hint at a side of Sir John's character that is rarely revealed in his correspondence.

With the Frenchmen hard at work Thynne next decided to build

1 The firste volume of the ecclesiasticall historie containing the actes and monuments of euerie kinges time in this realme &c wrighten by ffox and printed Anno 1570

2 The seconde volume of the ecclesiasticall historie containinge the actes & monuments of euerie kinges time of this realme &c wrighten by John ffox and printed a 1576

3 An olde wrighten bible in lattin lackinge the beginninge of genesis & exodus.

4 Chaumcers workes printed by Thomas Godfreye Anno 1532

5 Sermons of m John Calvine vppon the booke of Job, and translated out of frenst by Arthur Goldinge and printed in Anno 1574

6 An other olde wrighten bible in lattin.

7 Bowres of the state of princes in englishe wrighten.

8 A bible in inglishe written containinge those testamentes and prophites

9 The flower of the commandmentes of god with manie examples and authorities extracte of holie scriptures translated oute of frenst into inglishe & printed Anno 1521

10 A booke in wrighting hand containinge the names of the baylifs, mairos, and succesfors of london, with manie other notes woorthie of certaine thinges happeninge from richarde the firste vntill the 2 or 3 yeare of henrye the 6.

11 The legendarie in inglishe printed by John notorye in Anno 1503.

12 A cronicle in inglishe in wrighten hand

13 The bible in inglishe with an epistle of Edmonde benke to Edwarde the 6 printed 1549

14 Chaumcers workes printed in Anno 1561

15 A bible in inglishe printed Anno 1541

16 Peter martin in inglishe vppon the epistle of s paule to the romaines.

17 The workes of Sir Thomas moore printed 1557

18 Homelie Chrisostomi super Johannem filium sine eluadianum diffundatum iuxta offirium misse

19 The institution of religion wrighten in lattin by Calvine and translated into inglishe.

20 The common places of wolfganus musculus in inglishe with a preface of John inanmi to mathew of canterburie.

21 The moste fruictfull and learned commentaries of Docter peeter martir &c

22 The historie wrighten by Shminders translated oute of frenst into inglishe by Thomas pe nolles goosmithe and citizen of london

23 If abiamus euomitte.

24 The defence of peace translated out of lattin into inglishe firste imprinted published or sence farther abused in the inglishe tongue by william marstad 1535

25 The booke of fame of Chaucer, printed by reason the rurall of Alice chaucier translated oute of frenche into inglishe by william Caxton
Cato in lattin verse with the same in inglishe verse A booke of phrases in inglishe sueng

26 Bartend do translatione philosophie in inglishe

27 A dialogue of s Thomas moore knighte of veneratoñ of mayes &c printed 1530

28 The cronicles of England with the dedes of popes and emperoures and also the destruption of Inglande with diuers reason firste put in printe accordinge to the translation of Eusebius with the requeste of the lorde barkley translated polixemson into inglishe &c

30 The volume of the veruyles of the historires of troye translated oute of frenst into inglishe by william caxton and finnished by him Anno dni 1472

An inventory of Sir John Thynne's books

larger cellars under the house, and a start was made on excavating and laying the necessary foundations. The new work was to mark the end of an age. For at three in the morning on 21 April 1567 Longleat caught fire and continued blazing until late in the evening. By the time the flames had burnt themselves out the hall had been gutted, the west wing destroyed, and the remainder of the house severely damaged. The fire's cause is unknown, but for Longleat's owner it must have been a bitter blow. Twenty years' work had been destroyed in the space of a few hours. On the following day he ordered salvage operations amidst the rubble to begin, and extra labourers were employed to help pull down the scorched remnants of the walls and gables.

The Thynnes moved into their Corsley home. Friends sent gifts of trees and offers of assistance. But no amount of sympathy could rebuild Longleat and, after eight months' deliberation, Sir John Thynne gave the orders that would finally lead to the construction of the house we know today. Perhaps more than anything else this decision shows how inflexible he was in his determination to rebuild Longleat, not as a ghost of its former self, but as one of the most enduring symbols of the enterprise and vigour of Elizabethan England. He was a perfectionist, and all that he had learned during the years spent patiently modifying the priory was now to be fused into a single ambition, to create a house that would live on as evidence of his vision and success. Without ever realizing it, he was to build a house that ranks as one of the most beautiful in the country.

In December 1567 Adrian Gaunt began making a wooden model of the new Longleat, and work on the house started on New Year's Day 1568. Sir John's agents were sent out in search of the craftsmen and materials needed. An entire quarry of Bath stone was bought at Haselbury, twenty-five miles from Longleat, and the stone was hauled to the site on sledges pulled by oxen. Slate came from Cornwall and Wales, glass from Spain; the local forge was set to work making tools; timber was cut and stacked for seasoning; nails, panelling and other necessities were shipped up the Thames and then transferred on to waggons for the slow overland journey to Longleat. In March, Robert Smythson, a young and very talented master-mason, was sent down to Longleat by Humphrey Lovell, the Queen's Master-Mason.[45] Smythson's own team of men accompanied him, and so eager was Thynne to start work that he paid their travel expenses and the cost of bringing their equipment to the site.

Robert Smythson's arrival helps answer what is perhaps the most perplexing riddle connected to Longleat, the identity of its architect. Thynne, with the memory of William Spicer's abrupt disappearance still fresh in his mind, probably insisted that the final responsibility for Longleat should be his, and his alone. As far as we know Longleat never had a professional architect, and this, combined with the complexity of its design, makes its owner's achievement all the more impressive. Sir John's personality, his mistrust of others, his vanity and impatience, suggest instead that he drew up the initial plans, or that they were worked out in uneasy collaboration with Smythson and Lovell.

Thynne was determined that the house should be built in the new Italian style, and its classical character is self-evident, especially in the lines of Doric, Ionic and Corinthian pilasters grafted in turn on to the exterior of the three floors. The Renaissance concept of symmetry, of proportion and elegance, was of paramount importance but Thynne and his masons were still influenced by the rich imagery of traditional design. When the masons reached the roof, the classical façade was thrown out of balance by the apparently haphazard positioning of eight pepper-pot domes (of which only seven still survive) amidst the gables and guttering. The placing of a line of grotesque stone dogs on the balustrade, each with his tongue hanging out, where they look down into the inner courtyards, provided a further contrast with Longleat's external harmony. The final result of this unlikely marriage is the essence of the High Elizabethan style. A brilliant synthesis of the Classical and Gothic in an age when internal peace made a fortified castle unnecessary. But, for all its magnificence, Longleat was intended to be a family home, and today a direct descendant of John Thynne's still lives with his wife and family in one wing of the original house.

Longleat owes its construction, quite simply, to West Country muscle. At a time when heavy machinery was unknown, each piece of hand-cut stone had to be lifted into place by block and tackle. Plumb lines were used to ensure that the walls remained vertical and the estate's own woods provided the enormous oak beams that criss-cross the internal fabric, knitting the whole house together. In purely human terms it was a mammoth operation and a total of

112 joiners, glaziers, masons, plasterers, plumbers and bricklayers
were employed on the site. Many of the tenants from the surrounding hamlets did a gift day's work, hauling stone from the quarry or
helping the lime-burner prepare his kilns. Sir John relied on Smythson's skilled craftsmen, and a small band of Dissenting freemasons
he had hired prior to the fire to build the cellars; the masonic
symbols carved by these men on to individual pieces of the stonework
can still be seen on Longleat's walls. To begin with the Dissenters
worshipped secretly in a glade in a local copse but Thynne eventually
gave them permission to build a small thatched chapel on the edge
of Horningsham which still stands: the first Free Church built in
England.[46]

The cellar foundations provided an obvious starting point for the
new house. Progress was rapid and, by the end of the year, the south
and east wings – the former 210 feet long and the latter 180 – were
so advanced that one of the masons set to work building sixteen
chimneys. Each one was over seventeen feet tall, and after being
built at the quarry they had to be lifted on to waggons, taken to
Longleat, and carefully raised on to the roof in leather slings. For
this the mason was paid £8, but Thynne was so in debt because of
Longleat that he had to wait two years for payment.

Even within a half-hour ride of the house Sir John Thynne fretted
constantly. He seemed beset by minor irritations. The masons ran
out of stone and work had to be halted whilst the purchase
of a new quarry was negotiated. He quarrelled with Smythson and
Gaunt over their wages. They accused him of making them work
longer hours than anyone else on the site, ending their demand for
extra pay with a statement typical of all those who had financial
dealings with the avaricious knight: 'We think that in all England
there is none that hath received less profit and lesser thanks than we.'[46b]
An additional steward was taken on the pay-roll to assist George
Walker but the poor man, so confused he was by the activity on the
site, soon wrote to his employer informing him that 'I am utterly
unacquainted with the phrases of builders God knoweth.'[47] But
neither his ignorance, nor a threatened strike by Smythson's men,
could hinder Longleat's progress, and in 1572, five years after the
fire, the Thynnes were able to return. That same year Sir John
ordered his masons and plasterers to begin resheathing the gabled
exterior of the house with its existing Classical façade. At last, more

than thirty years after the purchase of the priory, he had discovered an architectural style that satisfied his instinct for perfection.

By the date of the family's return to the house the Great Hall had been finished, and at once became the focal point of the south wing. The kitchens, the Long Gallery, some parlours and bedrooms had also been completed; and once the roof had been leaded Dorothy and the children could eat sweetmeats and fruit in the new banqueting turrets. But even with the family in residence the work continued and, for the remainder of Sir John's life, they shared Longleat with the craftsmen who built it. Since then the house has inevitably been modernized, but today, standing in the flagstoned Great Hall, one can see the meticulous craftsmanship that is Longleat's hallmark. In this perfectly-proportioned room, perhaps more than anywhere else inside the house, one can distinguish between the accomplishments of Thynne the architect and the characteristic pig-headedness of Thynne the man.

Even as he approached his sixties Sir John Thynne remained as mercenary as ever. His income totalled £2000 a year and although most of this was spent on Longleat there were other demands on his wealth. Daughters required dowries, sons their independence and, being by far the most prosperous member of the family, he was constantly plagued for loans. The activities of a first cousin, Francis Thynne, were typical of the financial thorns that so aggravated him. After marrying an eleven-year-old girl and quickly deserting her, Francis ended up almost penniless in London and continually wrote to Sir John begging for money and occasionally threatening suicide for fear of imprisonment. Eventually he was jailed for debt and immediately wrote to his cousin: 'I am turned into the common gaol and am utterly despoiled if you be not good to me. I crave but small things. I beseech you to help me with some money to apparel me.'[48] Thynne sent him £20 (then a substantial sum) and promptly forgot about him. Charity was not part of his nature and he seems to have spent virtually all he earned either on Longleat or his own pleasures.

Inevitably there were exceptions and the most expensive was the only one which he could not avoid. The question of a Royal Visit by Queen Elizabeth had first been discussed two years after the priory had burnt down. The queen was determined to visit the house, and Thynne was equally determined that she should not. Her presence would mean endless expense and her temper was as volatile as his own. She would expect presents, plays, flattery, and a banquet. A two-day visit could cost a fortune. By embarking on her famous Royal Progresses the queen had evolved a method of keeping a watchful eye on the ambitions of her nobility at the same time as forcing them to pay for the maintenance of her lavish Court. When the Royal Visit had first been suggested Thynne was able to point out that Longleat was not yet built. By 1573 there were no such obstacles and he was informed that, like it or not, the queen was to be his guest in the following summer. As the date of her arrival drew nearer he foolishly hinted at the presence of an infectious disease in the house.[49] The queen lost her temper, declared Thynne a scoundrel, and after hastily withdrawing all objections to her visit he employed a cook, 'qualified both in skill and good behaviour',[50] and invested £160 in a present for Elizabeth of 'one jewel called a Phoenix set with one great emerald, fifty other diamonds and rubies and an apendant pearl.'[51]

Dorothy was as unhappy with her wardrobe as her husband was apprehensive at the visit's final cost, but she persuaded him to buy her a new russet taffeta and silk gown to wear when welcoming the queen. After some delay 'the trunk wherein was apparel for yourself and my Lady before the Queen's first coming into the country'[52] finally appeared. In mid-September, accompanied by one of Sir John's daughters as a Maid of Honour in her entourage, Elizabeth arrived at Longleat. Although the queen's stay was probably celebrated by a series of feasts, punctuated by hunting, music and jousting, no detailed record of her visit survives. But we do know it was a success, for a month later Thynne received news that 'Thanks be to God, her Majesty is well returned with good health and great liking of her entertainment in the western parts, and especially at your house, which twice since she hath greatly commended.'[53] The final bill for Elizabeth's brief visit was undoubtedly enormous. But it was a symbol of royal approval, a triumphant climax to all those hazy dreams, those distant aspirations, that had been nurtured in John Thynne's brain when he was still only a kitchen clerk.

But, despite the Royal Visit, criticism of Sir John's achievements still continued. And in the following year his peace of mind was further disturbed when Will Darell published what has become known as 'Will Darell's Knavery'. The 'Knavery' is a satirical address, supposedly spoken by Longleat itself and, if many of its pages are an exaggeration, they do at least capture the obsessive quality of Thynne's relationship with his home. 'But now see him, that thirty years almost, with such turmoil of mind hath been thinking of me, framing and erecting me, musing many a time with great care, and now and then pulling down this and that part of me, to enlarge sometimes a foot or some few inches, upon a conceit, or this or that man's speech, not all worth a woodcock's brains.'[54]

Darell be damned. Soon after the 'Knavery's' publication Sir John travelled the eighteen miles to Bath, immersed himself in the hot waters of the Roman baths, bought a new pair of breeches, and returned to the still uncompleted Longleat. The 'Knavery' seems to have goaded him into fresh action and in the four years that followed many of the rooms were panelled, a start was made on the west wing, and in tribute to three of his oldest friends the arms of the Earl of Suffolk, Sir William Cecil, and the Duke of Somerset were carved on the facing of the new minstrels' gallery.

Throughout this period Sir John and Dorothy spent part of each year at their recently-bought riverside mansion in London. Whenever they returned to Longleat the kitchen maids were kept busy slaughtering livestock and poultry to ensure that ample fresh meat awaited their arrival. 'There is a cramming and feeding against your coming,' wrote the farm bailiff on one occasion, 'twenty-four capons, twenty-four geese, twelve duck, with as many fowl as I can get able to feed.'[55] That this was possible is proof of the estate's prosperity. The farm was flourishing. Its flocks of sheep were added to annually by purchases at Salisbury market, which were then driven over the rolling chalk downland by drovers hired specially for the task. A bull was installed in 'My Lord's Byre', new barns built, and additional land ploughed and sown. The farm accounts, written with painstaking care by the bailiff on long rolls of parchment that crumble as you touch them, offer evidence of Longleat's self-sufficiency. Minor expenses stand out. The payment of 2d to a shepherd 'upon his paynes for helping the sheep that were enchanted.' The repairs to the park palings when a 'marvellous tempest of wind' blew many of them down.[56] There were droughts, storms, and sudden late frosts which blackened the ripening corn. But such calamities were few and, more than anything else, the accounts are a record of daily life on the land, in the mills and dairies that played so important a part in guaranteeing the estate its independence. Spanning the forty years of Thynne's ownership of Longleat, they give his career a sense of perspective and at the same time remind us that although Longleat's construction was his main achievement he never lost interest in the land that surrounded it.

In 1580 Sir John Thynne was sixty-five. Old age had mellowed him, and as a concession to his years he had bought a coach. But the visits to London became rarer. Many of his old friends were dead and he seems to have been content to remain at Longleat with his wife and family until 'whensoever God shall call me.' In preparation for that moment he had made a will. Its contents emphasize his astonishing success, for a total of £5000 was needed to meet the commitments listed in its pages.

To Dorothy he gave a third of his plate and Longleat's contents, as well as money, cattle, and a hundred sheep from those at Corsley on the day of his death. Land and an income were settled on each of his sons and dowries were provided for his unmarried daughters. To the faithful servants who had for so long borne the brunt of his temper he left a blue coat and six months wages. Finally he asked to be buried in the parish churchyard at Longbridge Deverill, a small village three miles from Longleat, and requested that a tomb be built there as a memorial to himself and Christian.

The end came unexpectedly. In early May he was confined to bed. But Tudor medicine had no cure for the illnesses of old age and nothing could be done for him. On the morning of the 21st he learnt that his own death had been reported in London. Later that day, perhaps content at cheating the world even on his deathbed, Sir John Thynne died. Beside him were Dorothy and some of his eighteen children.

In recognition of the financial precision that had brought John Thynne his fortune, and as tribute to his long-suffering stewards, the Longleat accounts tell the story of his final hours and burial:

To Butler the surgeon of Warminster for his paynes tending upon my Master in his sickness 20/-
To him for his paynes in wrapping of my Master and making his serecloth 13/-
Paid for one dozen of black lace for the coffin 15d, nails 11d.
To a tailor for sowing the black covering upon the waggon 3d.

To Kynge the poor man for turning the spit at the burial 2d.[57]

Longleat and its estates were to be inherited by Thynne's eldest son, a lean, troublesome, wooden-faced young man, also called John, who after annoying his father by seducing Lucy Mervyn, the daughter of a local squire, had made amends by his eventual marriage to Joan Hayward, the wealthy daughter of London's Lord Mayor. But Dorothy had no time for him, and the relationship between Longleat's heir and his stepmother had deteriorated to the point where neither would talk to the other. When he reached the house on the day after his father's death, Dorothy refused him entrance to her rooms. Although the will had not yet been read, she believed that the Corsley property was now hers. Determined to protect her legacy and the 'breath not being quite out of his body', she began contradicting earlier orders made by her late husband which concerned the Corsley estate: even going so far as to prevent the removal of some timber which was intended as floorboards for Longleat.

Sir John's brother had also arrived at the house. After he had removed the keys from his dead brother's purse in order to open the trunk containing the will, some money was found to be missing. None of this much pleased Longleat's new master but there was little he could do about it. Once the will had been read Dorothy began transferring her share of Longleat's contents to Corsley. That done she locked herself in her rooms with her family and friends and refused to move. Of her stepson's attempts to dislodge her she took not the slightest notice. She ordered deer to be slaughtered for her table, paraded in the evenings with her entourage on the roof, and successfully smuggled some harness and Sir John's favourite mare out of the stables and over to Corsley without anyone knowing about it. For two days Sir John Thynne's corpse stayed locked in the room where he had died and the house remained paralysed by the friction between widow and heir.[58]

Eventually Dorothy departed, leaving behind her Longleat's new and untried master, the shrouded body of her late husband and the magnificent stone outline of his greatest creation.

2

THE FRUGAL YEARS,
1580-1670

'For although I sit at home and weave clothes that hath
worn out their apprenticeship I will not be melancholy,
but with good courage spend my life and waste my spirits
in any course to please thee, except fighting.'[1]

Maria Thynne to her husband, Sir Thomas
Thynne, 1608.

John Thynne was twenty-five when he inherited Longleat. A man of
mediocre talents he was, like many a second generation, content
to enjoy the fruits of his father's remarkable success without con-
tributing or adding to it in any way. The fault was not entirely his.
His mother died when he was ten years old, and he had been brought
up disliked by his stepmother and overshadowed by his father.
Reaction was inevitable and whilst a student at Oxford he developed
a taste for dissipation and excess. Such behaviour, aggravated by
the seduction of Lucy Mervyn, caused his father to threaten dis-
inheritance. John mended his ways and the two men declared an
uneasy peace. But he rarely visited Longleat and after his marriage
to Joan Hayward set up house in London.

Sir John and his son had little natural affection for one another.
Their relationship seems to have been guided by John's determination to do nothing that might weaken his claim to Longleat.
Sir John never encouraged his heir to take an interest in the estate
or his plans for completing the house and John, rebuffed by his
father and ignored by his stepmother, turned increasingly to his
father-in-law for support.

In the summer of 1580 John and his wife, together with their
two-year-old son Thomas, moved into Longleat. Joan was timid,

dowdy and nineteen. Although her dowry had given the Thynnes additional estates in Shropshire she had been brought up in London and was unaccustomed to the inconvenience of rural life – on however grand a scale. Both found it hard to adjust to their new roles; Joan as mistress of a self-sufficient household and her husband as owner of an unfinished mansion dependent on an income from agriculture. They hankered after London gossip. Letters from friends are full of petty scandal, such as 'a great mischance at Court yesterday as one of the maids of honour was delivered of a goodly boy by my Lord of Oxford', and in the spring of 1581 news of a 'strange and mysterious earthquake all over London.'[2]

There were problems. John's brothers constantly turned to him for financial help. One hoped to sail with the explorer Sir Humphrey Gilbert and required provisions, another the price of an Irish estate. Life was further complicated by the feud with his stepmother. On one occasion the faint-hearted Joan fled Longleat in the middle of the night rather than be abused by Dorothy. News of Dorothy's eventual marriage to Carew Raleigh, Sir Walter's brother, must have been greeted with relief, for she left Corsley and never troubled Longleat again.

Others also tried to take advantage of John's inexperience. Two peers wrote asking for the loan of the family's London house, a local bishop requested corn, and unscrupulous neighbours tried to persuade him to sell them parts of the estate. The requests were not always subtle. Lord Audley, asking for the gift of a tender young deer, insisted on it being a doe rather than a buck because those who were to share the feast with him 'possess dainty mouths'.[3]

John's first duty lay with Longleat, but he lacked his father's enthusiasm for the house and although work on the half-built west wing pressed slowly ahead many of the masons and carpenters were paid off. Seemingly unattracted by either forestry or farming he turned to hunting, bought a pack of mastiffs, employed huntsmen and a falconer, and made the tenants sign agreements not to hunt over the land. John Thynne's indifference to his father's vision is regrettable. If he had finished Longleat when skilled craftsmen were at work on the site, when plans and models still existed and money was available, the north wing might have been completed at the same time as the remainder of the house. Instead the work ground gradually to a halt, and the present north wing was only added early in the nineteenth century. This lack of continuity has marred Longleat's interior. If the house had been finished by Sir John and his son, its unity, the balance between the exterior and the planned design of the rooms might be more apparent. Until quite recently some corridors led nowhere, dead-ends and sudden openings existed without purpose. The only rooms unaltered since their completion are those finished before Sir John's death. Fashion and private fancy has allowed the remainder to be modernized by successive generations until its Elizabethan character has been almost obliterated.

Whilst her husband spent his days in pursuit of hawk and hound, visiting London or the outlying estates, Joan was left to run the household. She wrote to him regularly when he was away asking for petticoats, herbs, fruit – even a midwife, 'for my time is due'.[4] She bore her husband four children in the twenty-eight years of their marriage and apart from a favourite daughter nicknamed 'Dol', found them an intolerable nuisance. Motherhood exhausted her and she worried incessantly. Her character, combined with her background as the spoilt and pampered daughter of a rich city merchant, left her ill-equipped to cope as mistress of a country house. Longleat's household depended for survival on its own ingenuity and inventiveness and Joan's letters reflect her fear at failing both her husband and the servants. A shortage of blankets or an inexplicable illness unnerved her completely. She fussed about the lack of food in the larders and whenever her husband was away fretted in case he caught smallpox or the plague.

But there was always much to be done and Joan's shortcomings failed to stop the housemaids pounding the linen, scrubbing the flagstones or replacing the rushes on the floor of the Great Hall. Longleat's heart lay in its kitchens. In buttery, brewery, still-room, dairy, slaughter-house and bakery, the seasonal task of provisioning the great house went on unabated. Hams were smoked and bacon cured, cheeses pressed and butter churned, fruits turned into syrups for sweetening, nuts and berries gathered and stored. The kitchens were dominated by an open fireplace, to one side of which a small terrier revolved the spit from inside a treadmill. Nothing was wasted; garbage was fed to the gulls, fat became candles, feathers mattresses, and Longleat's sheep provided wool for blankets and clothing. The days were long and the work hard. The sentimental notion that sixteenth-century England was a merry and agreeable paradise is an illusion. Longleat's accounts record the reality: the meagre wages, the sudden deaths, the weekly 1d payments to one of the housemaids for emptying the chamber pots.[5]

John Thynne was quick-tempered and quarrelsome, and unpopular both locally and at Court. He annoyed Salisbury's merchants by attacking one of them with a sword for outbidding him at market and irritated the bishop by seizing the corn of a clergyman whose rents were in arrear.[6] Such behaviour was typical, but the family's prestige guaranteed his immunity. Joan's dowry had increased his influence and eventually he was appointed High Sheriff of Shropshire. His presence in the county made him enemies as well as profit and on one occasion his arrival at Bridgnorth Assizes prompted Lord Stafford to remark that the only certain remedy for the pain in his stomach lay in a meeting with the 'peevish' Thynne, a mile out of town and armed with a sword.[7]

But the placid respectability of the Thynnes' life at Longleat was rarely disturbed. Early in 1588, when a Spanish invasion seemed possible, he was ordered to assist in raising 2000 armed infantry to meet the emergency. Many of the men were enlisted in the villages round Longleat and John was appointed regional commander of the Queen's Levies and asked to be in readiness 'prepared with horses and other furniture fit for service.'[8] In June he was ordered to investigate allegations that West Country millers were profiteering from the crisis by hoarding grain and speculating over prices.

A month later the English fleet left harbour and, as it converged in mid-Channel with the Armada, beacons were lit to send news of the conflict across England.

'O'er Longleat's towers, o'er Cranborne's oaks,

The Fiery heralds flew', wrote Macaulay three centuries later. For one of them, a tar-filled barrel on top of a pole, hurried the news towards Bristol from the hills above Longleat.

In 1589 the Privy Council ordered Thynne to appear before them to settle his dispute with Lord Stafford. Shortly before his death Sir John had warned his son to be wary of displeasing the Council. Instead of heeding his father's advice he angered them by failing to appear, sending instead a frivolous letter.[9] Other offences added to his growing reputation for deviousness. The illegal detention of a widow's goods was followed by a fraud on the Bristol navy yard: both were discovered. The Council grew impatient and eventually he was charged with mismanaging the queen's West Country estates, dismissed from his Stewardship of the Wiltshire Royal Manors and fined £300.[10]

In 1603 James I succeeded Queen Elizabeth to the throne. Shortly afterwards John was knighted. The title may have pleased him, but was only given because the king needed support from the country landowners. Later in the same year his eldest son, Thomas, married Maria, Lord Audley's daughter. John was bitterly opposed to the match and withheld his consent for over a year. The situation was confused by Lady Audley's belief that John had fathered her own eldest son, she being the same Lucy Mervyn that he had seduced in his youth. Eventually using charm, threats and flattery, Lucy Audley persuaded her former lover to withdraw his objections to the marriage.[11]

In the following year rumours reached John that he was to be kidnapped and then ransomed. Swiftly he fled Longleat, took obscure lodgings in London, stabled his horses elsewhere, and waited until the danger had passed. Soon after his return to Longleat the forty-nine-year-old John Thynne died. He was buried alongside his father in the family vault at Longbridge Deverill.

Joan's two unmarried daughters were recovering from smallpox and with some misgivings that the journey might prove too much for them, she gathered them up and departed for Caus Castle in Shropshire. She was to remain there, increasingly involving herself in the career of the musician John Maynard, who shared her roof and perhaps one daughter's bed. In 1611 he dedicated a book of lute music to her with the imposing title of *The Twelve Wonders of the World*. That same year she died.

At twenty-eight, with neatly curled hair, a gold ring in one ear and a thin pointed beard that reached down into a high ruffed collar, Thomas Thynne looked more like a courtier or diplomat than a genial English squire. The majority of his correspondence has unfortunately been lost and we know little about his career. Intelligent and capable, it would seem he inherited his grandfather's instinct for self-preservation. Soon after his father's death he was knighted and appointed Ambassador to the Netherlands. In turn

High Sheriff of three separate counties, as well as Member of Parliament for Wiltshire, he guided the family through a period when the growing divisions between monarchy and Parliament were moving towards open conflict.

Thomas remains largely an enigma, but his letters from Maria have been carefully preserved and tell us much about her character. She once described herself as being as 'melancholy as a red herring, mad as a pilchard, and proud as a piece of ling.'[12] Headstrong obstinacy would perhaps be more accurate. Left at Longleat, disgruntled and alone, to 'weave clothes that hath worn out their apprenticeship',[13] whilst Thomas was in the Netherlands, she asserted an independence that was rare in a woman of her status. Attempts by Thomas to prevent her hiring servants and managing his affairs met with an immediate response. 'I cannot but grieve a little to find that I, who hath been a willing companion and partaker in your hard fortunes, should now be made so great a stranger to the proceedings in your better estate. You hold such a contempt for my poor wits, that being a wife, you think me not of discretion to order your affairs but leave me here like an innocent fool.'[14]

Their quarrels were rare, for Maria was devoted to her husband and after his return from the Netherlands and the birth of their three sons, they settled down to a quiet and peaceful life at Longleat. Its isolation drew them together and whenever they were apart Maria would write lengthy letters to Thomas, always ending them with some declaration of her loyalty and affection. 'I will now end,' she wrote on one occasion, 'willing that my life, happiness and contentment may never end, till thy love to me hath end. Thynne and only thine.'[15]

Her letters suggest a remarkable honesty and lack of humbug. Amongst them is one whose sentiments are, to say the least, neither orthodox or commonplace. 'Myne own sweet Thomken, I have no longer again than the very last night written such a large volume in praise of thy kindness to me, thy dogs, thy hawks, the hare, the foxes, and all in commemdation of thy great care in thy business in the country. I can say no more in way of gratitude, the dogs shall be without interruption allowed to expel their excremental corruption in the best room, (which is thy bed), whensoever full feeding makes their bellies ache.'[16]

On another occasion, apparently alarmed that Thomas might catch the plague, she sent him a recipe for a cure whose principal ingredients were treacle and dragon's water. In that same letter she added: 'Know that I have not, nor will not forget how you made my modest blood fligh up to my bashful cheeks at your last letter. So that when we meet there will be pay and repay. So now laying aside my high collar, know in sober sadness that I am at Longleat.'[17] Thomas's letter provoking her mood has sadly been lost but there can be little doubt that the two of them were very much in love.

In 1611 Maria became pregnant for a fourth time. Legend has it that a month before the baby was due she had a premonition that she would not survive childbirth and ordered her portrait to be painted. It still hangs at Longleat and shows her sombre, aquiline face and the advanced state of her pregnancy. The dream became reality and she died giving birth to a stillborn child.

Thomas was only thirty-three and within two years of Maria's death he remarried. His second wife was Catherine Howard, the Duke of Norfolk's niece. Thin-waisted and waspish, with ruffled red hair, pert pink lips and an instinctive cunning, she was the very opposite of Maria. As Thomas grew older he fell increasingly under her spell. The cause of endless bickering and argument within the family, she was the driving force behind a lawsuit that dragged on in the Courts for twenty-five years after Thomas's death.

Thomas's marriage into the influential Howards increased his reputation. Soon afterwards, having first been warned to 'have in a good store of wine, beer, beef and venison,'[18] he played host to Anne of Denmark, wife of James I. In 1615, when the first of their four children was born, the queen asked to be made a godmother. The son was to be christened Henry but, in deference to the queen's wishes, the name Frederick was added in memory of her father, the King of Denmark. These two christian names have been popular with the Thynnes ever since, including amongst their number the present Marquess of Bath.

That same year the Lord Chamberlain wrote to Thomas telling him that the king was about to create additional peers and that it would be possible to obtain him a title. 'I know there is given by some for a baron four or five thousand pounds, but it may be that I shall get it for you for three which I think will be reasonable.'[19]

Longleat's builder, Sir John Thynne.

Longleat from the South in 1675, by Jan Siberechts.

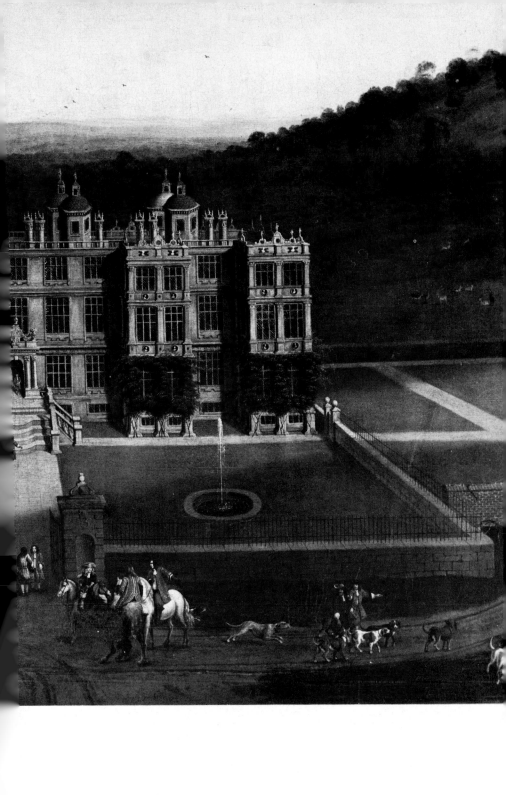

XV MAII·M·D·LXXII   ÆTAT MENS·XX·

An unnamed daughter of Sir John Thynne and his second wife, Dorothy.

Looking west over the southern side of the roof.
The cellars.

The two wives of Sir Thomas Thynne.
Maria Audley, Sir Thomas's first wife, shortly before her death in 1611.

Catherine Lyte-Howard.

Detail from one of Longleat's three surviving Elizabethan fireplaces.
Now in the Servants' Hall, this one was made by Allen Maynard in the 1560s.

Either Thomas was short of money or not anxious to be elevated to the peerage for nothing came of the offer and the family had to wait a further seventy years for a title.

Longleat's calm, its pastoral seclusion, was scarcely trespassed during the years Thomas was its master. The success of a salt pit on the Shropshire estates may have inspired him to open a lead mine in the Mendips, whose output was exported via Bristol. He proved an efficient businessman and the mine's profits were used to develop Longleat's timber plantations, needed now for pit props and smelting. Poaching and horse theft were occasional irritations, but the farms prospered and as Thomas grew older he was content to remain at Longleat with Catherine and his family.

Thomas's eldest son had died when still a boy and his second son, James, was now his heir. In 1626 England drifted into war with France. Two years later the twenty-three-year-old James announced his intentions to follow a 'soldierlike profession', sailed to the Low Countries and joined the Huguenot rebels in their struggle against the French. Encamped before Brabant he wrote to his father of what was perhaps his first experience of war. His company had been chosen to lead an attack on the enemy and early on a May morning he went into battle. Once within musket range he was ordered to supervise the building of two earth redoubts in case retreat became necessary. The French failed to counter-attack and the rebels occupied new positions without 'many being shot either by musket or cannon.'[20] It was a creditable start to his career. His father rewarded him with money and soon afterwards he set off for Rome, Venice and Turkey.

By the date of his return to England in the early 1630s James had matured into a well-travelled young soldier with a promising future. It would seem he met with few obstacles whilst courting and winning Lady Isabella Holland, the beautiful but eccentric daughter of the Earl of Holland. James was knighted after their marriage and the young couple joined Charles I's Court. Then, in 1639, his father died and Sir James Thynne became Longleat's new master.

Thomas's will stated that Catherine was to be sole executor of his estate, itself valued at £60,000. She was also left land worth £6500. Her son Henry Frederick received land and £4000 and her daughter

Elizabeth a legacy of £20,000. James's inheritance was limited to Longleat and its immediate estates. His brother Thomas was left only £1000.

James and his brother were in turn bewildered, shocked and enraged at the favouritism shown the children of their father's second marriage. James and his half-brother, Henry Frederick, were already in dispute over the ownership of the Gloucestershire estates and their father's bias made reconciliation difficult. The will requested Catherine to exchange part of the dower lands with property belonging to James and if she refused – as she did – to appoint Lord Coventry as her co-executor. James ordered an inventory of the dower farms and manors but his bailiff met with a conspiracy of silence. Gradually it became clear that Catherine had threatened the tenantry with eviction if they spoke.

The situation at Longleat became chaotic. The money left Elizabeth was hidden in a room in the house. Lord Coventry had the keys and refused to hand them over either to James or his stepmother. James broke down the door and installed himself amidst the plate, declining to part with so much as a pepper-pot.

James learnt from Longleat's steward what had happened in the week before his father's death. Bewitched by Catherine, Thomas had been persuaded to destroy and replace an earlier will. Whilst he lay bedridden, semi-delirious and in the 'extremity of his sickness', she sat beside him insinuating that the children of his marriage to Maria were all liable to hereditary miscarriage. To guarantee the succession she proposed her son, Henry Frederick, be appointed Longleat's heir. The entire story was a lie: James and Isabella were childless but his brother Thomas had two children. Catherine's deceit was only partly successful. Her husband refused to disown his eldest son, and in the end she contented herself with clauses bequeathing money and land to herself and her family.[21]

James was astounded at his stepmother's intrigue. He entered her rooms and threw her, her son and their belongings out of the house. Longleat's Muniment Room still contains seven boxes of papers dealing with the 'Long Suit' that followed. With Catherine's death in 1650, (somewhat improbably she was buried in Westminster Abbey) much of the argument between the two half-brothers became pointless. In later years they attempted – with little success – to patch up their differences. In 1641 Henry Frederick was knighted and he retired to Gloucestershire.

Sir James Thynne inherited Longleat when collision between King and Parliament was almost inevitable. Proof of Parliament's strength came in the summer of 1641 when he was prevented from purchasing a peerage in case the money went to the king. Such incidents were a warning, and may have influenced his decision to begin provisioning and reorganizing the estate so that by the outbreak of the Civil War in 1642, much had been done to safeguard Longleat's independence. A team of charcoal burners had cleared the woods, new livestock had been bought and barns and mills repaired. Many of Longleat's fifty horses, including 'stray nags' and Dutch coach horses, were sold for fear of requisition. 'I have sold the Old Grey Mare to one Bodnam', wrote the bailiff, 'but she gave him a hefty fall in the yard before he led her away.' Such mishaps interrupted a routine faithfully recorded by the accounts: the ringing of pigs, the building of haystacks, the purchase of coal and a cask of gunpowder. The estate deer were slaughtered and then salted down to prevent confiscation by the military or outright theft by gangs of armed poachers (one night fifteen buck were taken from the woods). Supplies of grain, malt and hops were bought in for storage, and the kitchen garden was walled. Salt, two barrels of herring and a supply of tobacco were delivered to the house. The wine cellars were restocked, and pewter plates and new coats for the servants arrived from Bath. An inventory revealed mice nesting in the blanket chests. The house steward began keeping a detailed account of 'All Sorts of Expenses, both Ordinaries and Extraordinaries, made in your Worship's house.'[22]

These preparations may have been unrelated to the war, which was declared in August. It seems unlikely; expenditure on livestock and fodder was unusually high, and the scope of James's plans suggest he intended to remain neutral. If this is the case, it was an unlikely decision. An experienced soldier, aged thirty-seven, by breeding, training and instinct a Royalist, his failure to take up arms and join the king at Nottingham was uncharacteristic of the man. His surviving correspondence offers no explanation and one can only assume a determination to protect Longleat – at whatever the cost. Both house and estate were undoubtedly vulnerable, being surrounded by cloth towns (such as Frome and Bradford-on-Avon) whose loyalties lay firmly with Parliament. Other events may have helped persuade him. Woodhouse Castle was razed to the ground, a mile from Longleat. His half-brother's Gloucestershire home was demolished, his land confiscated and an annual payment forced from him for the duration of the war. James's reluctance to join the struggle brought bitter reproaches from neighbouring Royalists; reproaches which grew louder when part of the estate was granted an Order of Protection by Parliament. But secretly he assisted the King wherever possible. Evidence suggests that, apart from a £2000 loan, he may also have lent Charles £11,000 to help purchase arms and cannon.[23]

The war gradually drew closer to Longleat. By the spring of 1643 a Roundhead troop was stationed four miles from the house. In April local opinion compelled Sir Edward Hungerford, a friend of James's and Area Commander for the Parliament, to order Captains Jones and Thistlethwayte to take 'thirty musketeers, Corporal Roland with ten horses, and go to Sir James Thynne's house at Longleat, and there seize all the horses, arms, money or plate you can find.'[24]

As the troopers clattered down Longleat's drive the communion plate and family jewellery was hastily buried beneath the cellars. The soldiers had orders to round up the cattle in the park, list all they seized and lock all that was too cumbersome to remove in a room in the house. Hungerford's orders forbidding theft and drunkenness were ignored. The two captains stole saddlery and harness, Captain Jones even abducting a mare from the stables. Their men broke into the wardrobe, cellars and larder, leaving the house as if struck by a whirlwind. But the damage was perhaps a small price to pay for Longleat's preservation and it was never visited again by either Roundhead or Royalist.

The Roundhead intrusion into Longleat proved that no house of its size and influence could stay isolated from the war. Shortages of both men and food affected life on the estate and made it increasingly self-contained. Farm labourers went off to join one or other army and girls were hired to help with the lambing. In summer the housemaids went into the fields to gather in the hay and harvest. Pigeons were added to the diet and, in 1646, over 1500 rabbits were trapped or shot on the heath and woodland surrounding the house.

Three years later the king was executed, the war ended and an uneasy peace returned to the countryside. James received many letters from those made homeless by the war. Some requested employment, others money. Typical was an appeal for £20 from a war widow whose husband 'was of the Royal Party and spent his whole estate in the King's service.' Distressed clergymen pressed their claim for a church living. Disbanded soldiers wrote asking for work as a gamekeeper or forester.[25]

James was generous by nature and it seems probable that he helped wherever possible. If superficially he appeared – as at least one begging letter asserted – 'blessed with happiness and plenty', in reality his private life was a continual source of sorrow and disappointment. His marriage to Isabella had failed. Perhaps the most remarkable of Longleat's mistresses, certainly the most notorious, she found it almost impossible to accept the limitations of marriage. Since childhood she had lived impulsively, obeying only her emotions and instincts. In her youth she secretly had an affair with a Lord Thurles when he was courting her closest friend, Elizabeth Preston. The result was an illegitimate son, sent surreptitiously to France. Lord Thurles and Elizabeth Preston were eventually married. Many years later, whilst writing to both Isabella and Elizabeth from Paris, where the boy was then at school, Lord Thurles muddled the envelopes. Only then did his wife learn of their deception.[26]

The Civil War seemed to encourage Isabella's independence. Early on she and James joined Charles's Court at Oxford. Once installed in the city she surrendered to frivolity, insisting on a liberty and self-expression quite remarkable for the wife of a West Country landowner. In the mornings, with a Mrs Fanshawe – whom one observer described as a whore – she attended chapel at Balliol dressed as an angel. In the afternoons, clad only in 'loose and very inadequate attire', she danced on the banks of the Thames. Reaction was mixed: some accused her of 'forgetting her honour', others were enchanted. One spellbound spectator of her performance wrote: 'Our grove is converted into a Daphne for the ladies and their gallants, and Lady Isabella makes her entry there in a jaunty manner, dressed in a fantastical costume, with a lute before her.'[27] Edmund Waller, the poet, put it more deftly in the first couplet of 'On My Lady Isabella playing a lute.'

'Such moving sounds, from such a careless touch!
So unconcerned herself, and we so much.'

Isabella's visit to Oxford unsettled her. She and James had no
children, there was nothing to detain her at Longleat, and once the
war was over she deserted her husband and moved to London.
Bills and scandal followed in her wake. James gave her generous
alimony, but was eventually compelled to print a public notice
disclaiming liability for her debts.

Once rid of her marital shackles Isabella enjoyed a series of short-
lived affairs, at least one of which resulted in the birth of further
bastard children. She is supposed to have spent much of her time
at an inn in Covent Garden kept by an equally infamous acquaintance,
'Oxford Kate'. After the Restoration she joined Charles II and Queen
Catherine at Court but her behaviour grew more reckless and she
was banished. 'It is a bad sign when such stars fall', wrote one
witness to her departure, noting that the queen had given Isabella
'a box on the ears which Lady Thynne then gave to Mr Gorman to
keep.'[28] In the early 1660s, dissipated by alcohol, prone to hallucina-
tions and apparently 'having met with her own apparition, habit
and every-thing, as in a looking glass',[29] she died. She was a tragic and
extraordinary woman. She produced no heir for Longleat and her
conduct and decline must have saddened James. Her memory
survived to haunt the family, for after James's death some of her
illegitimate children presented themselves as Longleat's rightful
heirs.

In 1660, the year of the Restoration, Sir James Thynne was
appointed High Sheriff of Wiltshire. Earlier in the year, at Assize
time, he had been granted permission to feed his guests meat
during Lent 'so long as public scandal be not made.'[30] (The cook's
accounts record its consumption, hence 'a quarter of beef, surloyne
and rumps, weighing 120 lbs.') The Records of the 1660 Assize
are still preserved at Longleat and amongst the entries are three that
vividly illustrate the gulf between the rural poor and the gentry.

'Mary Atkins, charged with the stealing of two shirts and some
pillows, to be hanged.

Elizabeth Atkins, her sister, to be whipped.

Warren Adworth, charged with the suspicion of stealing a pig,
to be hanged.'[31]

Warren Adworth's guilt was not proven, his annual income was perhaps £7; Sir James Thynne's exceeded £7000. It is perhaps hard for us to comprehend the severity of Adworth's sentence, but it does provide a contrast between the luxury enjoyed inside Longleat and the poverty beyond its walls.

In 1661 James made a further effort to improve the relationship with his half-brother. He wrote to Henry Frederick offering to surrender some land, 'not out of fear, or doubt of my cause, but in affection and strong desire to close up all those unhappy breaches and differences which hath so long been gaping so wide as to devour us.'[32] In response Henry Frederick attempted to take illegal possession of James's London house. Once again the two half-brothers resorted to the courts.

Such incidents were few. The exuberance of the Restoration, so different in character and tone from the austere years of the Commonwealth, led to a change of atmosphere at Longleat. In 1662 a new chaplain was appointed. The interview between James and the Reverend Joseph Glanville, who arrived with a woodcock, partridge and box of tobacco pipes as gifts, took place in the 'rushy parlour'. Once opened the box revealed four turkey eggs. Glanville was offered a local living as well as the chaplaincy and a salary of £30.[33]

The accounts mention extravagant dinners and it seems that James filled the house with his family and friends, amongst them his brother Thomas's son, Tom. One autumn Charles II and Queen Catherine visited Longleat, staying overnight with the entire Court. They came from Bath, and departure was delayed by the queen's insistence on hearing mass before entrusting her soul to a coach and country lanes. Little is known about the visit, only the overturning of the queen's coach on the return journey to Bath has been recorded for posterity.[34]

Isabella's death had caused James increasing concern over the succession. He was determined to bar her illegitimate children as well as Henry Frederick and his sons from inheriting Longleat. In 1665 he made a will leaving Longleat to his brother Thomas and his heirs. He was ill at the time and his recovery seemed unlikely. He was prescribed 'purgative and opening potions' and liberally bled by a Warminster surgeon, whilst the household prepared for his death. In this they were premature, for James's strength gradually returned and within three years he was fit enough to consider improving Longleat.

The spark came in a letter from the Bishop of Salisbury, who had staying his 'good friend, the ingenious Surveyor, Dr Wren'.[35] Christopher Wren had been born only nine miles from Longleat and at the age of thirty-six was already a well-known architect, famous for his plans for rebuilding London after the Great Fire. He was at once summoned to Longleat and prepared a set of plans for the front door, hall and staircase. James was delighted, the work was commissioned, and a start was made on an arch for the hall and a 'handsome rail and baluster' for the staircase. Although the work was eventually completed none of it remains at Longleat. Within thirty years the front door had been removed to Lord Weymouth's School, Warminster, where it still stands. Tragically the staircase was destroyed by Sir Jeffrey Wyatville in the early nineteenth century: the plans have all been lost.[36]

Wren's visit inspired James to further activity. Whilst entertaining Charles II a hole had been knocked in the wall of the upstairs salon so that the king could see the musicians at the far end of the Great Hall. The salon remained unfinished and James ordered it to be completed and the front hall and passages paved. A set of four stag heads was sent from Bavaria to grace the Great Hall, 'such as are large and graceful on moderate terms.' A garden terrace running the length of the south wing was also constructed.

James's health appeared restored as he entered his sixties. Just as the alterations to the house had seemed to open a new chapter in his life, so Isabella's death had ended another. In 1669 an old friend wrote to him from Newmarket (where the Court was staying) suggesting that he remarry, choosing as his second wife an old comrade's daughter who was the 'famed beauty in these parts.' 'What say you?' went on the letter, 'shall I speak a good word for you, for her father's sake you ought to love her a little?'[37] But James was too old for any further romantic adventures. His brother Thomas was dead, his nephew Tom his heir. In October 1670, whilst staying with Tom in Richmond, his health failed and he retired to bed. On the morning of the 12th, he died.

3

'TOM O'TEN THOUSAND'

*'Who'd be a wit in Dryden's cudgelled skin,
Or who'd be rich and senseless like Tom Thynne.'*[1]

John, Earl of Rochester.

In appearance and style Tom Thynne epitomized the Restoration rake. A wardrobe inventory mentions a gold-and-silver-hilted sword, a grey wide-brimmed hat, silk shirts and stockings, 'little pieces of point for Pantaloons', a lace-embroidered waistcoat, black velvet breeches and green frock coat. A private caprice was a seven yard gold-fringed scarf.[2] He inherited Longleat in his early thirties and a portrait painted soon afterwards suggests bravado, affectation and foppishness. The curly hair falling in ringlets over the shoulders, the Roman nose and petulant mouth complete the picture. Amongst his closest friends was the king's illegitimate son, the Duke of Monmouth, in whose company he frequented London's brothels and gaming rooms.

This description is not intended to imply caricature. But the facts are few, we know little about Tom's character. Shortly before Sir James Thynne's death Tom had written to him begging for money to help settle his debts, 'for I am left here without company and without support, not owned by my father, nor encouraged by anybody, and now I must give my creditors a verbal satisfaction, for I despair of giving them a real one.'[3] Longleat's accounts, the clothing, wine lists and banquet expenses, also suggest extravagance and indolence. In one year he bought 168 lbs of gold. In one month eighty dozen bottles of wine were purchased: within two months more was required.

After inheriting the estate Tom was appointed Colonel of the Regiment of Horse of the Wiltshire Militia and elected Member of Parliament for the county. But he rarely occupied Longleat, choosing to live in the family's London house in Cannon Row with few servants and Longleat's ex-gamekeeper, Captain Kidd, as his steward. Longleat he apparently regarded as a rural retreat suitable only for hunting and house parties. The estate provided an income whose total became his nickname, 'Tom o'Ten Thousand', but the £10,000 was spent on pleasure rather than improvement. He relied increasingly on bailiffs and agents and the years of his ownership led to a gradual decline in the efficiency of Longleat's management. But Tom's neglect could not detract from Longleat's splendour and Jan Siberechts' painting of the house, dated 1675, captures its beauty and tranquillity. The painting shows Longleat's south front; climbing roses hug its walls and two fountains rise from rectangular lawns. Servants in orange livery stand at the entrance to the walled garden. Outside the gates are huntsmen and hounds and Tom's coach with its team of six grey coach horses. Meadows and woods recede into the background to the north of the house.

Tom Thynne and his two sisters had been brought up in Richmond. After leaving Oxford he joined the entourage of James, Duke of York, the king's brother and heir to the throne. James was Catholic, and when he married the fifteen-year-old Mary of Modena, widely believed to be the youngest of the Pope's illegitimate daughters, Tom was amongst those who switched allegiance to the Exclusionist Party. The party's main aim was to exclude Catholics from the succession, and by the end of the 1670s it had gained widespread popular support. The Protestant Duke of Monmouth had emerged as its figurehead.

In 1680 Monmouth set out on what amounted to a royal tour through the staunchly Exclusionist West Country. Credited with a miracle, cheered wherever he went, he travelled from one stronghold to the next. It was the beginning of a five-year journey that was to lead him to the executioner's block. In his satirical poem 'Absalom and Achitophel' Dryden described the scene:

> Fame runs before him as the morning star,
> And shouts of joy salute him from afar.
> Each house receives him as a guardian God
> And consecrates the place of his abode.
> But hospitable treats did most commend,
> Wise Issachar, his wealthy Western friend.

Issachar was Tom; as wealthy, though by no means as wise, as

Dryden suggests. His enthusiasm for Monmouth and the Exclusionist cause seems unlimited. When Monmouth arrived at Longleat
flowers were strewn in his path and Tom gave him a lavishly-
equipped team of coach horses. Monmouth's rapturous welcome
at Longleat irritated the king. Aware that the Wiltshire Militia
might be used to help place Monmouth on the throne, the king
deprived Thynne of his command. Despite this setback to his
career Tom's expectations were high and in the summer of 1681
he married the fifteen-year-old Lady Elizabeth Ogle.

Red-headed and unruly, Lady Elizabeth was the only child and
sole heir to the Duke of Northumberland. Born a Percy, she would
one day inherit a vast estate of moorland and hills that stretched
across the Border country. She was also the most eligible widow
in the land. After her father's death she had been sent to live with
her grandmother, the dowager Duchess of Northumberland, at
Petworth in Sussex. At thirteen, without either her knowledge or
consent, she was married to the Earl of Ogle. Her grandmother
arranged the match, one of whose conditions was that Elizabeth
should continue to live at Petworth without her husband. The
marriage was never consummated and within a year Lord Ogle
was dead.

Shortly after Lord Ogle's death the dowager Duchess began
considering the choice of a suitable second husband for her grand-
daughter. When Tom Thynne's name was suggested, she accepted
at once. An influential landowner of indisputable wealth, his friendship with Monmouth could have far-reaching consequences. It
seems that Tom was equally eager to marry Elizabeth and to press
his case he gained the support of a Major Brett and Elizabeth's old
nurse, Mrs Potter. The major was promised the lease of a rectory
for his help and Mrs Potter £500 within ten days of the wedding.

On 14 July the Duchess, Elizabeth and Tom gathered secretly
in the parlour of Brett's Surrey home. Elizabeth was in a difficult
and obstinate mood. She had never met her proposed husband, her
year of mourning was not yet over and Tom insisted that no
clergyman connected with the Percys be present. Longleat's ex-
chaplain conducted the service and as disgruntled bride and ambitious groom stood side by side their protestations of mutual affection
must have sounded hollow and thin. Elizabeth promised Tom land;

he in turn agreed to give her an annual £2000 allowance. According to a statement made later by Major Brett, on the words 'With all my worldly goods I thee endow', Tom produced a hundred gold guineas, placed them on a prayer-book and held it out towards his wife. Without any hesitation Elizabeth snatched the money, wrapped it in a handkerchief and thrust it down her bodice. The married couple exchanged rings and parted.[4]

It was an irreverent and mercenary ceremony. Elizabeth's family were quick to dispute her dowry and Tom was forced to take them to court. Major Brett and Mrs Potter were ignored (later they brought an action against Tom's executors but failed to obtain judgement). But marriage encouraged Tom to begin renovating and modernizing Longleat. A suite of rooms was prepared for his bride in the west wing, the drawing- and dining-rooms were finished, and a back staircase for the servants and a new stable block were built. His fondness for Elizabeth appears genuine. Not so her grandmother, who regarded the marriage as a financial agreement. Elizabeth soon realized this, the two women quarrelled, and she left Petworth to stay at the British embassy in Holland.

At the wedding it had been agreed that Elizabeth should join her husband after a year. But it seems she was in no hurry to settle in Longleat, take on the monotonous duties of its mistress and install herself, like some bought chattel, in Tom's bed. Safe from an interfering grandmother and husbands she did not love, Elizabeth enjoyed the compliments and flattery that collected round her in Holland.

Amongst those who hoped to have an affair with her was a Swedish count, John Konigsmark. The twenty-two-year-old count had first met Elizabeth after Lord Ogle's death, but his wealth and influence were no match for Thynne's and he left London to fight in North Africa. Facts about Konigsmark are scarce and their accuracy is doubtful. Most published accounts of his life date from the mid-nineteenth century, a period much given to romantic sentiment, and the line between fact and fiction has become blurred. His biographers insist on his reputation as a lover and adventurer, describing him in such phrases as 'a person to dazzle any eyes, and to aspire to any prize that daring might win.'[5] It seems probable that at the age of eighteen he was wounded fighting with the Knights of St John of Malta against Barbary pirates.[6] A French countess remembers him in her memoirs as being nearly gored to death at a Madrid bullfight, dressed in black, his white plume studded with diamonds and wearing the favours of a Spanish princess.[7] Another account of his career mentions the wife of an English peer who deserted her husband and followed him round Europe dressed as his page.[8] In short he was a lady-killer and on meeting him again, it seems that Elizabeth fell hopelessly in love.

Either alone, or encouraged by Elizabeth, Konigsmark became convinced that Tom Thynne was the only obstacle to their eventual marriage. He issued Tom with two challenges to a duel. Both were refused, but it may be possible – for the reports are many and contradictory – that Tom sent Captain Kidd over to Holland to persuade the count, by force if necessary, that his interest in Elizabeth was unwelcome. Early in 1682 it was rumoured that Konigsmark had caused the break-up of the Thynnes' marriage. On 2 February, accompanied by his steward Captain Vratz, and a Polish groom, George Boroski, the count landed at Gravesend and secretly took up residence in London. The legends surrounding Konigsmark have obscured his unpleasantness. The visit had one purpose, the assassination of Tom Thynne.

Konigsmark was anxious to avoid implication in the murder plot and left the planning to his steward, a brave but stubborn German who seems to have had few qualms about the nature of his responsibility. On a previous visit to London Vratz had met a Swedish mercenary called John Stern. The friendship was renewed and Stern persuaded to help plan the attack. They hoped to employ an Italian assassin to commit the murder. Thynne would be ambushed at night by three footpads misled into believing they were taking part in a robbery and stabbed to death in the confusion. But the scheme proved difficult to implement and after further discussion they decided to ambush Thynne themselves, choosing a moment when he was alone in his coach.[9]

On Sunday 12 February Vratz, Stern and Boroski gathered at a Whitehall tavern. Vratz explained his plan to Boroski, gave him a blunderbuss and told him that he had been selected to kill a man on behalf of his master. The Pole was apprehensive and confused. For the past year he had 'not been guilty of one act either of drunkenness or uncleanness, of swearing or lying.'[10] He went into another room, repeated the Lord's Prayer and awaited divine guidance. When none came he decided that 'God had appointed that he should do the killing.'[11]

Tom Thynne was ignorant of his intended fate. He spent the Sunday with Monmouth and a group of friends riding in St James's Park. In the early evening he parted from Monmouth and paid a brief call on the dowager Duchess of Northumberland at her house in Pall Mall. After leaving he instructed his coachman to return to Cannon Row. As the coach rattled over the cobbles their way was lit by linkmen carrying torches. Behind them in the darkness and keeping well out of sight were Vratz, Boroski and Stern. The three men had been following Tom since early afternoon, waiting for an opportunity to launch their attack. Stern was slightly to the rear of the others. Fatigue, and the growing conviction that Vratz had purposely given him the slowest horse so that only he would be caught, made him feel that 'though he was not drunk, yet he was like one drunk, for he was almost stupid.'[12]

As Thynne's coach reached the eastern end of Pall Mall, Vratz, followed closely by Boroski, galloped forward. Reining in alongside the coach he ordered the Pole to shoot its occupant. Boroski aimed the blunderbuss at Thynne and pulled the trigger. To clear a passage and speed their escape Vratz shouted 'A race! A race!' and he and Boroski immediately disappeared towards Piccadilly. The gunshot and shouting woke Stern from his daze and realizing what must have happened he set off in pursuit. Thynne's own men gave chase but were quickly given the slip.

Tom had been wounded in four places and death was inevitable. Once the coach reached Cannon Row a doctor and Monmouth were called and the king notified. A London magistrate, Sir John Reresby, has left us a lively account of the events that followed the attack.[13] He was with the king when the news reached Whitehall and mentions in his memoirs that Charles first suspected an anti-catholic plot. As the story spread through London,

> All women wept, all Mankind grieved sore,
> Salt tears ran trickling like the Common Shore,
> And children with their infant voices rose.[14]

Grub Street sentiment was one thing, attempted political assassination another. Improbable rumours circulated. Monmouth had been the intended victim; a Scottish army led by the Duke of York was marching south; prominent Exclusionists were to be murdered as they slept. But once it became clear that the attack on Thynne was not part of a national conspiracy fashionable society began savouring the scandal. Some suggested that Lady Thynne had ordered her husband's murder. Tom and Monmouth had once shared the same mistress, a Miss Trevor who did 'full justice to a white bosom, ogled significantly and danced voluptuously.'[15] She had once discovered Monmouth in bed with another woman and, having been seduced by Tom under a promise of marriage, gave birth to a daughter who died in infancy. Perhaps she had planned revenge on both her lovers? Miss Trevor was found, declared innocent and the hunt continued.

After leaving the king Reresby was 'just stepping into bed' when Captain Kidd arrived asking for an immediate 'hue and cry' to be granted. Reresby agreed to the request and special constables were enrolled to assist the search. Hard on Kidd's heels came a messenger from Monmouth requesting that he join them without delay. Reresby dressed and was driven through the deserted streets to Cannon Row. The magistrate's motive for co-operation remains unclear. But he had a judicial duty to mount an enquiry and perhaps hoped to please both king and Monmouth by making an early arrest.

During the night Tom Thynne's condition rapidly deteriorated. He died at six in the morning, bleeding heavily from the stomach and surrounded by Monmouth and a group of close friends. Reresby issued warrants for the arrest of the unknown assassins and ordered a close watch to be kept on all ports. The magistrate received his first definite clues shortly after dawn. On the previous day a sedan chairman had carried Stern to the Whitehall tavern. He now arrived at Cannon Row, asked for Reresby and told him that when entering the inn to collect his fare he had seen Stern and two other foreigners loading pistols and a blunderbuss. A prostitute who had befriended Vratz's servant was the next witness to appear. After her departure Reresby and Monmouth organized a house-to-house search for the servant. His capture provided the breakthrough. He told them that Vratz had employed him to track the movements of Thynne's coach. The mention of Vratz implicated Konigsmark and the plot began to assume both shape and motive. Further questioning revealed Vratz's address, and bursting unannounced into his lodgings Reresby and Monmouth found the captain asleep. A parcel containing a blunderbuss and other weapons lay on a table. Vratz told Reresby where his accomplices were hiding and by midday all three men had been arrested.

Later that day they appeared before the king. Each was examined separately, Vratz first. He admitted being employed by Konigsmark and told the king that he stopped the coach intending to challenge Thynne to a duel, but that Boroski, mistaking his orders, had opened fire. Initially Boroski denied all knowledge of the murder. But, confronted by the captain's statement, confessed firing the blunder-buss into the coach. He swore that Vratz had ordered him to kill Thynne and, on being shown the weapons found in the captain's room, recognized a sword which he insisted belonged to Konigs-mark. Stern appeared last. He was nervous and frightened and stated that when Thynne had been shot he was innocently returning to his lodgings after riding with Vratz in St James's Park. He swore that he had played no part in the ambush and knew nothing about either a duel or murder plot. None of this impressed Reresby and all three men, 'whose cruelties are to be admired, and whose rewards will doubtless in little time be awarded them', were charged with murder and removed to Newgate prison.

The arrest of the murderers delighted the king. The crime lacked political significance and no Englishman appeared to be involved. After questioning Konigsmark's younger brother, a student at a London military academy, Reresby searched the count's last known address. He had vanished, no one knew where to, and Thynne's brother-in-law immediately offered a substantial reward for informa-tion leading to his capture.

On Monday morning, after hearing news of Thynne's death and Vratz's arrest, Konisgmark fled London and went to stay with a Swedish merchant in Rotherhithe. On Thursday he left for Graves-end, telling his host that he planned to board a ship sailing for Sweden. The merchant's failure to act earlier on this information remains unexplained. But on Sunday morning, suspicious of Konigsmark's behaviour and perhaps eager to claim the reward, he rode into London and told Captain Kidd that he knew where the count might be hiding. Monmouth's own steward was detailed to investigate and he reached the small Kentish port in the late afternoon, exactly a week after the murder.

After arriving in Gravesend Konigsmark had persuaded a local wherryman to put to sea in the hope of hailing a Scandinavia-bound ship. Afloat there was less chance of being caught and they remained in the Thames estuary for three days. The count paid the wherryman a generous fare, explaining that he was an apprentice jeweller incorrectly suspected of theft who had to leave the country before returning to clear his name. By Sunday no ship had been sighted. Konigsmark suffered sea-sickness and provisions were low. They returned to harbour and the count, disguised in a 'black old peruke, with his hair tied up like a woman's and the rest hung down his back under his coat, his own being very white',[16] installed himself in the darkest corner of a quayside inn.

Monmouth's steward's account of Konigsmark's capture was published as a broadsheet, now preserved in the British Museum. After reaching Gravesend he walked round the town questioning publicans and boatmen until he had established where Konigsmark was hiding. Eventually he entered the inn, approached the count and informed him that he held a warrant for his arrest. Konigsmark's reply was characteristically affected. He threw off his wig and said, 'Tis a stain upon my blood but one good action in the wars will wash it all away.' He seemed indifferent to his arrest, even suggesting that Tom Thynne's death was of little importance. On learning that the king intended to punish the guilty he passed 'a great many compliments and desired to be civilly used.'[17] Before being taken back to London he insisted on thanking his captors for their courtesy by distributing money for the purchase of beer and tobacco.

On arrival in London the count was led before the king. He was questioned, denied any knowledge of the murder plot and was sent to Newgate. There he lodged in the governor's house, ate and drank to excess and received a steady flow of fashionable visitors. Konigsmark had chosen his part carefully and played it with brilliance. By the date of the trial his light-hearted banter, charm and good-humoured innocence had impressed all who met him.[18]

Stern, Boroski and Vratz were neither so fortunate or subtle. They were visited in Newgate by Dr Burnet, a celebrated theologian and later Bishop of Salisbury, and an account of his visit was eventually published. Stern seemed close to insanity. He now confessed his guilt, adding that prior to the murder he had never been guilty of 'any act of cruelty or treachery, of blasphemy or rapes.'[19] He spent his time in prison writing a lengthy confession and singing Lutheran hymns. Boroski's mind was equally erratic. He had been reading aloud from a book of religious tracts in an attempt to keep awake. The result was partial hallucination and only after a vision – in which a woman he had known in Poland kept appearing – did he finally calm down. Vratz was made of sterner stuff. He told his visitor that he had no intention of making his confession to some 'meddling and inquisitive . . . divine'. As for Thynne, he was dead, and no English cleric breathing fire and brimstone could bring him back to life.[20]

The trial of the four accused took place in the Old Bailey. Konigsmark rejected eighteen jurors before a half-foreign jury was sworn in and it seems possible that the final verdict had been decided in advance. In a private conversation prior to the trial the king told Reresby that he expected Konigsmark to be acquitted. Reresby was approached by the principal of the military academy at which the count's younger brother was a student and offered money in return for ensuring an acquittal. John Evelyn's diaries mention that the jury was corrupt.[21]

Stern and Boroski were doomed the moment they entered the court. Vratz's assertion that he had been present at the scene of 'this hellish murder' proved his complicity. When Konigsmark entered the dock, the judge, Sir Francis Pemberton, refused as evidence an earlier statement by Stern that he had seen a letter signed by the count promising a reward to whoever killed Thynne. Pemberton's ruling revealed his prejudice and Monmouth, sitting in court with Thynne's family, protested. Pemberton had almost certainly been bribed. He ordered Monmouth to remain seated and the hearing continued.[22]

Other elements of the trial bordered on farce. When Konigsmark was asked to explain his absence from polite society during his stay in London, he replied that he was receiving treatment for venereal disease, could neither dance nor drink and did 'not care to appear in public until the course of his prescription was over.'[23] Potentially more damaging to his case was public knowledge of his feud with Thynne. The count insisted that on learning of the murder he had feared an attempt at revenge by Thynne's family and, although innocent, thought it wise to return to Sweden. Asked a motive for the crime he suggested that Vratz had acted independently, perhaps hoping to please him and speed his eventual marriage to Lady Elizabeth.

Pemberton did all he could to protect the count from cross-examination. In his final summing-up he labelled the three other accused as 'barbarous villains' who were 'not fit to look upon themselves to be accounted men' and advised the jury to acquit Konigsmark.[24] In his opinion the count's absence from the scene of the crime was adequate proof of his innocence. Late in the afternoon Boroski, Stern and Vratz were found guilty of wilful murder and condemned to be hung in Pall Mall, at the place where the murder had been committed, from gibbets erected specially for the purpose. Count John Konigsmark left the Old Bailey a free man.

Monmouth and Tom's family were astounded. Challenges to a duel were issued but the king forbade the meeting to take place, advising the count to leave the country. Three weeks after Thynne's death he boarded a ship for Sweden leaving his accomplices to their fate.

Dr Burnet again visited Newgate. Stern had begged for his life at the trial and been contemptuously dismissed as a 'common murderer' by Vratz. He was now in a religious trance and anxious to be executed instead of hung so that the evil within his body could be released. After leaving Stern, Burnet visited Vratz in the hope of persuading him to make a confession. He spoke at length of eternal damnation and 'Hell's great furnace'. Vratz, more concerned with his vanity than the character of eternity, announced that he was not such a fool as to believe that 'souls could fry in a material fire, or be roasted as meat on a great hearth', and demanded to be taken to the gallows in a coach rather than a cart.[25] His request was refused.

Boroski's short confession, scattered with such phrases as 'What a pity I should fall into this unexpected misfortune',[26] reveals his naïveté. He understood no English, the ritualistic precision of the legal system had escaped him and he was understandably dejected. He spent his last night in Newgate with Stern. Whilst Vratz slept peacefully next door the two men took it in turn to pray. In the morning Stern was discovered pacing his cell chanting psalms. Tears flowed down his face which he insisted were not 'tears of sorrow but flowed from the abundance of his joy.'[27] Shortly before noon the three men were placed on the cart and driven through the bustling streets to Pall Mall.

News that there was to be a public hanging in Pall Mall seems to have attracted a large crowd. The 'Bloody and Inhumane Murderers' were all foreign, and to add spice to the occasion the 'Horrid and Barbarous Murder' smacked of society scandal. Broadsheets announced the time and place of the hanging and, by midday, Pall Mall was so congested that Monmouth and Reresby had difficulty in reaching the gallows.

Vratz appeared to be smiling as the cart drew up beneath the line of nooses. Neither trembling nor complaining as the rope was placed round his neck, 'his manner savouring much of gallantry, but not at all of Religion',[28] he asked the hangman if he could dispense with the customary blindfold. 'Never', wrote John Evelyn, 'man went so unconcerned for his sad fate.'[29] Boroski, shivering with fear, stood silent as the noose was fastened. Stern verged on hysteria. He handed Dr Burnet his confession and mumbled that he was dying for the benefit of a man he had never met, a woman he had never seen and a dead man of whom he knew nothing.[30] The black hood was lowered over his head. After standing for fifteen minutes with the nooses round their necks the condemned men were asked whether they were prepared for the cart to be removed. Vratz assented. Soon afterwards Tom Thynne's three murderers were declared dead.

Two weeks later John Evelyn was taken to view Vratz's body. It had been embalmed – a process then in its infancy in this country – and was to be shipped back to Germany for burial. His flesh was 'florid, soft and full, as if the person was only sleeping.' He lay exposed in a lead-lined coffin, 'too magnificent for so daring and horrid a murderer.'[31] Stern had been buried, but Boroski's corpse had been hung in chains in the Mile End Road as a salutary warning to all foreigners entering London.

Konigsmark outlived his fellow conspirators by only five years. In 1687 he joined an expedition against the Turks and died at the Siege of Argos. His biographers disagree as to the cause of death. Some mention pleurisy; others, that he died in action. Women were the family's downfall. In 1694 his younger brother was assassinated after being seen leaving the bedroom of Sophia of Zell, George I's first wife and mother of George II.

Lady Elizabeth soon recovered from the death of her second husband. Four months after the murder she married the Duke of Somerset, an extreme autocrat whose daughters were made to stand in his presence and whose servants addressed him in sign language. As Duchess of Somerset she became a favourite of Queen Anne. The satirist Jonathan Swift was amongst her enemies and in the *Windsor Prophecy* published a scathing attack on her past.

> And, dear England, if aught I understand,
> Beware of carrots from *Northumberland*.
> Carrots sown *Thynn* a deep root may get
> If so they be in *Somer set*;
> Their *Conyngs mark* thou; for I have been told
> They assassin when young, and poison when old.

As for Tom Thynne, he acquired dignity in death. As one of Monmouth's staunchest supporters we may suppose he would have been executed for taking part in the rebellion of 1685. Instead he was buried in Westminster Abbey and a marble bas-relief depicting the ambush was erected.

Tom Thynne is remembered today as 'Tom o'Ten Thousand'. But a bawdy epitaph that circulated after his death offers an alternative summary of his career and character.

> Here lies Tom Thynne of Longleat Hall
> Who never would have miscarried,
> Had he married the woman he lay withal
> Or laid with the woman he married.[32]

4

PROSPECTS OF PARADISE

*'Providence makes way for the advantages of good men by
the ill designs of the bad.'*[1]

Lord Coventry to Sir Thomas Thynne on
learning of Tom's murder.

First reports from Longleat were discouraging. The gardens were a
quagmire, livestock had been sold, fields lay fallow and the stables
silent. Servants had been dismissed and others were owed four
months' wages. Tom had bequeathed the furniture to his brother-
in-law. Only a cane-backed chair and shove-ha'penny table too
heavy to lift remained in the house. Longleat stood empty, damp and
neglected.

During the weeks that followed Tom's murder Sir Thomas
Thynne, cousin and heir to the estate, waited impatiently for his
claim to be confirmed. Much depended on Tom's widow, the terms
of their marriage contract and the likelihood of her remarrying.
'No-one', wrote a friend, 'will let slip such a morsel'. Thomas felt
certain Lady Elizabeth would not sacrifice Longleat without first
disputing its ownership. Anticipating failure when a suitor crossed
to Holland 'to make love to the lady', he was surprised and delighted
when she became Duchess of Somerset.[2]

By the autumn of 1682 Longleat was legally Sir Thomas's property. In early December he was created 1st Viscount Weymouth
by Charles II. The choice of name remains unexplained. Although
the family owned land in Dorset their links with Weymouth were
tenuous and it seems probable that the king was responsible for its
selection. Shortly before Christmas, accompanied by fiddlers,
trumpeters and drums, the forty-two-year-old Thomas, his wife and
two small children left London by coach on the first stage of the
journey to their new home.

With his square boyish face, prominent nose and high forehead framed by a shoulder-length wig, Thomas's portrait suggests common sense and an even temper: rare virtues in the Thynnes. Methodical and self-assured, his talents were known and reputation secure. From the moment he inherited it was clear he intended to transform Longleat into a cohesive domain held together by efficient bailiffs and loyalty to a shared prosperity. It was an ambitious undertaking, but by the date of his death in 1714 the estate had been expanded to nearly 50,000 acres. Embracing both town and country, agriculture and commerce, cottager, parson, merchant and farmer, Longleat flourished during a period of national stability when the beginnings of enclosure and improvements in farming were adding to the rent roll and creating the comfortable, cultured world of the English country house. It was a crucial phase in Longleat's development and it is ironic that Thomas belonged to the one branch of the family that Sir James had wished excluded from the succession.

Thomas Thynne was born in 1640, the eldest son of Henry Frederick, Sir James's half-brother. Before entering Oxford he studied under William Burton, an 'excellent Latinist, noted Philologist, well skilled in the tongues, and an excellent Critic and Antiquary',[3] who was later to leave him his collection of coins and manuscripts – many of which still remain in Longleat. After the Restoration he joined the Duke of York's household as a Gentleman of the Bedchamber. At the age of twenty-six he was appointed Special Envoy to the Swedish Court. His official instructions cast little light on the years spent in Stockholm but do mention the provision of funds to buy secret information helpful to the Government. He sailed from Greenwich in the *Warspite*.[4] It seems that gale-force winds accompanied him. A letter from his mother, written in a barely legible hand on the day after he sailed, records her anxiety lest the *Warspite* capsize and her son drown.

By 1672 Thomas had returned to England to take up an appointment as Commissioner for Naval Prices in the Dutch wars, a post that allowed him to court Frances Finch, the twenty-five-year-old daughter of the Earl of Winchelsea. His brother James was amongst those who wrote to him after their engagement 'which is news that I cannot but think myself concerned in, and yet, although it was my fate to be amongst the last that heard of it, yet I can with great

71

confidence challenge a place amongst the first that wished it.'[5]
A letter from Thomas's tutor at Oxford warning him of indulging
the 'grosser appetites' was also received.[6] Thomas and Frances were
married by the end of the year. Although fair-haired and pretty,
Frances was excitable and easily unnerved. Her dowry provided
the Thynnes with £20,000, a London house and, perhaps the most
important of any extension to Longleat's original acreage, a 22,000-
acre Irish estate in County Monaghan.

Within a year of the marriage 'it pleased God to make my wife
last night the Mother of a very little but lively girl.'[7] A second daughter died in infancy. In 1676, after 'a sharp but not tedious labour' in
which it was first feared the child was stillborn, Frances gave birth
to a son. He was named Henry and described by Thomas as a 'weak
child, who by his sleeping and not much growing I am inclined
to think came before his time.'[8] As Henry grew older he tried the
patience of both his father and long-suffering tutor, Mr Repington.
Dull, fat and often ill, he turned into an indolent young aristocrat
who knew the lyrics of a thousand light operas, but – if we are to
believe Repington – he was dissuaded from singing them, 'his voice
being very unpleasant.'[9]

Before inheriting Longleat Thomas and Frances lived in Soho,
(then a residential London suburb which looked north across fields).
Thomas's three brothers and two sisters were regular visitors and it
seems they maintained a close and lasting friendship with one
another. Longleat is not mentioned in the few letters surviving from
this period, but their discussion about servants' wages, the cost of a
coach and need for economy, lends a surprisingly provincial flavour
to much of their correspondence.

Thomas's second brother, James, was a jovial bachelor whose
innumerable love affairs with married women withered as rapidly
as they blossomed. Hawk, horse and hound dominated his life. He
kept his own race-horses and employed a family of jockeys who
rode 'switch to spur'.[10] 'I hear', wrote Thomas on one occasion,
'your rider at Stonehenge had foul play showed him, though he
win both the plates, which is evidence of the goodness of your
horses, and therefore I doubt not that you had a good price for him.'[11]
In the mid-1670s James persuaded his brother to purchase a stud of
horses and race them at Newmarket in the Thynne colours. He was
preoccupied with their diet and welfare and amongst his papers are

recipes for medicinal purges. Thomas's own interest in horses was brief. After inheriting Longleat he decided not to keep hounds, a decision which James greeted with disbelief and never forgave.

Thomas's second brother was named Henry Frederick after their father. Portly, staid, a model of respectability, he was a successful civil servant who in turn was Keeper of the Royal Library, Secretary to the Chancellor, Clerk to the Privy Council and Treasurer to Charles II's widow. Thomas's third brother died while young.

This then was the family into whose hands Longleat had so unexpectedly fallen. Close-knit, influential and ambitious, headed by a brother they all respected and related by marriage to many of England's leading families, they could view their future prospects with composure and exhilaration. If fate had led them to Longleat, then they would transform it into paradise.

Thomas and Frances's hired coach took three days to travel the hundred miles between London and Longleat. Tom's murder had made Frances 'more fearful than I used to be.'[12] It was mid-winter, their coach had wooden shutters instead of windows and the long journey with two children exhausted her.

Their arrival at Longleat has passed into obscurity. The accounts mention no festive welcome, merely a gift of two fish pies from a local mayor. It was an inauspicious beginning to their new life. In later years myth and exaggeration must have collected round tales of that first winter. Longleat was still unfurnished, the roof leaked and Henry succumbed to a succession of minor illnesses. It was bitterly cold. A letter mentions a case of frostbite and the accounts record 'throwing the snow from the house top.' Had Thomas ventured far from the house he would have been confronted by an even bleaker picture. Many of the estate cottages were in need of repair. The park fencing had fallen and sheep and deer either strayed or were buried by drifting snow.

Thomas appointed a London agent, farm bailiff and steward for Longleat soon after moving into the house. He seems to have sought and acted on their advice and owed to them much of the credit for the estate's recovery. His mother had written suggesting he choose a steward who would be a 'companion and friend as well as merely useful in your great works.'[13] The appointment of Thomas Allen is proof he heeded her counsel. Allen's correspondence suggests wit and ability. His letters to Thomas and his neatly-kept accounts breathe life into the monotonous detail of Longleat's improvement.

In the spring of 1683 Thomas and his steward set to work. The fields were manured and a start made on draining the park. A woodman was employed to supervise a team of labourers who cleared the underwood, cut rushes, laid hedges and planted stands of saplings. The bailiff toured West Country markets buying livestock. Coach and heavy horses were bought, grooms and a coachman hired. A small cottage was built on the banks of the stream and a permanent fisherman employed to trap otters, pike and other predators. The gamekeepers began clearing the woods of vermin. The fish-still was rebuilt, two new granaries started and thatchers hired to reroof barns.

By early summer it must have been obvious to the cottagers that their new landlord intended improvement. Having subsisted on Parish Relief, spinning yarn and making buttons (outwork from the local cloth trade), they looked forward to regular wages, work for their children in Longleat's kitchens, stables and dairy, and some form of support (normally timber and flour) during periods of hardship.

But not all Thomas's tenants respected him. His politics were the opposite of Tom Thynne's and many of the cottagers continued to support Monmouth and the Exclusionist cause. Some did not hesitate to voice their dislike in public: 'Richard Arnett, warrener, deposeth that on or about the 7th of July he saw Robert Fitzclothier in the porch of George Clarke's house, where he did hear him say these words; 'Let my Lord Weymouth kiss my arse, and tell him so when thou seest him.'[14]

Such invitations were outnumbered by requests for employment. By the end of July some forty labourers were digging drainage ditches to improve the grazing in meadows near the house. Thomas Allen's accounts chronicle the progress, and even a random selection evokes energy and bustle.

'Widow Huntley for picking cowslips   7/6d
Solomon Hays, blacksmith for 8 cart horse shoes   5/4d
To Jane, dairymaid, for 5 days making butter and cheese 1/8d
John Rabbits, for going 39 days with a plough   17/-'[15]
The briefest list gives substance to the portrait of a vigorous and

thriving estate. A chandler, wheelwright, cooper and brewer are all mentioned as being employed for short periods. By autumn Longleat had acquired a new housekeeper and it seems the house-maids in her charge were soon walking the hedgerows to gather flowers and herbs. Once dried and stored their fragrance must have permeated the house's north-eastern corner where the still-room was situated. Bordered on one side by sculleries and on the other by the housemaids' room, the business of keeping its shelves laden went on whenever idle hands needed an occupation.

New maids, footmen, Brotherton the butler and a 'boy at the back door' (who also served as chimney sweep) joined the house-hold. Frances designed a special livery for the servants. The maids wore muslin caps and printed chintz dresses, whilst the footmen acquired mustard-yellow coats, black silver-trimmed waistcoats, knee breeches and silk stockings. On formal occasions they added to their dignity by placing a cocked hat, complete with silver braid and crested buttons, on their lightly-powdered and periwigged heads. The housekeeper's accounts record the purchase of sewing materials, bales of silk and flannel, medicines and bedding. The household settled down under Frances's direction, gradually assum-ing the stately calm of any well-administered country house.

Thomas seems to have been indifferent to Longleat's domestic management. Determined to redesign the interior of the east wing he sent Henry Frederick a copy of his plans 'which I pray you show Sir Christopher Wren and beg his advice in it, as he partly knows the house and is better able to judge it.' Thomas proposed reducing the length of the Long Gallery by building bedrooms at either end. Each bedroom would be entered by glass doors which, when open, would return the Long Gallery to its original length and allow ample space for dancing. 'Pray ask Sir Christopher', continued Thomas, 'what size he will have the glass doors of, barn doors are not proper for bedchambers. If he can contrive it better having the dimensions of all before him, I shall be thankful, either in money if he will take it, or by sending him a buck in the summer.'[16]

Thomas's scheme was never realized and it seems unlikely that Wren was consulted. Instead he spent £2000 replacing the Long Gallery's sixteenth-century leaded windows to improve his view of the gardens, a costly but minor alteration. The destruction of the panelled Elizabethan Long Gallery was delayed until the 4th

Marquess of Bath's passion for the Italian style led to the redecoration of the State Rooms in the 1870s.

Longleat's modernization was a slow and vexing process. For several months in 1683 Thomas and his family sought refuge from the confusion by returning to their London house. A professional architect was appointed to supervise the builders and eventually the roof was releaded, many of the rooms painted walnut or ochre and fireplaces installed. A start was made on converting part of the house into new kitchens and a chapel. A year later the architect reported that the 'chapel looks very well. Although neither painted nor wholly glazed and paved, t'will be very noble when finished.'[17] After completion it was consecrated by a local clergyman whose sermon was published as a pamphlet. Plate and furnishings were bought and Thomas decided to appoint a chaplain. The chance to combine spiritual duties with Longleat's secular pleasures inspired numerous applicants and, after some deliberation, a Dr King was given the post. Six years later failing health persuaded him to tender his resignation: an 'inconsistent temper' encouraged Thomas to accept.[18]

Thomas's attitude to his position as a landowner was characterized by good intentions. Shortly before inheriting Longleat he had written to his father, 'My whole life shall be a continual act of service.'[19] Although he tended to confuse service with improvement and improvement with extravagance, it seems both he and Frances believed they enjoyed a simple and frugal existence. Thomas's consumption of claret was unremarkable. His interest in the chase only cursory. Though he had once found it 'pleasant to be pleasing on the subject of ladies', he had taken the advice of a friend who assured him 'that past follies of that nature are now a greater trouble than they ever were a pleasure.'[20] The only diversion of which he never tired was gardening and, as he grew older, Longleat's gardens absorbed increasing amounts of his energy and income. Between 1683 and the end of the century he spent £30,000 (at least £200,000 in modern figures) on earth removal, planting and construction work of almost epic proportion. By the date of his death seventy acres of formal garden offered evidence of his ambition to surround the house with a paradise that matched its splendour.

Thomas was fortunate to possess the money and live through an age when gardening matured into an exact and considerable science. Labour was plentiful and cheap. Rare plants that had been imported from the Indies aboard ships of the East India Company were raised at Longleat alongside sturdy native stock. Root selection and grafting were practised, hot-houses and forcing-frames erected. Gradually the fruit bowl set before the family at each meal began to hold an exotic mountain of peaches, apricots, oranges and melons.

Longleat's gardens were laid out to the east of the house and combined two distinctive styles, the grand French garden originated at Versailles and the intimate Dutch garden. Initially they were designed and stocked by the Brompton Nurseries, whose hundred-acre site west of Tuthill Fields is now buried beneath the museums of South Kensington. Thomas Allen supervised the construction work and the Brompton Nurseries supplied a gardener. Thomas is likely to have given the appointment careful consideration. Prior to inheriting Longleat he had employed a gardener who was a Peeping Tom and spent much of the day 'being careful to walk before' Frances's window whenever she was alone in her room. Dismissal was the only remedy, but his replacement had an equally salacious reputation. Rumour reached Thomas that he had 'married two widows and left several bastards upon the parish.'[21] This was denied, but proved only a reprieve, for it was eventually discovered that he was removing and selling plants from the borders.

Discussion about the respective state of each other's gardens was always a familiar topic between Thomas and his brothers. A certain amount of rivalry can perhaps be detected in the race to complete various schemes. Thomas seems to have been obsessed by what he chose to describe as 'my water works'. To his dismay Henry Frederick completed a fountain in his Middlesex garden before even the piping had been laid at Longleat. He need not have worried, for his brother then discovered that his new fountain lacked sufficient water pressure to operate and would have to be rebuilt.

Despite setbacks Longleat's gardens took shape. The pond was drained and the stream temporarily rechannelled. A letter from Allen mentions that 'the terrace walks are raised and levelled. The Canals and the arches are finished on both sides, but the western part of the north wall of the garden is somewhat shrunk, the foundations settling, so that it must be new laid again. It is very difficult to procure teams in the country to fetch gravel. They are cutting the quick-set hedges in the Frome walk, leaving the crab trees growing upon the hedge.'[22] The accounts for 1694 record numerous purchases connected with the gardens: 2000 cabbages, 100,000 bricks, 62 spades and 15 bushels of fresh deer's dung amongst them.[23]

Charles II died in 1685 and was succeeded on the throne by the Duke of York, now James II. Thomas attended the coronation, returning to London in early June to be painted wearing his coronation robes. Henry was away at school. Frances, apprehensive about being pregnant for the first time in nine years, was alone at Longleat with the servants. It seemed as if nothing could disturb their lives. Summer loomed ahead. The gardeners were planting hedges round an orchard to keep out deer and the bailiff was preparing for haymaking. On 13 June the Duke of Monmouth landed at Lyme Regis in Dorset with four cannon, a handful of soldiers and only one purpose – to oust James from the throne. At his side rode Captain Kidd, once Tom Thynne's steward and Longleat's gamekeeper. Had Tom Thynne been alive he presumably would have accompanied them.

Monmouth's brief rebellion may seem irrelevant to Longleat's history. But to Frances and Thomas Allen alone in the house it acquired a very real significance. Thomas's correspondence includes many of the letters his wife and steward wrote to him during the four weeks the rebellion lasted. As Monmouth's army drew closer to Longleat, Frances became increasingly frightened. Allen, as methodical and calm as ever, seems to have been oblivious to the danger. Frances first wrote to her husband two days after Monmouth landed. 'This day we have been so alarmed with news from Lyme that I confess I was in some fear. However one thing I rejoiced at, that you I thought was in a safer place, for if there be danger I rather be here by myself than have you with me.'[24] Her courage was further tested when reports reached her that 'frighten so cowardly a creature as I.'[25] Estate tenants, known sympathizers with Monmouth, were seen handing out copies of his Proclamation within a mile of the house. A group of labourers left the unfinished gardens to join the rebels. Allen informed Thomas, adding, 'I believe Myles the warrener is gone over to the rebels. I can never find him at home of late.'[26] Armed rebellion, possibly another bloody and protracted civil war, seemed imminent.

As Monmouth's 5000-strong army marched north across Somerset two chests of silver and plate were packed and taken by Brotherton the butler to Salisbury. Frances was certain that Longleat would be attacked and burnt down, 'for I know of no forces near that the King has to oppose him. There were a few troops at Warminster yesterday, but they marched away again so I know not what condition we are in.'[27] On 23 June panic persuaded her to flee. She left for Salisbury with her daughter and maid, escorted by armed keepers and a groom.

Five days later Allen visited Frome, then occupied by Monmouth. He reported that the rebels were estimated at 30,000, 'but if there be so many, the greater part was asleep whilst I was there.' He watched Monmouth as he rode round the town, noting that 'they call him King as confidently as if he had the crown on his head.'[28] At the eastern end of the estate in Warminster the local militia mutinied and drank Monmouth's health in the streets. Longleat's coal merchant found six red coats hidden by deserters under a hedge. After completing his tour of the district Allen wrote to Thomas: 'Your mares now being horsed I think it were better if the stallions were removed and the bay mare also, for if the rabble hereabouts should take up arms they would be in danger of being lost. All other things have I secured, but horses are things which cannot be concealed.'[29] He armed a gamekeeper 'upon the black store horse, two of the ploughmen upon cart horses, and Nick the groom upon the Spaniard' with muskets from Longleat's armoury and ordered them to join the militia. His own horse he considered worthless but the remainder were rounded up and sent to Gloucestershire.[30]

The armoury became his main concern. Captain Kidd was familiar with its contents and likely to order confiscation. Allen pondered his response, deciding that if threatened with death he would surrender the keys as 'here are but 13 cases of pistols for them, 9 muskets, some old birding pieces, 38 pikes, 30 halberds and 3 suits of armour.'[31] His worst fears were realized when two rebels arrived at Longleat requesting admittance. After some delay they were allowed into a small parlour and each given a bottle of claret. Before finishing their wine news reached the house that Momnouth had left Frome. The rebels mounted and followed; their visit was so brief that its purpose was never mentioned. On the following day

Allen heard rumours that Monmouth's army was camped at King's Sedgemoor on an outlying part of the estate, 'and if so your Lordship will have but little hay this year.'[32]

The report was true, and confirmed beyond doubt when Longleat was visited by those commanding the loyalist force sent to suppress the rebellion. Amongst them was the Duke of Somerset. His wife Elizabeth was not yet nineteen, but he was her third husband. Her second had been Tom Thynne, once Longleat's master and Monmouth's closest friend. Perhaps the irony escaped Allen, for he fed his visitors venison which was 'the best entertainment the house could afford, and they seemed well satisfied with it.'[33]

Monmouth's hopes of capturing the crown were dashed amidst Sedgemoor's dykes and peat bogs. During the night of 5 July his army was routed and the rebellion ended. Three days later the fugitive duke was caught hiding in a ditch on the edge of the New Forest. Thomas rode down to Longleat as soon as news of the victory reached London. Frances seems to have been concerned lest the excitement cause her to miscarry and remained in Salisbury until convinced the roads were safe.

Two weeks later Thomas received a letter from his London agent. It was dated 15 July and contained an account of Monmouth's execution. 'Between eleven and twelve o'clock the late Duke of Monmouth was beheaded on Tower Hill. The Executioner made five strokes ere his head was severed. At the first he almost rose up on his knees, the second he turned his head though held by two or three people.'[34] Amongst those attending him on the scaffold was Thomas Ken, newly appointed Bishop of Bath and Wells and a friend of Thomas's since their student days at Oxford. Ken turned his head as the axe fell for the third time. At Longleat the details were withheld from Frances.

Captain Kidd was captured soon after the battle. He had been granted the only knighthood issued by Monmouth and insisted on being addressed by his title. It could not save him, nor could a plea for clemency from William Penn, the Quaker founder of Pennsylvania, who wrote to Thomas asking for his influence 'if not to get him pardoned, at least transported.'[35] Sentenced to death by the infamous Lord Chief Justice Jeffreys at the 'Bloody Assizes' and visibly shaken after watching eleven of his companions hung and disembowelled, Longleat's ex-gamekeeper pulled himself together and died bravely on the beach at Lyme Regis.[36]

The rebellion caused widespread suffering throughout the West Country. Areas bordering Longleat were occupied by regular soldiers, ordered to prevent further disturbance, who required billets, fodder and food and whose presence was a heavy burden on a countryside already devastated. Even Thomas looked forward to their departure. Hay and provisions became scarce and a visit by a troop of dragoons to a hamlet on the estate nearly ended in bloodshed.

At Longleat it was time to pick up the threads of an interrupted summer. Haymaking had been delayed as many of the estate labourers were still serving in the militia. The gardeners, bricklayers, masons and carpenters were owed two months' wages and threatened to cease work until a fund be raised to pay them. In a letter announcing her wish to visit Longleat Thomas's mother wrote, 'I suppose the late disturbance has set even your affairs into disorder, so that it will be some time to settle.' She arrived, accompanied by a cart-load of lilies, and was greeted by five of her children. It was an unexpected and delightful surprise, 'my great age not giving me hopes of ever doing it again.' She and Frances pottered round the gardens, 'now pleasant and full of flowers'.[37] One evening the women gathered to watch their men play bowls on a secluded lawn to the west of the house. Frances summed up all their feelings when she wrote, 'I am in high hopes now that we shall be quiet and may live at home in peace at Longleat.'[38]

But the strain of being pregnant through so disrupted a summer had yet to take its final toll. Thomas was staying with his brother James when news of the tragedy reached him. 'Having this day miscarried I can no longer forbear writing to my Dearest though I am still very weak. Since I miscarried I have slept in bed most part of the time. When I sat up I was full of pain, but now it appears that there was some cause for it.'[39] Three years elapsed before Frances's self-confidence allowed her to chance having another child.

A fresh crisis soon followed. Thomas began suspecting that his eleven-year-old heir was developing rickets. Frances, over-sensitive and emotional at the loss of her child, seems to have believed that Henry's ill-health reflected on her ability as a mother. Thomas wished Henry to be bled, still a common cure for a variety of diseases, but Frances was bitterly opposed. 'I think it better if he be left alone; for if he were a fat child full of humours or had fits it might be proper, but for one so lean I fancy it will make him leaner.'[40] Henry's treatment remains unknown, but instead of growing thinner he became the corpulent and thickset young man depicted in his portrait.

Frances's anxiety about her own health and then Henry's led to increased nervousness. Insomnia and loss of appetite resulted. Her doctor recommended she visit either Tunbridge Wells, which he hoped would 'ease the vapours in my head with which I have sadly been tormented of late',[41] or Bath, which he thought better for the prevention of future miscarriages. She finally chose Bath and, accompanied by two maids and a groom who paid the tolls and opened gates, she set out on the twenty-mile journey on an oppressive and muggy day when recent rain had muddied the roads.

Bath was not the elegant Georgian city it later became. The Pump Room and theatre were unbuilt. Cheap lodging houses crowded the narrow streets. Upon arrival Frances rented rooms and hired a sedan chair. Consultation with a doctor persuaded her to bathe in the baths before drinking the waters. A contemporary account describes her first immersion in the Roman baths. With a band playing, the cries of hawkers and street-vendors heard from beyond a veil of steam and her modesty secured by a voluminous canvas canopy that threatened to engulf her, Frances was unceremoniously lowered into the waters.[42] It was an event she chose to ignore, and her correspondence does not mention the progress of her cure. Gossip, the behaviour of 'people of quality' and visits to a popular sherbet shop seem to have occupied much of her time.[43] Perhaps we may date her recovery from the moment she discovered that Lady Albemarle, a fashionable London beauty, had lodgings reputed to be worse than her own.

By 1687 Thomas's income had reached £12,000. Into the offices of his London agent flowed rents from the Midlands estates, £4000 a year from Ireland – as yet unvisited by any Thynne – as well as income from Longleat. Common sense had guided its expenditure and the first stage of the estate's improvement was complete. Flour was being milled, sheep sold and twelve pairs of sawyers were at work in the woods. Trees planted by Thomas's ancestors had reached maturity and were yielding some of the best English oak planking 'for length and goodness seen at the Navy Yard stores these many years.'[44]

Thomas was a sympathetic landlord and did much to improve conditions on the estate. Pumps and drains were installed outside cottages. A widow was employed to educate many of the poorer children. Gifts of a few shillings to a 'woman with a past', a 'lame' woman and a 'poor man at the gates' record his response to pleas for charity. The accounts even mention the payment of 10/6d to a Mrs Gerard 'that she might give her vallantyne half of ginne.'[45]

Thomas, for all his generosity, never ignored his own comfort. He filled Longleat with porcelain, glass, carpets, paintings and an endless supply of books whose pages – though perhaps unread – reflected his interest in theology, agriculture and gardening. Many of his purchases still remain in the house. The leather-bound books are amongst the 30,000 volumes in Longleat's five libraries. Portraits by Kneller and Lely line the walls. Silver flagons, rare clocks, inlaid writing tables, Flemish tapestry and costly lacquered screens can still be seen by visitors to the house.

Perhaps it was to confirm his achievements that Thomas ordered the battlements lining the roof to be 'new railed and balustered.' The results are still visible, as are the statues carved by a mason to accompany the finished work. Alexander the Great, Henry V, Boadicea and the other stone figures chosen by Thomas to stand guard over Longleat symbolize an aristocracy whose prestige and wealth seemed immeasurable.

Once the work on the roof had been completed a start was made on building a basement dining hall for the servants. The household was gradually enlarged and Longleat acquired a French footman, 'though his speech scarce shows it for he writes with a good hand, let's blood well, has the character of a sober man and indeed appears to be so.'[46] Progress outside the house seems to have been handicapped by a series of disputes with the labourers. Thomas Allen was finally forced to dismiss the team hired to build floodgates for the ornamental canals in the gardens because 'they come to work when they please, and work just as they please, in spite of all eyes I can set upon them.'[47]

Apart from seasonal estate work and alterations to the house, Thomas's correspondence suggests that little else of importance took place at Longleat during this period of his life. Typical of letters to have survived is one from his brother James describing his rescue by two boatmen after falling in the Thames. The London agent's account of a whale, which having been sighted near London Bridge 'yesterday made his retreat to sea, not withstanding all endeavours to stop him',[48] has also been preserved.

Thomas's official responsibilities offered some diversion. He was Lord Lieutenant of Wiltshire, a post given to him by Charles II, and from which he was to be removed by James II, reappointed to by William and Mary and dismissed by Queen Anne; an alternation which must have taught him much about the inconsistency of royal favours. Occasionally he attended the local Quarter Sessions and of one afternoon's work wrote, 'We provided for some bastard children, the regular business of the Sessions in this most irregular age, whip't three petty larceny men, and burn'd one cow stealer in the hand.'[49]

In 1687 Henry developed smallpox, and to ensure that the disease did not spread through Longleat he was sent to lodgings in Bristol until he either died or recovered. Although the attack pockmarked his face it was 'kindly and favourable' and quickly over. After returning to Longleat a protestant exile from France called Maimbourg was appointed to teach him languages and Repington, who had recently disgraced himself by getting so drunk that on awaking he was ignorant of where he was and 'what was said or done', was ordered to take a rest from the exhaustive business of educating Longleat's heir.[50]

Shortly afterwards the trustees of the late Earl of Pembroke, owner of Wilton House near Salisbury, suggested that the thirteen-year-old Henry marry Pembroke's daughter. Although the match meant an alliance between two of Wiltshire's most powerful families, Thomas was determined to prevent it. The girl's father had killed two men in drunken brawls and her aunt had been Charles II's mistress. 'I thank the trustees for their obliging offer', he wrote, 'but as my son is younger than the lady, we think him much too young to be disposed of.'[51]

The trustees changed tactics. Where flattery had failed would a detailed account of the financial benefits accruing to the Thynnes through the dowry succeed? Thomas's reply terminated all further discussion. 'My son's inclination shall be the chief ingredient in my decision rather than the rent. I would add that neither the Religion nor the Parents are what I would willingly allege to. What the father was you have heard, and what the mother is the whole world has heard too loudly.'[52]

Thomas's involvement with the Pembrokes did not end there. In 1689 the Protestant William of Orange succeeded James II to the throne. In December 1688 Thomas and the new Lord Pembroke, acting as representatives of the House of Lords, had travelled to Henley to deliver a letter to William inviting him to take over the government. Thomas's blunt rebuff to Pembroke's trustees was too recent to be forgotten and the two peers made poor companions. William's attitude to the two men made matters worse. Pembroke was greeted with affection and Thomas ignored. It was a wound to his vanity that never healed, and after William and Mary's coronation he began patronizing the non-jurors (the 400 clergymen who refused to take the loyal oath) and forbade prayers for England's new monarch to be read in Longleat's chapel.

Early in 1689 Frances announced that she was pregnant. Although anxious to avoid another miscarriage she was determined to enjoy the promise of a perfect spring. The orchards were in blossom and the gardens coming into flower. She wrote to Henry Frederick inviting him to Longleat and asked that he bring her a pair of clogs for walking in the park. Henry Frederick found Thomas contented and active, and the two brothers spent much of their time together touring the estate and planning further improvement. They negotiated a timber sale, laid out a nut grove and yew walk and instructed the bailiff to build a new poultry house under the shelter of the garden wall with 'perches set up for them to roost on, and at the bottom coops made to fatten them in.' The pleasures of Longleat must have delighted Henry Frederick, for after returning to Middlesex he described its 'condition' as 'so excellent it makes my mouth water.'[53]

By mid-summer continual sunshine had resulted in a drought throughout the West Country. The water level in Longleat's canals fell so low that the fish had to be moved. Thomas returned to the house after a visit to London and discovered that twelve men were being employed to water the trees in the park. He ordered

Thomas Allen to reduce the garden staff to three in an attempt at economy. Allen replied that if he obeyed his employer's instructions the gardens would 'decay so fast that were it not for the walls it would be hard to find them.'[54] It was Allen's last surviving letter to Thomas. He had served as steward for seven years and was shortly to retire.

It proved an eventful summer for Thomas. The drought, Frances's pregnancy and the need to appoint a new steward must have taxed his time and patience. In August his mother died. Later in the month he was asked to advise a Kentish cousin, John Thynne, whose fourteen-year-old daughter had been abducted from the family coach whilst returning home from church. A Mr Pye had ambushed her, bundled her into a waiting coach and disappeared towards London. John gave chase, eventually catching up with his daughter and her kidnapper inside Westminster Abbey. The abbey was full ('it then being in prayer time') and Pye was apparently attempting to persuade the dean to read the wedding service. But John 'called out to the people, and many knew me and would not suffer it.' Father and daughter were reunited. It was only when John's daughter announced her intention to elope unless permitted to marry Pye that Thomas was consulted.[55]

In October Frances gave birth to a second son. Called James, she nicknamed him 'Button' and insisted that he be fed on a daily supply of asses' milk sent from the dairy. One of Thomas's two married sisters was also expecting a child and shortly before the baby was due her midwife suddenly departed, 'leaving her apprehensive and uncomfortable, and without her greatest support when she most needs it.'[56] The only volume of her private accounts to have survived covers this period in her life. Its pages reveal a tragedy typical of the age.

'December 28th,
To a cradle rug for the chylde   6/6d
January 27th,
Given to a midwife to stay with me till Mrs Rowley came   10/-
Given to Mrs Rowley when I was brought to bed   £8 12s 6d
January 29th,
Given to Dr Onely for christning of ye chylde   8/-
February 2nd,
For 6 yards of flannell for clothes for ye chylde   4/6d

February 6th,
For a pound of burying crepe for ye chylde   3/10d
For a coffin   6/-
Given to Mr Skinner for burying ye chylde   1/6d.'[57]

Frances's correspondence does not mention the tragedy, but we can guess her reaction. Mr Maimbourg's eleven-year-old daughter also died in February, turning Longleat into a 'most melancholy house'. In a letter to Thomas, Frances described how she had fallen victim to a fever 'which meeting with a very weak body, without either spirits or blood, has since overcome her, so that she is now alive, having neither sense nor motion, and cannot live many hours. God grant such spectacles may be a warning to us.'[58]

After his daughter's death Maimbourg resigned and Repington returned to complete Henry's education. A flute teacher, dancing-master and fencing-instructor provided occasional tuition, but even with their assistance the task proved almost impossible. On Henry's seventeenth birthday Frances described him as 'much grown, but not in years.' Repington's letters suggest an intractable temper and an inclination for playing the flute. Eventually Thomas decided to send him to Italy. He was given an allowance and together with one servant and Repington, dispatched to Venice. He succumbed to toothache on arrival and consumed copious amounts of gin in an effort to dull the pain. From Venice they travelled inland to Padua and Verona, but Repington found Henry uncontrollable. He and the servant had become inseparable companions, taking every opportunity to evade Repington and get drunk. Repington despaired, dismissed the servant and returned to England.[59] In 1696 Longleat's twenty-year-old heir married the daughter of a rich lawyer and bought a London house.

Whilst Henry was in Italy Longleat's calm was disturbed by a domestic scandal typical of those that flourished below stairs in all country houses. Frances was certain that one of the housemaids 'looked much bigger than she used to.'[60] The girl admitted her pregnancy but refused to name the father. Frances explained that if the man was a bachelor he might be persuaded to marry her before her condition became too obvious to conceal. The argument succeeded, the housemaid burst into tears and announced her seducer to be Brotherton, Longleat's virtuous and respected butler. Frances was astounded, but after being questioned Brotherton confessed his guilt and agreed to a prompt marriage. A groom was sent to Warminster to fetch a marriage licence but, before his return, Brotherton had packed, removed a horse from the stables and vanished. Behind him he left a brief note and his keys of office.

Thomas's London agent was asked to employ a replacement. No one could be found 'without the character of a drunkard' until a footman applied for the post who rode well and was a good sportsman, 'but what time your Lordship will allow for such things who cares not for them himself, I know not.'[61] The accounts suggest he was promoted and employed for a probationary six months. Soon after arriving at Longleat he was ordered to list the contents of the cellars; only then was it discovered that Brotherton had been diluting the wine and either selling or drinking the balance. Amongst Thomas's correspondence is a contrite but undated letter from Brotherton, begging forgiveness and asking to be reinstated in his post.

In 1694 the agreement between Thomas and the Brompton Nurseries for the maintenance of Longleat's gardens expired. The construction work had been completed, orchards planted and many of the flower beds established. Thomas now appointed a head-gardener called Vance to complete the work, and under his direction Longleat's gardens expanded and matured. Out of a £300 salary the new head-gardener was expected to pay for much of their upkeep, but he struck a hard bargain, for Thomas had to provide 'at his own cost and charges the following necessaries relating to the said gardens. Diet and lodging for Vance, and an apartment for keeping his seed, materials, roots, fruits etc, and also diet and lodging for his two servants. Dung, sand, and earth for manuring the ground. Firing for the Orangery in winter. Boards and planks to wheel upon in the winter time that the ground may be dug without spoiling the plants. That some convenient long shed be made that a magazine of dung and earth may be laid under it to be kept dry. Pots and stakes for the espaliers and hedges, with all sorts of flower sticks. Ladders of several sorts to gather the fruit and prune and dress the trees. Gravel and turf to be brought as near the garden or place where it shall be used, as conveniently can be. A horse to be kept to roll the walks etc. Also tubs and pots for evergreens and flowers.'[62]

The list of equipment is indicative of the growing sophistication

Lady Isabella, wife of Sir James Thynne.

Tom O'Ten Thousand.

LORD
WEYMOUTH

Thomas Thynne, 1st Viscount Weymouth, in his coronation robes. This portrait,
by William Wissing, was painted in 1685 at the time of the Monmouth rebellion.

Frances Finch, 1st Viscountess Weymouth, by Sir Peter Lely.

of Longleat's gardens. The best guide to their design, and of other country-house gardens, are Leonard Knyff's topographical drawings, engraved and published early in the eighteenth century. Knyff's work is detailed and complex. Features displayed in some of his drawings are so spectacular that it has been suggested he intended them to gain him entry into the homes of a flatterable nobility so he could sell animal paintings. Letters, contracts and contemporary descriptions relating to Longleat prove otherwise. Not only are they accurate, but also in scale.

The main body of the gardens began with a terrace stretching along the east side of the house. 14 yards wide and 215 yards long it enclosed grass verges, paved walks and a line of 2500 flower-pots balanced along a parapet. Beyond it lay the full glory of Thomas's most satisfying achievement – a vast, dreamlike, interlocking system of lawns, paths, parterres and orchards, divided by the canal and bounded by a wall. Designed in the ornate formal style, one enclosure leading into the next, each walk and knot a tribute to symmetry and proportion, they symbolized man's mastery of the surrounding countryside. In the walled Grove, a formal wood of beech and chestnut was laid out with rides converging on a central point. There was even an ornamental wilderness; caged by iron palings it was a mere curiosity, a tamed world to be regarded from a vantage of safety.

To a visitor the gardens must have seemed like a giant jigsaw. Created by dividers and set-square they formed an intricate combination of geometrical designs. There was a bowling green and a maze; there were gravel walks – perhaps coloured pink, blue or yellow – knot gardens filled with urns and statues, and box or yew hedges clipped into unicorns, dragons and all the mythical creatures of a hedgerow Ark.

The gardens were dominated by Thomas's 'water works', and a reservoir was built to supply the fountains and cascades that constantly splashed into the carp-filled canal waters. The water was piped in hand-bored alder wood piping and the accounts mention extensive payments for the work. Beyond the cascades and 'grass terraces, slopes with verges to them, alleys with borders of standard evergreens and flowering shrubs' lay a fir plantation, a hazel copse and a small orangery where delicate fruits could be warmed during the winter months. The orchards were equally capacious. An inventory for one of them lists cherries, plums, pears, nectarines, walnuts and peaches as growing within its walls.

The original vegetable garden had been washed away by floods and it was now replaced by an eleven acre kitchen garden. In appearance it was as formal as any parterre. Even the currant bushes stood in regimental squares, 'trimmed up stiff and stately as Lords and Ladies at the Court of Hague.' A typical extract from Vance's accounts records the planting of '2 quarts egg peas, 2 quarts sugar peas, 1 quart crown peas, 1 quart divers peas.' The new kitchen gardens were situated half-a-mile from the house on the edge of Horningsham and quickly proved a temptation to the villagers. The accounts mention the purchase of padlocks and the employment of a nightwatchman. It seems Thomas was as wary as his head-gardener. Across one bill for cauliflower seed he scribbled 'I will not pay 1d of this bill.'

In 1699 when Izaak Walton's son, a cousin of Bishop Ken's, wrote to Thomas asking if he could visit Longleat, 'your house being the most remarkable in the neighbourhood',[63] the gardens had reached maturity. Grapes, melons and roses awaited his inspection. Before leaving Frances entertained him to a meal in a small summerhouse built so she could nurture two lemon trees.

Ten years later Thomas's precocious twelve-year-old grand-daughter wrote asking for a basket of currants. Her letter ended with a poem that offers some insight into the delights and hazards of Longleat's gardens:

> So may Longleat in future years
> Become renowned for plums and pears.
> And apricocks on every boughe
> Stand thick, as leaves upon them now.
> May cherries without fear of hail,
> Or their worse enemy the clay,
> With lovely burthens load yr trees
> And every eye, and every palate please.[64]

In 1688 Thomas Ken and six other bishops were imprisoned in the Tower of London for forbidding James II's Declaration of Indulgence to be read from their diocesan pulpits. Three years later Ken was deprived of his see of Bath and Wells for refusing to take the oath of allegiance to William and Mary. It was then:

When I, my Lord, crushed by prevailing might,
No cottage had where to direct my flight,
Kind Heaven me with a friend illustrious blest,
Who gives me shelter, affluence and rest.'[65]

In exchange for £700 raised by Ken from the sale of his posses-
sions Thomas offered him lodgings in Longleat and an £80 annuity.
Ken accepted, and rooms on the top floor of the house were prepared for his arrival. Longleat was to remain his home for twenty
years.

Ken had served nine months in the Morocco Seas as chaplain to
the Earl of Dartmouth before being created a bishop. Earlier in his
career, when a canon at Winchester, he had refused lodgings to
Nell Gwynn, Charles II's mistress. But the king obviously forgave
him, for after Ken's return from Tangier Charles II declared that
no one should 'have the see but the poor little black fellow that
refused his lodging to poor Nelly.'[66] Humble, austere, known for
his devotion, Ken's presence in Longleat had a profound influence
on his benefactor. Thomas acquired a reputation for 'good deeds'
which, as one acquaintance maliciously observed, 'pleased him
extremely, having affected to be thought so all his life, and which
the companions of his youth would by no means allow.'[67] Ken
encouraged him to begin giving bibles to the poor and the two men
founded a London Charity School. He paid for the building of a
new church, offered impoverished relations rooms in Longleat
and drew up plans for the foundation of the two Grammar Schools
bearing his name.

On Ken's advice George Harbin, a non-juror of 'brisk and
cheerful disposition',[68] was employed as Longleat's chaplain.
Initially he was appointed for only three months but quickly he
became indispensable to Ken and popular with the household. A
box of Harbin's papers has been preserved and amongst its contents
is a small folio of poems. Their subject matter – the attractions
of Longleat's house and kitchen maids, and titles – 'While On
Those Lovely Looks I Gaze', would seem to deny both piety and
chastity.[69]

In 1697 Thomas was incapacitated by gout. Recovery seemed
unlikely, but within a few weeks his brother Henry Frederick
congratulated him on his 'great improvement in health; which I

believe is what yourself nor your friends did ever expect to see. My own condition is very different from yours, for I am confined to my chamber by the gout in several places. The frequent return of which is weakening my joints so much that I fear a little more time will deprive me of the use of my hands as well as feet.'[70] After convalescing Thomas travelled north to Chatsworth, a house which compared with Longleat he thought had little 'beside wilderness to recommend it.' In the following year he visited the Irish estates.

In 1694 a Polish baron had written to Thomas asking if he could lease 4000 acres and the Irish estate town of Carrickmacross in order to settle 200 Protestant families from Silesia. Thomas consented, but the agreement was cancelled when the baron announced his intention to demolish the town and rebuild it in the Polish style.[71]

After returning to England Thomas sent his Irish agent instructions for building the Viscount Weymouth Grammar School, Carrickmacross. 'I intend the school house shall be slated and made a convenient house, which will draw scholars and benefit the town, therefore the timber must be oak.'[72] But Thomas was an absentee landlord and ten years elapsed before he discovered that his agent had embezzled the building fund and repaired an existing building. The school was eventually built and its syllabus, which included 'Oratory, Virtue, Surveying, Antiquities', suggests its pupils must have quickly become familiar with the stern language of the 9th Statute. 'The master shall make diligent enquiry after such as shall break, cut or deface, or anywise abuse the desks, forms, walls or windows of this school, and shall always inflict open punishment on all such offenders.'[73] Thomas also founded the Lord Weymouth School, Warminster. The school is still in existence and may be entered through the doorway which Wren had originally designed for Longleat.

In 1702 Queen Anne succeeded to the throne; Thomas was appointed to the Privy Council and created Secretary of State for Trade and the Plantations. It was not his political début for, in the 1670s, he sat as Member of Parliament for Oxford. It seems to have been an experience that dulled his political appetite. In one letter he had written resignedly to James, 'This afternoon, Committees, being as tedious and as of little consequence as the debates in the house.'[74]

Much of Thomas's ministerial work was connected with trade between England and the North American colonies. Very little of his official correspondence has survived, but whilst in office he was responsible for introducing Lord Weymouth's pine into England. Its slender, tapering trunk and quick growth made it invaluable for ships' masts, and it had first been discovered growing in Maine a century earlier by a merchant called George Weymouth. Once known simply as Weymouth's pine, the prefix 'Lord' was added and large quantities planted at Longleat. Soon after they were planted many of the saplings were destroyed in a storm. A local clergyman wrote to inform Thomas, adding that the gale reminded him of the 'earthquakes and shocks that we heard of so often last year from Italy. Some people ventured out to keep down their thatch from flying, others were forced to get in again to escape from being overwhelmed.'[75]

Even as a member of the government Thomas seems to have devoted part of his time to Longleat's improvement. Letters to his steward and to Frances suggest he quickly wearied of London life. Frances's instincts remained domestic and maternal and, as Thomas grew older, he preferred to remain at Longleat with his wife and family. His brother Henry Frederick died in 1703 and, in the following year, his own son James died whilst at school. The tragedy provided him with an excuse to tender his resignation for the 'loss of his younger son had quite unfitted him for business, and he was unwilling to receive the profits of a place, the duties of which he was in no condition to execute.'[76]

The deaths of his brother and his son mark the beginning of the final period in Thomas's life. It was perhaps to console Frances and dispel Longleat's gloom that soon after James's death Thomas hired an elephant. The massive creature duly arrived at Longleat, broke twenty-one flagstones entering the house, and was led into the Great Hall with two men on its trunk and a further eleven on its back. Its performance astounded the household. According to George Harbin, who wrote an account of its behaviour, after waving different coloured flags 'he used his trunk like a pair of pincers: for being commanded, he took up a 6d and held it by closing his trunk, in the opposite parts of which are protuberant pieces of flesh that joining together hold things as close as if they were fingers.'[77]

In 1706 Thomas's only surviving brother, James, was invited to Longleat, 'for the country air will do you more good than any

Chemical Doctor.' James's gout had nearly crippled him and he considered himself so decrepit as to be fit company for only his closest friends.[78] Soon after James's arrival Thomas's hands became paralysed by gout but, despite their infirmity, the two brothers 'stomped' round the gardens; Thomas with both arms bandaged and James on crutches. They were joined by Henry and his two daughters who delighted their grandfather and great-uncle by dancing on the lawns.

Within two years both James and Henry were dead. Thomas had outlived all three of his brothers and both his sons. His nephew Tom, Henry Frederick's son, became heir to Longleat. In 1709 Tom married Mary Villiers, daughter of the Earl of Jersey. Seven months later he lay dead from smallpox and his young bride was pregnant. Tom's funeral accounts have been preserved. They mention the velvet-covered 'outsize' elm coffin he was buried in, and the nine gallons of sherry and twelve of port consumed at his funeral. 'Mr Thynne's death', wrote a friend to Thomas, 'is so melancholy a subject that words cannot express my hearty concern. Therefore I shall conclude this, beseeching to send Lady Mary a son, which may be a small comfort to her.'[79]

When Lady Mary gave birth to a son both Thomas and Ken were temporarily bedridden. Ken was now a national figure. The *Divine Poems* and hymns such as 'Awake, my soul' had given him a reputation that still endures. Although old age persuaded him to refuse reinstatement as Bishop of Bath and Wells, he accepted a royal pension. In March 1711 he fell ill, dying in his room at Longleat on the morning of the 19th. He was buried at dawn, without ceremony, beneath the east window of Frome church.

A year later Frances collapsed and died. Twice after her death Thomas was offered an earldom but, certain that the title would not long survive, it was declined on both occasions. The remaining years of his life were spent quietly at Longleat. Since inheriting the estate he had saved it from probable ruin. He had created the gardens, modernized the house and regenerated the woodland and farms. In August 1714, at the age of seventy-four, he died in his bedroom overlooking the gardens. Paradise had reached its appointed end.

5

DOWNHILL ALL THE WAY

'Can costly robes or beds of down,
Can all the gems that deck the fair,
Can all the glories of the crown,
Give health or ease the brow of care?'[1]

Thomas Thynne, 2nd Viscount Weymouth.

Thomas Thynne was only four years old when his great-uncle died and he became Longleat's heir. He had never known his father and his mother, Lady Mary, widowed at nineteen, was now twenty-three. Her portrait still hangs in Longleat. It captures her beauty but ignores the extravagance and vanity that helped shape her son's temperament.[2] Within a year of her first husband's death she married George, Lord Lansdown, and together they were appointed Thomas's joint guardians until he turned twenty-one and inherited Longleat and the family estates.

Lord Lansdown's interest in his stepson was minimal. Indolent and reckless, a dramatist and minor poet, he co-authored an opera and wrote a number of unremarkable plays with such titles as 'Once a Lover, Always a Lover'. In 1712 he was appointed Treasurer of the Royal Household. His one excursion into politics ended in disaster. After Queen Anne's death in 1714 he sided with the Jacobites in their attempt to place James Stuart, the Old Pretender, on the English throne. It was an ill-considered decision. George I was crowned king, the rebellion quickly quelled and Lansdown arrested for inciting an uprising in the West Country and imprisoned in the Tower of London for three years.

Thomas spent his childhood in London. His mother seems to have been indifferent to his welfare and he was cared for by a spinster nurse to whom he was devoted. But his behaviour was affected by the lack of paternal influence and, by 1718, when Lansdown was released and the family decided to make Longleat their home, he was already displaying signs of the arrogance and obstinacy that help explain the contradictions of his later life. In appearance he was short and thin, with an angular nose and sallow complexion. His mother and great-uncle had not expected him to survive infancy and, although they were proved wrong, he did suffer from occasional ill-health.

Information about Thomas's childhood is scarce but his early education was strict and rigorous. He was given his first riding lessons at the age of two. Aged four a governor was employed to teach him Latin and mathematics. He was, as his many tutors were fond of declaring, a 'young nobleman'. Longleat was legally his and his mother and stepfather were only permitted to live in it because the trustees thought it foolish for the house to stay empty. Letters written much later suggest that Lady Mary and Lord Lansdown tried to mislead Thomas into believing that they were the owners of Longleat, and that he would only inherit when they were both dead. The purpose of their deception remains unexplained and discovery of the truth must have soured the relationship between mother and son. When Thomas reached the age of twelve his mother and stepfather suddenly reversed their attitude to his upbringing. Excessive discipline surrendered to total freedom and his behaviour grew unruly and his temper worse. Only the hours spent with Longleat's grooms or gamekeepers afforded any pleasure and their instruction was the only learning that never faded. All other advice was ignored and 'consequently he will suffer no honest man to live with him: which is a very reproachful and ill-boding character for a young nobleman.'[3] Only in one surviving letter to his mother can hints of loneliness and misery be detected.

After the 1st Viscount's death the trustees had discharged many of Longleat's servants, including the steward, farm bailiff and ubiquitous George Harbin. For four years the house stood empty. The depredations of time fulfilled Thomas Allen's prophecy and the seventy acres of garden became an unrecognizable wilderness. The estate's management was transferred to the trustees and London agents. They were rare visitors and, without either a bailiff or steward, little could be done to halt the inevitable decline in the estate's prosperity.

Longleat's ailing fortunes were ignored by Lady Mary and her husband. The accounts suggest they behaved like extravagant caretakers. Harbin returned to his post. A cook, butler and house-keeper were employed. The Lansdowns filled the house with fashionable acquaintances, installed a permanent band and organized daily dances in the Long Gallery. For nearly three years they enjoyed Longleat's hospitality at Thomas's expense.

Soon after her arrival Lady Mary was asked to prepare an inventory of Longleat's contents. The final result has survived and evokes the mood of luxury and well-upholstered affluence that pervaded the house during the years of their occupation. Her own bedroom contained a hand-painted six-leaved Indian screen. Bolsters, goose-down pillows and an embroidered silk counterpane covered her bed. The butler's room boasted a green mohair bed, silk quilts and an assortment of ten chairs. The laundry maids had rugs, mirrors and fireplaces in their attic dormitories. The inventory mentions a total of 104 rooms: amongst which was the armoury and whose contents are listed as,

70 pikes, 4 ½-pikes,

24 halberts,

21 muskets old, 14 ditto new,

3 fowling pieces, one old gun, 3 carbines,

3 swivels, 5 blunderbusses,

33 pistols, 24 pairs of holsters,

4 buffcoats, 34 belts or bandoliers,

a flaming sword, a basket hilted sword,

9 body plates, back and breast,

6 caps, 7 armes, 10 wooden frames, a cleaning frame,

a wooden wheel for cleaning, a bumm shell.[4]

Other rooms were less functional in content and even the smoking room, with its leather-backed ebony and oak chairs and its table carved from a single slab of Cheddar stone, made some concession to comfort. The kitchens are listed as containing a range, bellows, dog wheel, fire screen and much of the equipment needed to prepare meals for the Lansdowns and their guests; many of whom found life at Longleat so congenial they remained in residence for several months.

Amongst the visitors was Lord Lansdown's niece, Mary Granville.

Her memories of Longleat are likely to have been bitter, for it was in the chapel that her uncle forced her to marry a 'snuffly and sulky'[5] sixty-year-old Cornishman whose sole virtue was his wealth. She was soon widowed and eventually married an Irish cleric, Patrick Delany, Dean of Down, whom she had met through Jonathan Swift. Mrs Delany's interests were wide. She cut out flower mosaics and portrait silhouettes (some of the latter are preserved at Longleat) and in later years became friends with George III and Queen Charlotte. She was also a compulsive letter-writer and her published correspondence provides a superb portrait of social life in the eighteenth century, with its scandals and intrigues. Throughout her life she stayed regularly at Longleat and her letters chart Thomas's wayward progress with candour and lack of sentiment.

In 1722 Lord Lansdown left Longleat and moved to Paris, where he was to remain for ten years. His marriage had failed and he had grown tired of his stepson. Left alone with his coquettish and weak-willed mother Thomas became increasingly unmanageable. He contradicted her instructions and undermined her authority with the servants. Amongst Thomas's correspondence is a letter from his stepfather which suggests Lady Mary considered disowning all responsibility for her son's future. But their relationship gradually improved and, in an attempt to regain his mother's affection, Thomas asked the trustees to appoint her his sole guardian. This they refused to do. Lord Lansdown was replaced by the Countess of Orkney (once William III's mistress) and the trustees agreed to provide her and Lady Mary with £100 annually for Thomas's maintenance.

The trustees also decided to appoint a tutor, Mr Ince, in the hope that he might instil a measure of discipline and learning into Longleat's heir. The diffident and unassuming Mr Ince was totally unfitted for the task. He could devise no threat of punishment to match Thomas's disobedience. A nursery was converted into a schoolroom but Thomas's attendance seems to have depended on his mood. After six months he informed his trustees that a tutor was unnecessary. In reply the long-suffering Mr Ince wrote, 'Does anyone believe that a person of his age should be abandoned to his own will and humour? Can he himself be persuaded that a good education will be enough for him? Or does he imagine that it is to be obtained

Silhouettes by Mary Granville

without the assistance of an able and faithful Governor? If not, life must inevitably be very unhappy, and his Great Fortune will only serve to render it so more illustriously.'[6]

In desperation the trustees decided to send Thomas to Eton in the hope that a public school might succeed where a private tutor had failed. Before his resignation Mr Ince wrote to Thomas to explain their decision. 'You are not yet of a time of life to be left to your own conduct, and yet you will bear no contradiction. You yourself know you are too young and ignorant to be turned loose in the world, and yet nothing will satisfy you yet you will be your own Master: that is, you are resolved to give yourself up to your ungovernable passions and to such pleasures as are not proper for you.'[7]

Thomas's behaviour grew steadily worse. His language became so obscene that Mr Ince was once more compelled to write to him. 'I am told your Lordship is very frequently heard to swear, and that in a very scandalous manner, and that you often take pleasure in such discourse as no modest ear can hear. This is now commonly reported of you. God forbid if it be true, for if it is you are on the way to utter ruin.'[8]

Thomas's years at Eton seem to have blunted the worst of his arrogance. The trustees were determined to contain his independent streak, and once his formal education was complete negotiated his marriage to Elizabeth Sackville, the fourteen-year-old daughter of the Earl of Dorset. It seems unlikely that Thomas was consulted. Bride and groom remained apart and, after a brief return to Longleat, Thomas embarked on a prolonged European tour. Elizabeth died three years later. The news reached Thomas in France and his reaction remains unknown. But he had only met his wife on their wedding day and it seems unlikely that her death was allowed to interrupt his travels.

In 1731 the twenty-one-year-old Thomas became master of Longleat. Mrs Delany visited the house soon afterwards. If she still thought him 'liberal without distinction, warm in his temper, for he cannot bear contradiction and has not discernment to be reasoned with', she at least took the sting from her judgement by mentioning that he was 'affectionate and good natured'.[9] Thomas's first action after inheriting Longleat was to persuade his mother to move elsewhere. He gave her an allowance and house in Berkshire which she promptly sold. She and Thomas never reconciled their differences and she died in 1735, at the age of forty-five, in the same week as Lord Lansdown.

It soon became obvious that Thomas's childhood visits to the stables and woods had not been forgotten. The park and rough woodland that surrounded Longleat made it a sporting paradise and he began renegotiating existing tenancy agreements to improve the hunting. A steward, huntsmen, keepers and grooms were employed. A pack of hounds was bought and kennels built to house them. The stables were repaired and the huntsmen issued with a blue uniform. The head groom hired a fourteen-year-old 'brisk and handy' stable lad to help tend Thomas's hunters. 'I clothes him very well. He will only want a pair of boots and another pair of shoes, and now and then a 1/- to pay his washing, for I am not to give him any wages the first year.'[10] Following the 1st Viscount's death the woods had become the preserve of poaching gangs who now regarded them as a private larder. The gamekeepers were ordered to combat their depredations by seizing 'all manner of guns, bows, greyhounds, lurchers and other dogs: as well as fishing nets, anglers leaps, ferrets, tunnels, hare pipes, snares or other engines for taking game.'[11]

Response to Thomas's unexpected interest in horse and hound was not always favourable. Even Mrs Delany voiced doubts at his fondness for kennel and stable. Although some of the cottagers turned his enthusiasm to advantage by requesting employment as huntsmen or keepers, others resented his interference in their sporting rights. Trout were poached from Longleat brook. A local ruffian stole a lurcher from Salisbury market and used it to great effect in the woods. Only when, in the space of a week, he cut an ear off one of Thomas's hounds, was seen entering the gardens at night with ferrets and nets, felled an elm under the pretence of building a barn and committed 'other crimes too tedious to mention' was he finally arrested.[12]

Thomas seems to have been indifferent to the improvement of Longleat's farms and woodland. When his stepfather had moved to Paris the trustees had wisely leased the estate until Thomas came of age. Although this had halted the deterioration of the land it produced little income and, soon after inheriting, Thomas was compelled to repay a substantial loan borrowed by the trustees for his maintenance. In turn he was owed arrears of rent by a handful of tenants and the accounts record several instances of his accepting goods in settlement of their debt. When the tenant of a smallholding on the estate died owing £100 Thomas took possession of his livestock and implements, namely,

'Two waggons, valued at   £16
one bull   £3
5 cart horses   £24.10.0d
102 dry sheep   £45
2 cows with calf   £6
2 barren cows   £7'[13]

(The contents of the farmer's cottage were valued at £4.11.0d. At auction today they would probably fetch in excess of £1000. They included a grandfather clock, 20 pewter plates, 3 brass candlesticks, 2 brass ladles, a dresser, warming pan and porringer.)

It seems possible that many of the problems faced by the tenantry during the eighteenth century had their origins in the gradual enclosure of the open fields round Longleat. Thomas was the first member of the family to reap the advantages offered by enclosure and much of the rough pasture and moorland bordering Longleat was absorbed into the estate. But enclosure robbed the cottagers of the common land which traditionally provided timber, game and grazing for their stock. Many suffered serious hardship and Thomas received innumerable pleas for money or assistance. The accounts suggest that, irrespective of the original request, gifts of flour or meat were his most usual response. Two bricklayers with a total of nine children who wrote asking for employment were sent a piece of beef. Flour was given to a woman whose husband had abandoned her and her eight children. When, in mid-winter, a group of unemployed clothworkers wrote describing the problems caused by the 'state of trade being every day worse and worse, and the scarcity and dearness of all things necessary for food still increasing,'[14] Thomas responded by allowing them to cut turf as a fuel. His apparent indifference to their plight was not due to miserliness. On the contrary he imagined himself as being 'always ready to relieve those in distress.' It was a question of attitude, for where the 1st Viscount had regarded the cottagers' welfare as an almost moral obligation, Thomas lacked either the income or inclination to tackle their problems. His negligence led to a worsening of relations between landlord and tenant. Poaching and theft increased, outstanding rents became harder to collect and disputes over boundary and sporting rights multiplied.

In 1732 Mrs Delany set about arranging a marriage between Thomas and Louisa Granville, the nineteen-year-old daughter of Lord Carteret. As friend of both families she was ideally placed to match-make. Thomas needed domesticating and, although Louisa's 'fortune was small, she had been bred up in magnificence, and knew how to spend a large one gracefully.'[15] At first Thomas ignored his aunt's attempts to lead him to the altar, but Louisa was not only 'sensible, discreet, of a complying temper, gentle, mild and withal very lively'[16] she was also pretty and they eventually became engaged. Her parents were delighted at being able to 'dispose of their daughter in so advantageous a station'[17] and raised no obstacles to the marriage. The only influential opponent to the match was Sarah, Duchess of Marlborough. Writing to her grand-daughter she astutely noted Thomas's 'debts and charges upon his estate'. In the same letter she hinted that she could conceive of no reason why anyone, least of all the 'agreeable' Louisa, should wish to make Thomas their husband.[18] Her doubts remained unanswered. Thomas and Louisa were married in the summer of 1733. Shortly afterwards, with a band playing and bell-ringers lining the steps, Thomas escorted his bride through Longleat's door. Mrs Delany was thrilled at the success of her scheming. She witnessed their arrival at Longleat and decided they had 'a prospect of as much happiness as matrimony will allow.'[19]

Marriage and Louisa's influence led to change in Thomas's behaviour. But he remained unpredictable. Amongst the papers preserved in Longleat's Muniment Room is a small unbound and battered notebook headed 'A Bill of Work done for the Right Honourable Lord Weymouth at Longleat, from December 15th 1733 to January 16th 1734 by me John Line, Carpenter.' Scattered through its pages, amidst an absorbing miscellany of estate-built furniture which included a linen press, wooden plates and a half-tester bed, are a series of payments to Longleat's two house carpenters:

'For Benjamin, three days up at ye live creatures in ye Grove   5/-
Robert, five days a making a house for ye leopard   8/4d
Robert, one day for making a perch for ye parrot   1/8d

Benjamin, one day for making a house for ye bear   1/8d

Benjamin, three days for making a house for ye woolves   5/-'[20]

Thomas lived through an age when the aristocracy had ample funds to indulge caprice and the inmates of Longleat's menagerie are indicative of his eccentricity. The 1st Viscount had briefly owned two bustards (now extinct in this country), and Thomas rebuilt the aviary used to house them and purchased two vultures and an eagle. The two carpenters also built a cage for the bear in the cellars so that it could be led into the Great Hall in the evenings to entertain the household.

Immediately after his marriage Thomas hired a theatre company to stage plays in the Long Gallery. But when Louisa announced her pregnancy the merriment ceased. Poor Mrs Delany, even when she and others of the guests 'had it in mind to have a little dancing'[21] they were forbidden to do so in case excitement caused Louisa to miscarry. Disgruntled, Mrs Delany retired to her bedroom (its fireplace smoked) and took her daily exercise by walking back and forth in the Long Gallery. Over the dining table she discreetly observed Thomas and Louisa's relationship. 'He is excessively fond of her, which I do not wonder at, for if any man's heart is to be won by merit, she has a good title to his. I never saw more complaisance and sweetness of manner than she has in her whole behaviour.'[22] Thomas's precautions were rewarded and in 1734 Louisa gave birth to a son and heir, also named Thomas. A year later a second son was born.

Marriage and fatherhood provided Thomas with the security and domestic contentment that his own childhood had lacked. With Louisa he proved gentle and thoughtful. Outbursts of temper or obstinacy became infrequent. He began to take an interest in the improvement of the house and estate. Scaffolding was erected up the Grand Staircase and the ceiling plastered. Benjamin and Robert spent a month making 'stretching frames for pictures and taking down and putting up ye pictures and glueing the panels.' Amongst paintings commissioned by Thomas was a set of canvases by John Wooton. They were hung in the Great Hall – where they remain – and tell the story of a waif found by the hounds in Longleat's woods who was rescued, brought up as a stable lad and killed separating two fighting stallions.

Improvements to Longleat were limited by Thomas's income.

To save money he levelled part of the formal gardens and returned the land to pasture. But he did lay out a three-quarter-mile drive between Horningsham and Longleat's south front and today this drive is the main approach to the house. A pigeon-house and smithy were built and a farrier, falconer and ratcatcher joined the labour force. A local publican, reduced to poverty by rain-water flooding his cellars, spoiling his beer and driving away his custom, was found employment in Longleat's cellars.[23]

Thomas and Louisa appeared to have spent part of each year at their London house. Mrs Delany thought Thomas's time in London mis-spent. He was impressionable, inclined to drink and 'easily worked upon by those who have his ear.'[24] With Louisa it was otherwise. She 'bore away the belle' at a royal ball by appearing in a brocaded silver dress. Amongst Mrs Delany's favourite afternoons was the one spent with Louisa and a group of other society ladies at a Mrs Donellan's where they 'sang and played, and squabbled about music most extravagantly.'[25]

By the summer of 1736 Louisa was again pregnant and in December she gave birth to a third son. The birth proved difficult and her health deteriorated. By Christmas Eve she was delirious. 'She has had nine blisters, but to no purpose but to torment her, for they have injured her very much.' She died on Christmas Day, leaving behind three small children, a husband 'who is like a madman' and the legend that her own ghost haunts a corridor on Longleat's top floor.[26] Sightings of the 'Grey Lady' remain undocumented, but they are founded on the possibility that Thomas murdered her lover by pushing him down a staircase. There is no proof of Louisa's infidelity and only one fact lends substance to the story. In 1915 a jack-booted skeleton was found at the foot of a shaft near where the murder is said to have occurred.

But, her ghost aside, Louisa was dead. Although Mrs Delany thought Thomas would soon recover, 'for he is a man, and one who is more subject to joy than grief',[27] she could not look at Louisa's portrait without remembering 'what mirth, what happiness, seemed to surround her last time I was in this house. She was good and innocent, and no doubt is in a happy state.'[28] She was twenty-two.

Mrs Delany's optimism about Thomas was misplaced. Louisa's unexpected death plunged him into a mood of despair and loneliness from which he never recovered. She had given his strange and un-predictable life its only period of happiness, and without her support his petulance and temper quickly reasserted themselves. Memories of Louisa seemed to pervade Longleat. Eventually he could stand it no longer, moving into a small fourteen-room manor house in Horningsham with his three children, old nurse and three servants. The death of his youngest son at the age of four only increased his sorrow.

Longleat's entire household was dismissed. The house was emptied and the windows shuttered. Thomas lost all interest in the estate and, without either bailiff or steward, its income fell rapidly. In 1739 he was forced to sell forty-six cottages and some land in order to repay his debts. The following year he signed a Bill of Sale pledging the entire contents of both Longleat and his Horningsham home as security for an £8000 loan.

The final years of Thomas's life were spent cloistered in Horningsham with a 'gentleman' companion. He squandered much of his income on Louisa's two sisters, giving them presents he could ill-afford. It was suggested that he might marry again, but his obvious indifference made such a move impossible. He was Grand Master of the Freemasons, Keeper of Hyde Park, Ranger of St James's Park and Keeper of the Mall, but it seems he took no interest in any of these appointments. Only his stables continued to provide enjoyment. In 1741 one of his horses won the 100 Guineas at New-market. And even after his death Longleat's stables still contained 'trotters, amblers, coach, cart and work horses, and some fast race horses.'[29]

Mrs Delany's correspondence suggests that Longleat's future was ignored. A leaking roof and storm damage to the west wing remained unrepaired and, had Thomas reached old age, the house might easily have fallen into partial ruin. He spared it hardly any attention when preparing his will. The house was to be left to his eldest son, but the remainder of the estate was to be divided equally between both sons, with the elder having the option to purchase the other's share. He subsequently added a codicil requesting to be buried on the south side of the church in whichever parish he died 'in as private a manner as possible.'[30]

Thomas died at the age of forty-one in January 1751 and was buried in Horningsham churchyard, thus breaking the tradition that

Longleat's owners should be buried in Longbridge Deverill. An inventory of his Horningsham home was ordered after his death. Amongst its contents were listed 600 bottles of port, a 'saw for cutting off human bones' and a pair of scarlet breeches with '2 half-guineas, 6/- in silver and the keys of St James's Park in them.'[31] Amongst his papers was a short poem. Written during the years of self-imposed exile it seems a fitting epitaph for a wasted life:

> 'The sceptered King, the burden'd slave,
> The humble and the haughty die.
> The great, the good, the just, the brave,
> In dust without distinction lie.'

6

PICKING UP THE PIECES

'Why seek ye there in Courts of Kings
Alas, the search how vain!
For happiness which fairly springs
On Longleat's flowery plain.'[1]

John Cole, Longleat steward, 1770–1779.

In 1754, three years after his father's death, the twenty-one-year-old Thomas Thynne, 3rd Viscount Weymouth, inherited Longleat and its estates. The house had been unlived in for fifteen years and its contents were mortgaged. The accounts suggest that damp had caused substantial damage to the attic joists and to the plasterwork in many of the rooms. Thomas ordered the shutters to be removed and the roof made watertight. Once the work had been completed he moved in. It was a hard decision. During his father's declining years the farmland on which his future income depended had gradually deteriorated. His immediate prospects were so bleak that his trustees advised him to leave England and settle in France. His father's eccentricity had undermined local respect for Longleat's proprietor and Thomas, impecunious and inexperienced, seemed unqualified to attempt restoration of the family's dwindling fortunes.

No early portrait of Thomas survives, nor does any of his correspondence, but it seems he was ambitious and eager to begin his task. Mrs Delany, bedridden by a cold on her first visit to Longleat since Louisa's death, found time to reflect on its new master's behaviour. 'He is perfectly polite and easy in his house, very conversable and cheerful, you would think he had been master for years instead of weeks.'[2] She made no secret of her wish that he choose a wife – a hope shared by many a society matron with unmarried daughters – but their efforts to hurry him into wedlock met only with failure. Indeed his apparent lack of interest in the opposite sex caused George II to decide that Thomas 'could not be a good kind of man, as he never kept company with any woman, and loved but play and strong beer.'[3] It seems Thomas's gambling was rarely a success. His losses mounted and he found it increasingly difficult to pay for Longleat's modernization and the reclamation of the farmland.

Thomas possessed the Thynnes' most enduring defect, extravagance. Once the house had been repaired he turned his attention to the gardens. The small portion that remained intact was almost unrecognizable. The walls had collapsed, the fountains had been destroyed and weed choked the canals. But the decay of Longleat's gardens was timely, for during the forty years since their creator's death a new attitude towards gardening had evolved and the geometrical intricacies of the formal garden were no longer fashionable. As early as 1712 one commentator had remarked, 'We see the marks of the scissors upon every plant and bush. One cannot but fancy that an orchard in flower looks definitely more delightful than all the little labyrinths of the finished parterre.'[4] The Romantic movement had silenced the scissors, and the formal garden was now regarded as a foreign innovation that had ignored the natural undulations of the English landscape. A simple garden that imitated England's pastoralism became fashionable. The middle of the eighteenth century marked the beginning of fifty years of inspired demolition and regeneration that gradually transformed large chunks of the countryside into rolling parkland. The most successful exponent of this new style was 'Capability' Brown and in the spring of 1757 he arrived at Longleat.

Lancelot Brown was born in 1716, the son of a Northumbrian smallholder. After working as a gardener at Stowe in Buckinghamshire he set up his own landscaping practice and began obtaining the private commissions that finally brought him to Thomas's notice. By the date of his death, a wealthy squire and Huntingdon's High Sheriff, he had perfected an art of which Cowper, slightly mockingly, wrote,

> 'Lo, he comes!
> The omnipotent magician Brown appears!
> Down falls the venerable pile, the abode
> Of our forefathers.
> He speaks; the lawn in front becomes a lake;

Woods vanish, hills subside and valleys rise;
And streams – as if created for his use
Pursue the tract of his directing wand;
Now murmuring soft, now roaring in cascades
E'en as he bids. The enraptured owner smiles.
'Tis finished! and yet, finished as it seems
Still wants a mine to satisfy the cost.'

But Brown was a practical man. The landscaped garden was easy to plan and relatively inexpensive, particularly when measured against the cost of maintaining the formal garden. He designed it to enclose both park and woodland. Sheep were its lawn-mower and plantations of oak and beech its shrubs. It was gardening on the grand scale, but Brown's enthusiasm for his task placed the English country-house garden in a setting that still endures.

Whilst staying at Longleat Brown rode round the estate with a theodolite and notebook, taking measurements and making sketches. In the evenings he translated his plans into a contract. He and Thomas signed an agreement by which Brown was to 'alter and take away the terrace on the east front of the house. To lay the two canals next the serpentine river into one. To alter the sharp turns on the serpentine river, and to make the cascades.'[5] He also agreed to remove the gardener's privy or 'necessary house', which, in an age when main drainage was unknown, must have been both primitive and aromatic.

It was a formidable operation. The work was sub-contracted, Thomas providing the labour and equipment. In effect Brown intended laying out a broad river, easily mistakable for a lake, which would provide a 'picturesque' replacement for the gardens. He worked to a uniform theory (most of the 130 country-house gardens he landscaped share the same characteristics) and had little sympathy for any natural obstacle that interfered with his plans. The construction of a lake was undertaken without any regard for its cost or complexity. Steep hills became gentle slopes, narrow streams winding rivers, and everything else was turned into pasture. The result was 'graceful, placid, and extremely neat.'[6]

A year later Brown returned to Longleat to inspect his work and make certain that the lake's water level could be raised to sluice out the house drains and flood the water meadows in spring. He also agreed to make a walk from the south entrance to the kitchen garden.

'Adorned with shrubs, trees of several sorts, and turf' the Pleasure Walk typifies the contradictions inherent in landscaping. The manufacture of a romantic walk, complete with clearings and wide enough for a coach, made by artificial means to blend with its natural surroundings, cost Thomas £1200 he could ill-afford. For whenever the landscape did not measure up to Brown's standards he improved it. One critic described his habit of crowning hilltops with isolated and unnatural stands of trees as that of a 'cabbage planter'.[7] At Longleat Brown planted large plantations of beech and Lord Weymouth's pine, both in the park and on the high ground overlooking the house.

In 1760, when Mrs Delany next visited Longleat, she was astonished to find no evidence of the £30,000 spent by the 1st Viscount on his gardens and 'water works'. 'They are succeeded by a fine lawn, a serpentine river, wooded hills, gravel meandering round a shrubbery, all modernized by the much sought after Mr Brown.'[8] Brown returned to Longleat twice, building new roads and a half-mile ha-ha and levelling the meadows round the house. His work at Longleat cost Thomas £8000, but its character remains. Standing at Heaven's Gate, an open promontory four hundred feet above the house and a mile from it, one looks out over an ocean of turf which stretches in a gentle downward slope to where the lake's waters mirror the stone outline of the house. It is a superb first view of Longleat, and no less perfect for being man-made.

'Capability' Brown died in 1783. On hearing the news George III said to his gardener, 'Brown is dead; well Mellicant, you and I can do here what we please.' It is proof of his genius that whilst alive they could not.[9]

In 1759 Thomas married Elizabeth Cavendish, the twenty-five-year-old daughter of the Duke of Portland. Mrs Delany was delighted, and so lost for words she compared Thomas to bricks and mortar. 'I have great satisfaction in the match. I think there is a good foundation in Lord Weymouth. The superstructure was attacked, but being in time well repaired and supported, I hope the building will defy all future assaults. Many false and evil reflections have been made by those whose nets he has happily escaped.'[10]

Not everyone shared Mrs Delany's feelings on the subject. Lady Caroline Fox informed a friend that 'all the misses are enraged at

Lord Weymouth's match with that ugly dismal Lady Bentinck . . .
'tis les beaux yeux de la cassette to be sure that charm him, nothing
can be less pleasing than her appearance. He is a very pretty man.'[11]
Although Elizabeth lacked the pert glamour of the fashionable
eighteenth-century beauty she was by no means as dowdy as has been
suggested. During the course of a long life – she died in 1825 aged
ninety-one – she bore her husband fifteen children of whom two
died in infancy and a further four were two sets of still-born twins.
Only much later in their marriage, when the rigours of child-bearing
had blunted her looks, did Thomas turn elsewhere for the pleasures
he had once enjoyed in a bed 'about fourteen foot high on wainscot
pillars with fine carved cornices all compleat.'

Marriage encouraged Thomas to be less extravagant and his
gambling reached a temporary halt. His annual income stood at
about £15,000 and he spent most of this money on improvements
to the house. Whilst still a bachelor he had bought a house in Bath,
but it was now converted into lodgings and the income used to help
settle his debt to 'Capability' Brown. Expenditure at Longleat was
high and there was rarely any money to hand when it came to
preparing the annual accounts. Thomas and Elizabeth were determined to make Longleat comfortable and self-contained. They
enlarged the household and appointed a housekeeper, butler and
cook. Mrs Delany viewed these improvements with relief, for she
thought they might persuade Thomas to become 'devoted to a
domestic life, which I hope in God will fix him fair and sure.'[12]

Thomas's finances were controlled by his London agents from
their offices in Parliament Street. They collected the rents from the
Irish and Midland estates and paid wages to those who worked on
them. They appointed clergymen to church livings, dealt with his
banking and legal affairs and arranged the mortgage repayments on
his father's loan. In effect they administered what was virtually an
independent kingdom with its own first family and hierarchy.

Only Longleat retained its autonomy. The household was headed
by the steward, whose offices were in the west wing overlooking
the stables. He employed and dismissed servants, paid the wages
and bills, prepared the accounts and collected rents from the tenant
farmers and cottagers. The head groom, forester, gamekeeper,
gardener and Clerk of the Works were in control of their own depart-
ments. The groom and head coachman were responsible for the

horses and the upkeep of the carts and coaches kept in the stables. (Amongst the latter was the State Coach – still preserved in immaculate condition and last used in 1964 – which Thomas bought for 2000 guineas from Barkers of Chandos Street). The Clerk of the Works supervised any building or repair work that needed to be done on the estate; typical of a week's work by his men was the sinking of a new well and the re-roofing of a widow's cottage. The gamekeeper's expenses were consistently high. Gun dogs had to be fed, powder and shot bought and eight under-keepers were needed to rear pheasant and trap vermin. The accounts mention the purchase of a pair of trained truffle dogs. Professional informers were used to apprehend poaching gangs. William Arnold, the most efficient of these unpopular men, was 'assaulted by 3 poachers, given apparel of all sorts worth £5.5.2d, entertained by Widow Maley at the Red Lion on your Lordship's account, and paid £20.17.7d for a year's informing';[13] only £10 less than the head-keeper's salary.

The bailiff was in charge of the labourers who worked on the home farm. They ranged from a turkey boy to four dairymaids. Many of the local cottagers were employed in part-time jobs, tending to their own smallholdings for the remainder of the year. In summer these men, without whose muscle 'Capability' Brown could never have landscaped the gardens, assisted with haymaking and harvesting. In winter they worked in the woods, grubbing out brushwood and planting saplings into new plantations. From them the steward bought hurdles, faggots and poultry. William Stoker, who before being appointed an under-keeper was typical of the semi-self-employed cottager, supplemented the meagre income from his own land by training gun dogs and selling geese to the kitchens. Another cottager scythed thistles in the park for three months in the year. These arrangements suited the local community, for they allowed the countryman to retain his traditional independence whilst remaining assured of seasonal employment.

Longleat's internal management was left in the hands of its cook, butler and housekeeper. The French cook was the best paid and his £60 salary reflects eighteenth-century fondness for a well spread table. The house fed upwards of fifty people a day. The preparation of vegetables, baking of bread, turning of the spit and polishing the copper and silver was the province of six kitchen and two scullery maids. Although the estate produced most of the meat, game and vegetables for the house, fruit and other necessities were supplied by local tradesmen. Thomas was notoriously reluctant to settle his accounts and his steward's correspondence includes several letters begging for payment of £200 or £300 bills. In his *Memoirs of George III* Horace Walpole mentions that 'no kind of principle entered into Lord Weymouth's plan or practice; he ruined his tradesmen without remorse, and with equal indifference frequently saw bailiffs in his house.'[14] But Longleat's self-sufficiency moderated its owner's extravagance. In a cobbled courtyard outside the kitchens were the slaughterhouse and fish-still; the estate angler's daily catch was stored in the latter until required. A travelling brewer was an occasional visitor, staying in the house until he had refilled the oak ale casks that lined the domed vaults of the beer cellars.

None of the butler's accounts has been preserved so his duties remain obscure, but he was aided in his work by an under-butler and five footmen. The third member of the awesome trinity that dominated life below stairs at Longleat was its housekeeper. Her sitting-room was close to the still-room, but her kingdom extended throughout the house and her authority over the housemaids was almost unlimited. Many of them were cottagers' daughters and after marriage (often to a groom or gardener), they would leave Longleat, set up house and practise the domestic skills they had learnt whilst serving the Thynnes. A housemaid's wage stood at about £6 a year, but each was given a new dress at Christmas and a share in the tips left them by house guests. In return they were expected to scrub floors, lay fires, fill hip-baths, dust, clean, polish and attend to the innumerable minor tasks so vital to the comfort of Longleat. Elizabeth employed her own French lady's maid. The children had a nurse, nursery maids and, as they grew older, either a governess or tutor. But none of the family's personal servants shared in the life of a common housemaid who, sleeping in an attic dormitory, rising at dawn and retiring at dusk, was the domestic backbone upon which the country house relied for its survival.

Even though their hours were long and wages poor, Longleat's servants enjoyed a carefree and ordered existence. Medical attention was provided. Meals and clothing were guaranteed and the humblest laundry maid shared many of her employer's privileges, for the distinction between one social class and the next had not yet evolved into the rigid hierarchy of the Victorian household. The rich diversity of English life saved the aristocracy from arrogance and the number of servants employed in the house was not yet measured in terms of status. Other employees would occasionally join the household for a limited period. A skating-master, a group of professional musicians, a bookbinder and candle-maker are amongst those mentioned in the accounts.

If any of Longleat's servants was inessential it was surely the ornamental hermit employed by Thomas to suggest the melancholy of the then fashionable Gothic revival. Perhaps the proximity of Stonehenge, which by the middle of the century was the epitome of 'sensations pleasing awful',[15] persuaded him to hire the unfortunate recluse. His conditions of service are likely to have been similar to those imposed on the hermit at Pain's Hill in Surrey, who was provided with a Bible, hourglass, mat, hassock, spectacles and bread and water, agreed to remain in residence for seven years, wear sackcloth robes and in no circumstances cut his nails, hair or beard, or exchange one word with the servants.[16] Little is known about Longleat's hermit. He was housed in a dank cave beneath Heaven's Gate (its final traces have only recently disappeared), soon vanished from his cell and was discovered drowning his distaste for the contemplative life in a Warminster inn. His presence was purely decorative and the fashion for keeping tame hermits was one of the fatuous extravagances to which any affluent society is occasionally prone.

In 1760 George III ascended the throne. Thomas was appointed a Lord of the Bedchamber, a post which he seems to have regarded as a stepping-stone into politics. In many ways his background and attitudes were typical of those of the landed Whig aristocracy dominating political life during the early years of the king's reign. He became a member of an influential political group known as the 'Bloomsbury Gang' and a close friend of its leader, the 4th Duke of Bedford.

Mrs Delany's belief that marriage would domesticate Thomas was quickly proved wrong. His gambling resumed and debts multiplied. In the *Memoirs of George III* he is portrayed as an 'inconsiderable, debauched young man much attached to the Bedfords.'[17] Walpole has left us with perhaps the most perceptive assessment of Thomas's character. Describing him as ambitious but lazy, as someone whose 'vanity made him trust that his abilities could reconcile intrigue and inactivity',[18] he also accused Thomas of unprincipled cunning. By 1765 Thomas's gambling losses were a matter for concern. At one point he considered fleeing to France to avoid his creditors.[19] It was left to the Duke of Bedford to extricate him from the threat of bankruptcy. Bedford's influence was sufficient for Thomas to be offered the vacant post of Lord Lieutenant of Ireland. He accepted with alacrity, pocketed the annual salary and allowances of £19,000 and resigned. His period in office lasted less than four months and he never set foot in Ireland. It was a characteristically ingenious example of eighteenth-century political manoeuvring. His financial reputation was saved and three years later he was created Secretary of State for the South and appointed to the cabinet.

Thomas could not have picked a worse moment to embark on a political career. The long-standing quarrel between George III and the radical MP John Wilkes had reached its climax. Thomas became responsible for the maintenance of law and order in the south at a time when London was threatened by mob rule. He was ill-suited to the task. Gambling occupied much of his time and a newly-acquired taste for Burgundy impaired his judgement. But he was an astute parliamentarian and a 'prompt and graceful speaker' – ('though it is said that to profit by the latter it was necessary to follow him to White's, to drink deep of claret, and to remain at table to a very late hour of the night').[20] In 1770 a dispute with Spain over the Falkland Islands provided him with the opportunity to resign. As the only member of the cabinet in favour of declaring war on Spain he perhaps realized that his 'extreme indolence and drunkenness made it impossible that he should execute his duties in time of war.'[21] Thomas had been a mediocre and ineffective minister and had he not resigned when he did it seems likely that he would have been replaced.

The first few years of the new decade marked a low ebb in Thomas's fortunes. *Town and Country Magazine* began publishing an infamous series of portraits of peers and their alleged mistresses and, in 1771, Thomas's silhouette was amongst those included.[22] Elizabeth had just been congratulated by the king on the birth of a second son, and we can guess at her reaction on learning of her husband's affair with Harriet Lambe, a noted courtesan. But in an age when the private vices of the nation's leaders were not regarded with anything like the public indignation they are today, such a liaison is unlikely to have caused much stir outside the family. Two years later followed the publication of an anonymous satire on the habits of the aristocracy which stated that Thomas remained a drunkard and gambler. Longleat's forty-year-old proprietor was undoubtedly heading towards ruin. His family and friends – and perhaps Thomas himself – began to realize that his excesses were likely to result in bankruptcy and political disgrace. 'He was', as one observer noted, 'no-one's enemy but his own. The love of gaming and wine absorbed all his attention and faculties, and having absorbed his estate into the bargain, necessity in some degree restored him to himself.'[23]

Thomas remains largely an enigma. Walpole's opinion of him may be biased, his private papers have all been lost and we know little about his family life and nothing of his relationship with Harriet Lambe. A handful of his contemporaries have left us accounts of his behaviour and it seems he managed to moderate his drinking in an attempt to regain lost prestige. In 1774 he prepared a speech for George III which attacked the 'turbulent and seditious' North American colonies, then steadily preparing for war. A year later he was reappointed to his post of Secretary of State and returned to the cabinet.

To some extent our ignorance about Thomas's private life is offset by interest in those of his official papers to have been preserved. Amongst them are a series of fascinating letters dealing with the fate of the American colonies. In 1776, by the death of a great-uncle, Robert Carteret, Earl Granville, Thomas inherited a 700,000-acre estate in North Carolina.[24] After the Declaration of Independence Granville's American agent, Hugh Finlay, fled to Canada and it was from there he sent Thomas's London agents his report on the state of the Carolina estates. 'I note with pleasure that Lord Granville left his whole fortune to Mr Thynne. Long may he live to enjoy it in health and happiness. I did not see the papers but doubtless his English estate is great, his American estate – a Kingdom in point of extent – will be of immense value when the tenants, and those who occupy land without grants shall be obliged to render common justice to the proprietor: but that will not be done until a law is passed for the purpose, and that law will not be passed in North Carolina without much difficulty.'[25]

The war made it unlikely that Thomas would ever gain any financial benefit from his inheritance. Many of the tenants farmed more land than they leased and others refused to pay any rent, declaring that they had bought their farmland from the Indians or a Virginia property speculator. Thomas's legal right to the land made little difference to the attitude of the courts. 'Let nothing', wrote Finlay solemnly, 'be expected from the justice of a jury born with prejudices not to be overcome by reason, and led away by the specious pretexts of a set of petty lawyers whose interest is to multiply vexatious suits.'[26]

Thomas could, and did, make speeches attacking General Washington and the American rebels, but he could not protect his uncle's legacy. Finlay could catalogue the 'goodness of the range', the fertility of the soil, the rivers teeming with fish, the buffalo, deer, elk and beaver,[27] but descriptive utopias produced none of the income that Thomas urgently needed to pay off his worsening debts. He was being sued by one creditor for £5000 and owed another £20,000. His lawyers vainly attempted to mortgage Elizabeth's marriage settlement and in the end Thomas was forced to sell the contents of Longleat's wine cellars to help settle his debts.

His hopes of receiving an income from North Carolina receded still further when an adventurer named Henderson stated that he had purchased the estate. He intended founding a new colony, to be named Transylvania, and was quick to encourage large numbers of settlers to take up residence. Extracts from his original advertisement are still preserved in a letter at Longleat. They make no mention of Thomas, merely stating that 'A company of gentleman have, for a large and valuable consideration, purchased from the Chief of the Cherokee Indians, by and with the consent of the whole Cherokee nation, a considerable tract of their land.'[28] Thomas's correspondence mentions an attempt to dislodge Henderson and his 'unprincipled company of freebooters',[29] but by 1779 he had lost all hope of turning 700,000 acres of Carolina into the brightest jewel in the Thynne crown.

His financial predicament gradually worsened and it seems his advisers suggested he should resign from the government, return permanently to Longleat and concentrate on improving the estate and increasing his income. The king tried to dissuade him, noting that 'I owe it to my own feelings as well as to the public, to try and persuade Lord Weymouth not to flee from the public business.'[30] But neither Thomas's loyalty to his sovereign, nor the fact that he was once again able to 'present a dignified appearance in public, and to express himself in the House of Lords with elegance, quickness and some knowledge',[31] deflected him from his course. In 1779 he retired from public life and returned to Longleat.

Longleat's steward throughout the 1770s was called John Cole. His portrait still hangs in the house. Robust and good-humoured, he sits quill in hand at a cluttered desk. A spaniel lies curled at his feet. His office windows are wide open and in the background the stable lads can be seen saddling and grooming the horses. Cole's correspondence suggests that he had a gift for depicting Longleat as the one place where Thomas might recover his self-confidence, forget his mistress and reduce his debts. His earliest surviving letter to his employer in London, written in mid-winter during a 'great frost', when Thomas's affair with Harriet Lambe was at its height, mentions that 7000 bundles of faggots had been given to the cottagers to prevent pilfering from the timber-yard. Cole's letters range in subject-matter from pigs to the protection of hares. They offer proof of a healthy and full life, of a vigorous and thriving estate to which Thomas might retreat should he weary of London life.

But in the same year that Thomas finally returned to Longleat John Cole retired. Thomas Davis, his replacement, shared Cole's enthusiasm for his work. In the remaining seventeen years of Thomas's life the two men were responsible for extensive improvements to the quality of Longleat's farmland and livestock. During those years a revolution in farming methods began to transform English agriculture. Thomas acquired a special interest in sheep and forestry. Were it not for a newspaper article written in 1782 and headed 'One of those little bits of information Historians like, and know how to make use of', and which listed Burgundy as Thomas's 'principal amusement'[32] it would seem that his years of dissipation were over and he had become a dedicated and responsible landlord.

During the latter part of the eighteenth century agricultural improvement was regarded as a fashionable occupation for the country landowner. Thomas and his steward did all they could to keep pace with the pioneering work being done in other parts of the country. New strains of grass were sown in the park, root crops planted and the dairy redesigned. Thomas wrote an account of the 'progressive improvement of a flock of sheep of different kinds, kept together and folded for three years at Longleat in order to ascertain their respective merits for Wiltshire husbandry – and afterwards fatted and killed together.' For this he received a prize from the Bath Agricultural Society. Amongst his papers is a small piece of decayed yellow wool labelled 'Bred by Lord Bath from a Spanish ram and Ryeland ewe.'[33]

Thomas's main interest was forestry. The number of books on the subject in Longleat's library would suggest that he was well-read and knowledgeable. He helped plan each season's planting programme and charts listing the numbers of each type of tree planted have been preserved. In 1784 nearly 600 acres of rough woodland were grubbed and turned into plantations. In the five years that followed over 300,000 trees were planted on the estate. By the date of Thomas's death in 1796 the numbers exceeded a million. The work was seasonal and during the winter provided employment for every able-bodied labourer in the area. The results of their endeavours have since reached maturity and the woodland which now surrounds Longleat is perhaps Thomas's most satisfying legacy.[34]

The change in farming methods on the estate led to an increase in Thomas's income. The rents were raised and he was able to pay off the mortgage taken out by his father. The increased profits were partly the result of enclosure and whilst Thomas was landlord he was able, by careful purchase, to increase the acreage of his Wiltshire estate. The old open-strip field system had become an anachronism (one of Longleat's tenants farmed 186 acres divided into 289 plots scattered in different parts of the estate). Enclosure was inevitable, but it caused a change in the relationship between landlord and tenant that was to have a far-reaching effect on life in the countryside. The dispossessed cottager became dependent on full-time employment for his livelihood whilst the power of the landlord increased.

In 1784 a common close to the house was enclosed (later it was flooded, turned into a boating lake and renamed Shearwater). Three years later a private Act of Parliament was passed whose

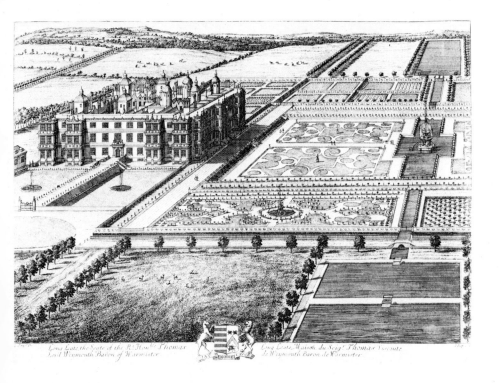

Long Leate the Seate of the R.^t Honble Thomas
Lord Weymouth Baron of Warminster

Long Leate, Maison du Seig.^r Thomas Viscomte
de Weymouth Baron de Warminster

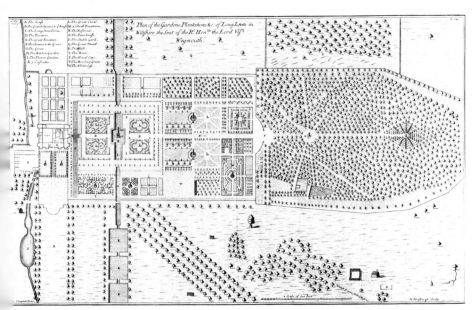

Plan of the Gardens Plantations &c: of Long Leate in
Wiltshire, the Seat of the R.^t Honble the Lord Vis.^t
Weymouth.

An engraving of Longleat's formal gardens in about 1704, by Leonard Knyff.
An early eighteenth century plan of Longleat's plantations and gardens.

John Cole, steward at Longleat during the 1770s, in his office in the west wing of the house.

Two watercolours from Humphrey Repton's Red Book of 1804.

The house from Heaven's Gate.
Shearwater.

The Great Hall in 1853 by D. Sargeant.

purpose was to 'divide and lay in severally all the open and common fields of Warminster and Corsley, and also to divide and enclose all the open and common meadows, common downs, common pastures and common places.'[35] Davis was author of the Act for, as Thomas told him, 'If we employ any one of the Warminster attornies we shall affront the others, and if we employ a London attorney we shall affront them all.'[36] The cottagers who had traditionally farmed the newly enclosed land were paid compensation, but once spent they had no option but to seek employment. Thomas's forestry programme would seem to have been a genuine attempt to assist those worst hit by enclosure and, as the estate grew larger, he was able to expand the work force. At one point Davis was employing two men to kill snails and four more to water trees in the park. A coal shaft was sunk on an outlying part of the estate. Only a thick seam of marl, valuable as a fertilizer was found, but rather than dismiss the men the marl was mined and carted to Longleat.

Thomas was as philanthropic as his income allowed. He paid the funeral expenses of a footman who committed suicide in the house and granted a small annuity to the family of a bricklayer who fell to his death whilst repointing the external masonry. He gave beer to the ploughmen, Christmas boxes to the tradesmen and the accounts mention endless minor gifts, ranging from cough drops to parrots to '2/- to an idle boy as an encouragement for going a soldier'.[37] But although he spent a substantial amount on the estate he seems to have been indifferent to the improvement of Longleat's interior. When Fanny Burney visited the house she found it 'much out of repair, and by no means cheerful or comfortable. Gloomy grandeur seems the proper epithet for the building and its fitting up.' Only the ground-floor State Rooms did she consider 'handsome', and the 'queer antique little old corners, cells, recesses, passages that led to nothing, unexpected openings and abrupt stoppages' with which Longleat abounded, only amused her.[38] Thomas's failure to modernize the house was due to a shortage of capital. The Soane Museum contains three designs by Robert Adam for the conversion of the Long Gallery into a library, but the work was never started. Whenever Thomas had any spare money he spent it on his collection of telescopes and scientific instruments (the collection is still preserved in the house), and even Walpole acknowledged that

'Lord Weymouth's head was admirably turned to astronomy and mechanics.'[39]

In August 1789 Thomas was created 1st Marquess of Bath and his eldest son inherited the courtesy title of Viscount Weymouth. A month later George III and Queen Charlotte interrupted their return journey from Weymouth to Windsor, where the king had been indulging his fondness for 'sea-bathing', to spend two nights as Thomas's guest at Longleat.

The detailed account of the visit to have survived gives a fascinating glimpse of the extravagance and style once enjoyed by Longleat's occupants.[40] Preparations for the royal visit began well in advance. Thomas invested 500 guineas in a four-seater coach with a 'green saloon, carpets, velvet and lace trimmed seats'. Flowers festooned the inside of the house, carpets were unrolled and an 'ingenious' London caterer sculpted a set of confectionery figures to decorate the dining-room. 3 oxen, 6 deer, 17 sheep and 'all kinds of game, poultry, fish and every good thing which the season could provide' lay ready in the larders for consumption by the 125 people who were to be staying in the house.

The arrival of the king and queen, their three daughters and the remainder of the royal party was announced by the hoisting of flags and pealing of church bells. Estate tenants carrying white poles lined the three-quarter-mile drive. The royal coach drew up before Longleat in the afternoon and once Thomas and Elizabeth had greeted their visitors dinner was served. Meals seem to have symbolized protocol and pomp. The royal family sat at one table, the Thynnes and their more distinguished guests at another. The royal family were served from one sideboard, everyone else from another. As the king lowered himself into a crimson and gold arm-chair all voices lowered to a whisper. Behind him stood a butler, and behind the butler a page. The eight-course meal was served on a rare soft paste Sèvres dinner service which Thomas had specially bought for the occasion. After an hour-and-a-half of the 'utmost good humour, pleasantry and cheerfulness' the queen informed the king that all had eaten. They both arose and exchanged the dining-room for the drawing-room. For the next two hours, whilst Their Majesties sipped coffee in isolated splendour, Thomas, Elizabeth and the remainder of their guests sat in the Great Hall playing cards.

They then returned to the dining-room and tackled another meal.

The royal family was accompanied by an entourage of equerries, pages and ladies-in-waiting – Fanny Burney amongst them. Longleat was so cramped that they had to be fed in shifts in five temporary dining-rooms. Etiquette forbade them to begin eating until after their sovereign had finished his first course. The fine social distinction between lunch and dinner must have bewildered Longleat's French chef. On the only complete day the king spent in the house dinner was served in the nursery and lunch in the steward's room at one o'clock, lunch for the pages and dinner for the servants at two. The royal dinner was served at four, the equerries at half-past, the pages at five, the ladies-in-waiting at five-thirty and the house servants at six. The forty-five-strong royal party was scattered throughout the house. Fanny Burney thought some of the rooms the 'dimension of college halls'. The view from her bedroom made her giddy, the climb up the stairs left her breathless, and her enjoyment finally palled when a proud housemaid announced her bedroom to be one in which Bishop Ken had put on his shroud before dying.[41]

When the household awoke on the following morning Longleat was already surrounded by a boisterous crowd come to admire their monarch. After being escorted round the house, the king was taken on to the roof by its steward and asked his opinion of the scenery. Sudden rain interrupted his reply and, 'after many thousands had found happy shelter under the spreading branches of the venerable oaks', the king and Thomas stood side by side at the Long Gallery windows to acknowledge the cheers of the 30,000 loyal subjects gathered beneath them. It is debatable which of the two men had the greater influence on their lives. The king's powers were on the wane. But as Lord Lieutenants of the county the aristocracy appointed the magistrates that protected their own interests. As landowners they founded the turnpike trusts that regulated the flow of goods through the countryside. And as the major rural employers they controlled the income and aspirations of most working people. In the England of 1789 there were few country folk who lived far beyond the borders of a country house and its estates. And yet all seemed content. That same summer a French mob destined to guillotine its king had celebrated the storming of the Bastille. But the good-humoured crowd gathered outside

Longleat to proclaim their loyalty had no thought of revolution. When the sun came out the royal family were driven the length of the drive and the crowd waved and cheered. They could only be persuaded to disperse when the king and Queen Charlotte were taken to inspect the dairy and pheasantry. On the following morning, after the king had remarked that 'everything at Longleat is very good', the royal party departed. 'Thus ended one of the most brilliant spectacles which the beautiful and venerable seat of Longleat had perhaps ever witnessed.'

Thomas's creation as Marquess of Bath and the royal visit mark the summit of his career. The years that followed were less auspicious and he was forced to negotiate an £80,000 loan. The size of the 'Great Loan' suggests that Thomas intended further improvement, but as he grew older the years of dissipation began to take their toll. The accounts record the permanent employment of a sedan chair in the house and it seems possible that gout may have caused him to become completely lame. He died in 1796 whilst visiting London. A 700-man mounted escort returned his corpse to Longleat and he was buried in the family vault at Longbridge Deverill.

Our ignorance about Thomas's private life makes him something of an enigma. In many ways he was typical of the eighteenth-century nobility. He possessed their virtues and defects, their addiction to improvement and extravagance. If he failed to obtain political success he succeeded in rescuing the estate from near ruin. He left behind the woods, 'Capability' Brown's gardens, nine children, his title and his debts.

7

THE WAYWARD SONS

'Talk to our children of your interests, of your affairs, and try and get reacquainted with theirs. Be their friend as well as their respected father.'[1]

From a letter by Isabella, 2nd Marchioness of Bath, delivered to her husband after her death.

Thomas Thynne, 2nd Marquess of Bath, was thirty-one when his father died and he inherited Longleat. A portrait, painted in middle-age, suggests a kindly but unassuming man with a long jaw and prematurely grey hair. Although shy and occasionally unsure of himself he was prone to none of his father's excesses. During the forty years he was Longleat's master he rebuilt part of the house, completed the gardens and consolidated the estate. His plump and jovial wife, Isabella Byng, daughter of Lord Torrington, was his closest companion. She was generous and strong-willed, sustaining his plans and involving him in her own schemes to improve conditions in the estate villages. During their marriage she bore Thomas eleven children, of whom three brought scandal and unhappiness to an otherwise respectable family.

In 1796 the stormy years lay well ahead. Thomas assumed his father's title and soon afterwards his brother John, later 3rd and last Lord Carteret and George III's Vice-Chamberlain, gave a celebratory dinner. The guest list has been lost but, whilst downing 200 bottles of claret, port and sherry, those present consumed oysters in dripping, 8 dishes of shellfish, 6 cod, 6 pairs of sole, turbot, carp, 4 hams, chines of mutton, 12 chicken, 10 turkeys, lamb, 2 rumps of beef, 2 tongues, 2 udders, 4 pigeon and truffle pies, 4 venison pies, 12 duck, woodcock, partridge, 10 lark, 12 sweetbreads, 12 dishes of asparagus and innumerable vegetables and puddings. On a sheet of paper attached to the bill the butler who itemized it wrote 'Only 2 chickens and a plate of pies remained; that same evening the Noble Lord had for his supper, venison, hare, crayfish, lobster, a half-bottle of port.' Shortly afterwards Thomas and Isabella left London for Longleat.[2]

Thomas's first task was to settle his father's debts. Thomas Davis had been retained as steward and the two men began a thorough examination of the accounts. The results proved worse than either had thought possible. Longleat's annual income totalled £23,000 but the 1st Marquess had been overspending by £6000 a year for the past ten years. Local tradesmen were owed £2500 and £4000 was repayable annually on the 'Great Loan'. His father's will requested Thomas to give an annuity to both of his brothers and substantial marriage settlements to each of his four sisters when they finally married. The international situation made matters worse. England was at war with Napoleonic France and to offset its cost the government had introduced additional taxation. A large portion of this money was raised from the aristocracy. Thomas's annual contribution stood at £1600 and included taxes on dogs, wig powder, windows and every servant, horse and cart employed on the estate.

Davis's correspondence suggests that trimming Longleat's running costs and raising capital occupied much of Thomas's time. It seems he had a financial talent that few of his ancestors had possessed. He leased church livings, sold timber and sheep, and began selling out-lying parts of the estate in the hope of being able to purchase land nearer to Longleat when all his debts had been settled. The accounts provide ample evidence of his ability to satisfy his creditors and maintain the household. Renegotiated tenancy agreements, rent receipts and detailed assessments of expenditure and income are included amongst the many surviving bundles of paper that deal with Thomas's early years at Longleat.

It soon became apparent that he intended modernizing the house. Davis had already complained that 'no door or window can be kept tight against the driving rain'[3] and many were replaced. He bought coal stoves, branched candelabra to provide better light in the main rooms and Longleat's first 'apparatuses for water closets'. But he was still dissatisfied and in 1805 (the year of Trafalgar) embarked on a building programme that by 1815 (the year of Waterloo) had cost him nearly £100,000.

Behind Longleat's façade lay a complex warren of enclosed

courtyards. The north wing had fallen into ruin and the interior of the house was muddled and unsatisfactory. There were no corridors on the upper floors and it was necessary to go from room to room when circuiting the house. Thomas hoped to remedy these faults and build a new north wing in the same style as the remainder of the house. His choice of architect was unfortunate. Jeffrey Wyatt (later Sir Jeffrey Wyatville) was a fashionable but uninspired architect who is best remembered for the million pounds he spent on rebuilding Windsor Castle for George III and George IV. Had Wyatt been content to rebuild the north wing his reputation at Longleat would remain secure, but he was paid a commission on all expenditure he suggested and, once the work had been started, submitted plans for a new stable block and Grand Staircase. Thomas accepted them. Wren's seventeenth-century staircase was destroyed and a group of farm buildings to the north of the house removed to make way for the stables. The results still remain. The enormous stable block, with its courtyard, towers and belfry, may have been an improvement on those it replaced. But Wyatt's work inside the house was less successful, for in making Longleat more comfortable much of its Elizabethan character was lost. The Grand Staircase typifies Wyatt's alterations. Featureless and formidable it lends the house a grandeur and solemnity that was never intended. Once finished Wyatt inserted the necessary corridors and knocked two of the courtyards into one. He also designed the South Lodge and Shearwater's Gothic boat-house (since destroyed) and encouraged Thomas to begin renovating the State Rooms.[4]

The year before Wyatt began his work Thomas had invited Humphrey Repton to complete 'Capability' Brown's gardens. Unlike Brown, Repton was a member of the social class for whom he worked. He was an amateur gardener who could paint and draw and had begun his professional career in an attempt to recoup his losses in business. Success was immediate and, by 1806, he had landscaped nearly a hundred gardens and published *Sketches and Hints on Landscape Gardening*. Repton's masterstroke was the production of the famous 'Red Books' which were drawn up for the potential client and suggested a selection of improvements. Each was bound in red leather and contained several hand-painted water-colours, some of which incorporated the legendary 'before and after' flaps that were Repton's trademark. The accompanying text was handwritten in flowing Gothic script and the book, which could cost as little as £10, must have persuaded many a landowner to undertake the far more costly alterations suggested within.

Longleat's 'Red Book' has been carefully preserved, and in it Repton took care to establish the difference between 'Capability' Brown and his own attitude to landscaping. 'To place a palace in the middle of a grass field is one of those excesses of innovation to which all kinds of reform are ever liable. A park is an appendage of magnificence rather than utility, and its decoration should partake of the character of a palace. It should consist of covered seats, a pavilion, or a prospect room, rather than objects of mere use, such as a hay barn or cottage. Because the latter may be found in any grass field, but the former denotes a superior degree of importance.'[4] The 'Red Book' contains the original plan of the boat-house as well as sketches of a terrace at Heaven's Gate where picnics could be eaten and the view admired. Its author had no time for the dull rides through plantation and shrubbery that many of Brown's imitators had laid down in homage to the master 'without any change or diversity of feature'.[5] He abhorred quantity as proof of quality and compared Longleat's lawns to Salisbury Plain.

Repton had originally been invited to Longleat to advise Thomas on the management of the water and a site for the new stable block. His introduction to the 'Red Book' sums up his guiding principles: 'Where such good taste has laid a fair foundation it remains for me to finish the superstructure rather than to display novelty by alteration! For the variety of its scenery, the natural beauty of its situation, the magnificence of its character, combine to make me consider Longleat as one of the most splendid concerns with which I have had the honour to be consulted.'[6] Such sentiments were intended to clinch a lucrative contract that would require years to complete. But at Longleat, although much was suggested, little was carried out.

Repton, for all his talent, was a snob. The stream that had given the house its name, water to the monks and power to the mill and fountains was, in his opinion, 'beneath the dignity of the place, and rather ought to be carried in a culvert underground than shown in the shape that nature has allotted.'[7] Thomas agreed and nearly 200 labourers were employed to divert a subsidiary stream flowing to the west of the house back into the main channel. A tree-clad island was constructed in the middle of the lake and £2000 spent on creating an illusory river blocked by cataracts and ledges of specially-placed rock. By forming a chain of small ponds linked by weirs and by planting willow and alder at each junction, Repton hoped to disguise the changing water levels and suggest a non-navigable river flowing through the grounds. His water-colour of the final result depicts a small yawl heeling before the breeze on Longleat's largest lake, Half-Mile Pond.

Once Repton had corrected the imperfections in the water supply he turned his attention to Longleat's approaches. 'I will take the opportunity of observing that however sublime may be the prospect from the edge of a precipice, the scenery loses much of its beauty unless it can be viewed with perfect safety. There are many parts of the approach from Warminster which are grand and magnificent but they are too terrific, and although I am aware that terror always forms some part of the true sublime, nothing can delight the eye where danger presents itself to the mind.'[8] Repton's philosophy failed to convert Thomas and Longleat's Warminster approach remains unchanged. Thomas Davis summed up his own attitude by writing 'I fear Mr Repton is a timid horseman, what would he say to the Devonshire Hills?'[9]

Few of Repton's plans for Longleat became a reality and when he died in 1818 the grand age of landscape gardening drew to a close. Even before his death he had foreseen that the nineteenth century was likely to produce a new breed of landowners who 'will wish only to improve the value rather than the beauty of their newly purchased estates.'[10]

Like Repton, Thomas was acutely sensitive to social change. As well as being a family home Longleat symbolized the traditional values of English rural life – values that were increasingly threatened by industrialization. Thomas's roots were embedded in three centuries of ownership and he was determined to strengthen the links between the Thynnes and the local population. Longleat's park gates were kept open and the local community encouraged to visit the estate and picnic by the lake. When the north wing had been completed he opened the house to the public once a week without charge. Legend records that on one occasion shyness persuaded him to hide from a party of visitors touring the house. Shortly afterwards a cupboard door opened revealing an embarrassed

Thomas Thynne, Marquess of Bath and Lord Lieutenant of Somerset, to the bewildered public gaze.

Amongst Thomas's papers is a poster, dated 1813, announcing his willingness to pay a reward to anyone 'giving information leading to the taking and conviction of the Foul Murderers of William Webb and Mary Gibbons.' Webb was an unmarried tenant farmer who had been found dead on his kitchen floor. A silver snuff box and some money were missing, a fallen dresser and broken furniture indicated a struggle. The body of his maid, Mary Gibbons, was finally discovered at the bottom of a well in the garden. Initially the murder seemed incapable of solution. Thomas's correspondence includes a letter from an amateur detective who knew the 'secret parts and haunts of your neighbourhood' and offered to solve the crime in return for a small fee. Thomas declined and invited a team of Bow Street officers to head the investigation.

The first suspect they arrested proved to be a farm labourer who had sold his gun at a local pawnbroker's, the second an unknown customer at a nearby inn. Eventually a musket and a blood-stained hammer were found hidden beneath bracken near the dead farmer's house. The discovery prompted a neighbour to report seeing two men, known to be courting local girls, walk past the house on the day of the murder. The men were arrested and later confessed. Shortly afterwards Thomas received a bill, postmarked Bow Street, asking for £30 to cover '14 days trouble.'[11]

Crimes as casual and brutal were rare in the villages round Longleat and, in some ways, Webb's murder can be regarded as a symptom of the poverty and hardship that affected the area during the first half of the nineteenth century. The enclosure of the commons and the movement of the cloth trade into the new industrial towns of Lancashire and the Midlands had led to serious unemployment. In 1816 parliament passed a Game Act by which anyone seen carrying poaching equipment could be transported and a poacher who even threatened a keeper hung. Thomas encouraged emigration – particularly to Canada – and spent over £1000 of his own money buying tickets for newly-married couples who could not afford the fare. During the severe winter of 1819 he distributed a ton of beef and three tons of flour to Horningsham's poor.

Although Thomas paid for the building of new schools and a church and was a founder-member of an anti-smallpox society, he inherited his father's love of luxury. In the 1820s he appointed a Paris agent and began buying furniture and *objets d'art* for the house. Amongst items mentioned in the accounts and still on view today are Talleyrand's writing-desk, a Louis XVI 'drum' clock and a *bonheur-du-jour* table by Severin. In one year alone he spent over £3000, even acquiring a new organ for the chapel. He added to the family collection of scientific instruments and for a short period had a standing order with a London bookseller for every new book as it was published. It would seem to have been a haphazard way of adding to Longleat's library. One parcel included books on Egypt, drainage, the philosophy of natural history, gas lighting and building a theatre.[12]

Thomas was easily influenced by Isabella and much of his generosity was inspired by her constant concern for the welfare of the cottagers. In 1829 she paid for, published and gave to every household on the estate a copy of a selection of William Cobbett's writings on self-sufficiency. The title page of *Domestic Economy* bore her dedication: 'To the Cottagers of My Neighbourhood, this little compilation written in the solitary hours of my ill-health, in the hope that it may be of some use when I am no longer here to assist you.'

It was an unlikely gift. Longleat's blue-blooded mistress and Cobbett had little in common. Cobbett, a Radical MP and author of *Rural Rides*, the man who defined freedom as 'the full and quiet enjoyment of your own property. If you have not this, if it be not secured to you, you may call yourselves what you will, but you are slaves',[13] would have had scant respect for Isabella's mixture of sentiment and philanthropy. She included his advice on keeping a cow, geese and pigs, but chose to ignore the fact that enclosure had robbed many of her readers of the pasture needed to graze their livestock. But the book was a charitable and sympathetic attempt to improve life on the estate and her visits to cottage parlours helped forge closer links between the family and their tenants. She did not flinch from including Cobbett's words on brewing, nor his brilliant attack on the evils of tea drinking. 'Tea drinking fills the public house, corrupts the boys by giving them idle habits, and does little less for the girls, to whom the gossip of the tea-table is very pernicious.

At the very least it teaches them idleness, and the everlasting dawdling about the slops of the tea-tackle gives them nothing that requires strength and activity.'[14]

In 1817 Thomas's eldest son, Thomas, Lord Weymouth, reached the age of twenty-one. Four of his seven brothers were still children but one had joined the navy, another the church and a third the army. One sister was married to an earl and the other two were shortly to marry the Earl of Harewood and Duke of Buccleuch. Thomas and Isabella must have been delighted as they witnessed their children's first flowering into marriage and manhood. Only Weymouth seemed indifferent to a career, but he was young and wealthy and they hoped to persuade him to stand for parliament. But it was Weymouth who initiated what Isabella later described as 'the melancholy change in our family'. In 1820, without first consulting either parent, he eloped with and married Harriet Robbins, the black-haired and beautiful daughter of a local toll-gate keeper.

For two months there was complete silence. Weymouth's disappearance seemed as mysterious as it was final. But eventually a letter from Italy arrived at Longleat. 'You know the remorse I feel for having given so many miseries to so good a father . . . a sort of fate hurried us on . . . I saw myself surrounded by misfortunes which I find at last were of my own making . . . My mind was in a state of confusion and despair, and I am ashamed to say I tried to attach the blame on you. I did not dare open the last letter from you for a long time, but when I did I flew to anything to drive away reflection.'[15]

The breach between father and son was too wide to be easily mended. The father was angry, bitter and in no mood for reconciliation. Before leaving England Weymouth had nearly been imprisoned for debt and his reputation for drunkenness was well-known. To Thomas it was as if his own father's vices, which he had grown up with and learnt to despise, were now being visited on his heir in an age much less tolerant of impropriety in its ruling class. Weymouth had gone one step further than his grandfather. He had formed a 'discreditable connexion'[16] and, by marrying Harriet, broken every rule in the unwritten code of behaviour that governed the lives of the aristocracy. If mistresses were still suffered, even acknowledged, a toll-gate keeper's daughter was unacceptable to a society now smothering itself with convention in an attempt to preserve its character. Whilst Weymouth and Harriet remained man and wife they would be regarded as outcasts from the world of the English country house to which Weymouth belonged.

Having chosen exile the young couple rented a house outside Paris and settled down to a life together in one of the few cities capable of turning a blind eye to their social differences. We know nothing at all of Harriet's character but remarkably enough, for many such marriages ended in tragedy, she and Weymouth were happy.

Thomas refused to forgive their behaviour and ordered his lawyers to begin reading through the entails, settlements and trusts whose sparse legal language had been formulated to ensure that Longleat would be passed on to his son. He made his position clear in a letter to a friend. 'I feel pity as much as anger for Weymouth's conduct. I think he is not entitled to any indulgence from me, or a greater share of the inheritance than he can legally obtain.'[17] Thomas was determined to bar his son from inheriting Longleat. But his lawyers soon established, so cunningly had primogeniture and the centuries preserved Longleat from division, that there was no legal loophole by which Weymouth could be excluded from the succession.

The years of estrangement continued. Contact between Weymouth and his family was rare and he and Harriet spent much of their time travelling through France and Italy. His marriage settlement provided an income, but it soon proved insufficient and two years after leaving England he wrote to his mother requesting she use her influence to have it increased. Thomas reluctantly agreed and, in a letter of thanks, Weymouth attempted to close their differences by promising that he now led a 'good, quiet life' and still hoped that 'some day we shall meet and be happy, and then you will have as much reason to rejoice in your son as you had to blame him.'[18]

In 1823 Thomas was created a Knight of the Garter. The appointment was greeted with dismay by many peers and the reason for his elevation remains unknown. Thomas did not answer Weymouth's letter of congratulation and four years later, still 'determined not to relinquish the hold on my rights',[19] he placed the entire affair in legal hands with the request that the succession be disputed in court. The result was costly, tedious and indecisive. At one point his lawyers crossed to France and met Weymouth in Boulogne. In return for the surrender of his title to Longleat they offered him £10,000, the Irish estates and £3000 a year. Weymouth rejected each proposal, insisting that Longleat was legally his and that after his father's death he intended to return to England with Harriet and occupy the house.

In 1825 Isabella went to Paris and stayed with her son. She was the first member of the family to meet Harriet and, before leaving, forgave them both their 'unkindness and misconduct'.[20] Weymouth's brother, Lord John Thynne, now a sub-dean at Westminster Abbey, was less willing to accept the situation. In an attempt to increase his share of the inheritance he started a rumour suggesting that Harriet had deserted Weymouth and that his brother was an alcoholic. The rumour lacked foundation and brought further bitterness and argument to an already disunited family.

Isabella died in 1830. Amongst her husband's papers is a letter she wrote to him and which was given to him after her death. 'I cannot bear the idea of being snatched from this world without bearing some testimony to the affection that has entirely filled my heart for my beloved husband. Accept my grateful thanks for all the kindness and happiness you have bestowed on me for so many years, which has been returned by the warmest affection that one mortal is capable of for another.'[21] It was a long and emotional letter, but Weymouth's conduct was mentioned only briefly and Isabella ignored the uncertainty that clouded Longleat's future.

The final years of Thomas's life were marked by a gradual disintegration of the family. Isabella had been loyal to both her husband and children. She had held them together and without her support Thomas found it impossible to control his sons. Weymouth had set a precedent which his younger brothers seemed eager to imitate. By 1833 one brother, Charles, had amassed debts of £20,000 and another, Edward, owed £7000 to his wine-merchant and tailor. Thomas agreed to their settlement but further extravagance led to a series of lawsuits during which he was forced to send a notice to *The Times* disclaiming all liability for his sons' insolvency.

Charles eventually made amends by taking Holy orders but Edward's debts continued to mount. By 1836 they totalled £60,000, he was separated from his wife and a 'beggar to his brothers'.[22] Thomas had no confidence in his son's ability to placate his creditors and resigned himself to the possibility of Edward's imprisonment. He grew melancholy and dejected, isolating himself at Longleat for much of the year. He ignored Edward's requests for assistance and, on one occasion, refused him entrance into the house. Edward had no one but himself to blame. He was violent, quarrelsome and churlish. His father's correspondence includes a number of his letters. Written on two-inch strips of cheap paper they reveal the arrogance that had hastened his ruin. 'My wife has refused any assistance which would have enabled me to regain my position in the world and save me from inevitable disgrace. Yet I cannot express the astonishment I feel that she should so entirely forget the respect she owes me.'[23] Perhaps it was to be expected. Edward had physically attacked her and spent her marriage settlement on presents for his mistress; behaviour which his father thought 'no woman of any character or spunk would submit to.'[24]

Edward's quarrel with his wife and father was overtaken by events. Lord Weymouth died in Paris in January 1837 and his second brother, Henry Frederick, became heir to Longleat. Thomas was understandably relieved. Henry Frederick, now a retired naval captain living in London, was respectably married to the daughter of an English peer. Thomas invited his son to Longleat, but past experience made the invitation cautious. 'I ask for nothing more than that you should pay strict attention to your own conduct, to ensure to yourself and your nearest connections the enjoyment of a rational mode of life.'[25] It was the last of Thomas's letters to have survived. In recent years his 'peculiarities' and health had caused increasing concern and at least one acquaintance believed that he had clung on to life to outlive his son. He died five weeks after Weymouth and was buried beside Isabella in Longbridge Deverill.

A portrait of Henry Frederick, 3rd Marquess of Bath, still hangs in Longleat. Dressed in naval uniform, his healthy features and straightforward expression suggests obriety and moderation. He was forty years old when he inherited Longleat and twenty of those years had been spent at sea. He had joined the navy as a midshipman at thirteen and in 1821 was appointed captain of the sloop *Frolic*. Other commands followed and he saw service in the Mediterranean and South Atlantic. His lieutenant's examination papers have been preserved and state his ability to 'splice, knot, reef, take in and set sails, moor and unmoor, work and manage a ship in the various situations she may be placed.'[26] His log-books and the few letters from men who served under him make no mention of discontent aboard his commands and he seems to have been a fair-minded and competent captain.

But he had never expected to inherit Longleat. He rarely visited the house and admitted to being happiest aboard ship. Friends thought he would 'undervalue rather than overvalue the difference between being the inhabitant of the finest palace in England'[27] and the South London house where he lived with his wife and four small children. He moved into Longleat with hesitation and soon felt ill-at-ease and uncomfortable in the unfamiliar surroundings.

Although Weymouth's death had removed the doubts which threatened the succession the family's legal advisers had reservations about Henry Frederick's right to inherit. They thought Weymouth's widow, Harriet, might be pregnant and suggested that the new marquess refrain from taking his seat in the House of Lords until nine months after his brother's death. Secretly their suspicions went deeper and they tried to persuade Harriet to submit to a medical report on her condition. 'She could of course consult any friends she might have about her, and if she is surrounded by persons of indifferent character they might lay a pretence of keeping herself in the family way and at the proper time produce a boy, which she would have no difficulty in procuring.'[28] Their suspicions made no allowance for Harriet's bereavement and their attitude towards her seems to have been abusive and offhand. They reduced her income and refused her a loan to buy paintings belonging to Weymouth, stored in Longleat and sold at auction after his death. Only one letter of hers has survived and the only evidence that she was once married to Longleat's heir are a miniature portrait inlaid into a snuff-box and a charcoal sketch that hangs in the Old Library. She never returned to England, eventually marrying an Italian count and dying in Rome in 1875.

After moving into Longleat Henry Frederick and his wife, also called Harriet, began redecorating the nurseries. Their occupation of the house was brief. Henry Frederick died three months after his father in June 1837 and his six-year-old son succeeded to Longleat and the family title. His death marked the end of an era. A few years later Thomas Davis, Longleat's steward since 1779, followed him to the grave.

8

THE GOLDEN AGE
1852–1896

'Lord and Lady Bath have little intercourse with those of their fellow creatures who move on a lower plane. They are finished and noble specimens of the English nobility, patrician to the tips of their finger-nails.'

The Foreign Resident, 1886.

Fifteen years after the 3rd Marquess's death his eldest son, Alexander, reached the age of twenty-one and inherited Longleat. The novelist W. M. Thackeray met the young 4th Marquess in Paris shortly afterwards, describing him as a 'high bred, high fed, petted and not over-wise young-man-about-town' whose 'greatest religion' was brandy and water.[1] Thackeray's judgement was perhaps severe. Alexander's period of insobriety was brief and in the words of a contemporary magazine he gradually 'froze down into the very exemplar of an immaculate, unemotional, self-possessed British aristocrat.'[2]

A portrait, painted in middle-age against the background of a sombre sky, shows an aquiline face, a neatly-trimmed beard and a distant, almost aloof, expression. Contemporaries thought him pedantic, even arrogant, but his public manner concealed shyness and occasional eccentricity (he kept kangaroos in the pheasantry at Longleat and made a study of their breeding habits). He succeeded to the family title in 1837, the year of Queen Victoria's accession, and his occupation of Longleat spanned all but five years of her reign. He lived through an age when the nobility's wealth and prestige seemed illimitable and when Englishmen of all classes imitated the conduct of their peers. He was fully aware of the privileges that his rank and position conferred. His obituary in *The Times*, still preserved amongst his papers, described him as a 'highly cultured, scrupulously honest English gentleman of the best type' who, although shy, 'remained unto the last, under a cloak of reserve bordering on hauteur, one of the most kindhearted of men.'[3]

In many ways Alexander was a contradiction. Brought up at Longleat by his mother and imbued first by her and then at Eton and Cambridge with the mid-Victorian ethos of duty, responsibility and self-improvement, he spent much of his income on luxury and extravagance. Whilst a devout Christian and generous to the cottagers, his children and friends found him stern and remote. Widely regarded as a distinguished bibliophile and art connoisseur he once declared that his favourite occupations were shooting and smoking. He held strong political opinions but refused public office. His character symbolized the attitudes of the landed aristocracy; that small but influential group of blue-blooded peers described by Disraeli as pursuing their way and maintaining their dignity 'with all the weight and rumble of a family coach . . . a large square block in the heart of English society, massive, majestic and dull.'

Alexander spent his childhood at Longleat. Aided by a succession of agents his mother administered the estate on behalf of the trustees. She adapted easily to her new life and when her son inherited the estate in 1852 Longleat's capital reserves stood at over £50,000. The rents were all fully paid ('in a manner unprecedented in the annals of Longleat'[4]) and, having reduced the labour force, she encouraged emigration to America and Canada. She moved out of the house when Alexander came of age, dying in 1892 at the age of eighty-eight.

Soon after his twenty-first birthday Alexander embarked on a Grand Tour of Europe. It was perhaps the most formative period in his life. In Italy, surrounded by the *palazzi* and churches of Florence, Venice and Rome, he developed a life-long passion for Renaissance art and the rich imagery of Italian design, a passion that culminated in his eventual decision to redecorate Longleat's State Rooms in the Italian style. It was an unlikely fascination, countering the prevailing interest in Gothic art and architecture, and it marks a further contradiction in the character of this supposedly impassive and dour young aristocrat. After returning to England he was sent to Lisbon by Queen Victoria on a special mission to confer the Garter on the

King of Portugal. In 1861, at the age of thirty, he married Frances Vesey, the attractive twenty-six-year-old daughter of the Viscount de Vesci.

Several portraits of Frances still hang in Longleat. She was tall and elegant with pale skin and slightly auburn hair. Whitwell Elwin, a Norfolk clergyman and close friend of the Thynnes, thought her 'high-minded and charming.'[5] The one diary and small portion of her correspondence to have survived suggest a light-hearted and amusing young woman whose character was the opposite of her husband's. She belonged to a gregarious and united family that delighted in practical jokes. In a letter written to her father before her marriage she described a new rector as a 'wonderful eccentric man. He preaches fine sermons and is very cracky.'[6] She was witty, entertaining and extravagant, but her apparent carelessness hid a determination to marry well and marry money. Of one prospective suitor she enquired, 'I want to know if he has family diamonds and much plate.'[7] She nearly married Lord Longford but his aversion to mothers-in-law and firm decision to marry only a girl whose mother was dead led to the end of their attachment. Although Whitwell Elwin thought Alexander 'endowed with all the characteristics for conferring and receiving happiness',[8] it seems that Frances hesitated before accepting Alexander's proposal. They were married in London, returned to Longleat by train and spent their honeymoon riding, fishing and touring the estate. Shortly afterwards she wrote to her father. 'I am so happy with Bath. His good qualities come out more and more everyday, and one finds out so often things one would never have dreamt of him doing.'[9] Alexander's infatuation for Frances astonished many of his friends and it was still noticeable after fourteen years of marriage. When Disraeli stayed with them in 1874 he commented that he had never met a man 'so entirely absorbed in the existence of another.'[10] Perhaps Alexander realized that his wife's vivacity was the best antidote to his own instinct for solitude. By encouraging impromptu house parties, dinners and outings, she saved him from fastidiousness and persuaded him to change his habits.

A year after their marriage Frances gave birth to a son (two other sons and three daughters were to follow). To celebrate the birth of an heir to Longleat it was decided to hold a fête in the park. Marquees and a stable tent for 300 horses were erected. Three bands were hired and a special piece of music entitled 'Bright Star of Longleat, Hail! Hail to thy Coming!' composed for the occasion. A harvest supper for the farm labourers and a tea party for the cottagers were planned but Henry Jones, Longleat's agent, soon discovered that the 'poor infinitely prefer a distribution of bread, beef and beer to any other form of entertainment' and the arrangements were cancelled. The tenantry and local tradesmen, together with their wives and families, were invited to the celebrations and danced quadrilles and polkas to the music of the Wiltshire Yeomanry band before sitting down to an 'elegant and substantial cold collation including wines, sherry, port, champagne, Sparkling Moselle and Burton beer.'[11]

Some 1000 guests attended the fête. The occasion cost £1200 and was an indication of Longleat's prosperity. A lead mine on the Shropshire estate was returning an annual profit of £5000, rents were rising and the farms flourishing. By 1883 Longleat's annual income totalled £68,000. The middle years of Victoria's reign constituted a prolonged period of expansion and profit for British agriculture. With prices high and labour cheap, Alexander was able to improve Longleat's livestock, drain and manure fields and resow much of the permanent pasture. He completely rebuilt the home farm, adding a new dairy and cheese room. A foundry was built and many of the farm waggons replaced. The poultry flock was increased to take advantage of the new markets opened up by the arrival of the railway at Warminster, and Alexander's correspondence mentions an attempt to grow root crops using varying amounts of guano, salt and phosphate as a fertilizer. The accounts record the purchase of new machinery, including a steam plough, a turnip cutter and a steam-driven saw bench.

The improvements to the estate and investment in equipment increased Alexander's income. But it seems that much of the money was squandered on unnecessary extravagances that must have undermined the traditionally intimate relationship between the Thynnes and the local community. He laid out a new croquet lawn, a cricket pitch and skittle ground, built a rustic cottage at Shearwater, a summer-house at one end of Half-Mile Pond, and a temple and summer-house in the Pleasure Grounds. The wrought-iron gates at the South Lodge, with their subdued tracery and gilded coronets, were also erected soon after his marriage.

Many of Longleat's refinements were perhaps paid for out of the income from the Irish estates and, in 1865, Alexander decided to pay a brief visit to Carrickmacross, the largest town on the estate. The visit had already been cancelled twice. The potato famine of the late 1840s and the mass emigration that followed had not been forgotten. High unemployment and hostility towards absentee landlords further aggravated the situation. Before leaving Longleat Alexander received a letter from his Irish agent warning him of the hazards that lay ahead. 'Do what we may, and come what time you will, mud must and will be stirred up by the visit. It is very important to have as little of it as we can, otherwise there might be worse than mud thrown.' Ten years earlier the Thynnes' apparent indifference to the welfare of the tenantry had led to several cases of arson in which buildings were burnt and machinery damaged. Alexander's agent advised him to be prepared for petitions, deputations and an endless recital of local grievances. A supper for the farm labourers and a 'hot beef and potato' meal for 200 paupers were arranged to coincide with his arrival. Carrickmacross was decorated with flags and bunting and Alexander's coach escorted into town by a band. Soon after his arrival he gave a dinner for 250 tenants at which champagne and 'four removes of the most recherché character' were served. In an after-dinner speech he requested that a similar meal be given to the inmates of the workhouse and offered to pay the trans-Atlantic passage of all those who worked on the estate and wished to emigrate to America. But the account of the dinner published in the local paper suggests that his agent stole much of the limelight. In an ebullient and lengthy speech he listed the improvements initiated by 'our Noble Benefactor', amongst which were 'glass windows that opened.' Before taking his seat he commented on the lack of religious dissent in the town and remarked that he had recently seen the 'wife of the vicar of the Established Church and the parish priest stand up to dance and foot it with a right good will to a country dance of an Irish jig time.' It seems John's visit was a success.[12] He stayed in Carrickmacross for a week, returning to Longleat with four pairs of fossilized elk antlers found in a local bog and which still hang in the Great Hall.

In 1881 a magazine called *The World* included an article on Longleat. 'Long before reaching the Hall a white gate is opened with a curtsy by a ruddy faced little country girl, who darts out from a neat gate-keeper's lodge by the roadside . . . Life at Longleat is made very easy, smooth and luxurious to the visitor. A perfectly appointed and managed household, trained servants who move about noiselessly and anticipate every want of the guest.' Behind such statements lay awe and envy. Longleat seemed to represent a way of life that the new middle classes were eager to imitate. An increasingly class-conscious society had placed the nobility on a pedestal and external influences were slowly fashioning new standards of etiquette and conduct that had little connection with the once unpretentious country house. *The Servant's Behaviour Book* is perhaps a typical example of the mid-Victorian desire to define respectability by suggesting a code of behaviour:

'Never talk to another servant, or person of your own rank, or to a child in the presence of your mistress, unless from necessity; and then do it as shortly as possible, and in a low voice.

Never take or carry a small thing into the room in your hand . . . any small thing should be handed on a little tray, silver or not, kept for the purpose.'

Longleat gradually adapted to its changing role. Although the estate still provided fresh meat, game and vegetables for the larder, the house was no longer dependent on its own self-sufficiency. The cherries bottled in brandy, the pot-pourri and distilled rose-water stored in the still-room were evidence of sophistication rather than essentials. As the character of the servants' work changed it became less vital to Longleat's survival. Frances dressed extravagantly, for experience had taught her that 'one can never have enough gowns',[13] but she never employed a seamstress at Longleat and her clothes were made by a fashionable London dressmaker. Even the servants' livery was supplied by a London outfitter and Longleat's two sewing-maids spent their days mending and ironing vast quantities of linen, including 100 tablecloths and 500 napkins.

During the late nineteenth century Longleat employed nearly 50 indoor servants, 30 gardeners, 50 farm workers, 14 grooms and coachmen, 50 woodmen, 20 gamekeepers and 50 labourers in the Clerk of the Works' department. Not all were necessary and Longleat performed many of the functions of the modern welfare state. Several villages were owned in their entirety by the Thynnes and over the centuries the family had granted allotments, sunk wells and built churches and schools. Many of the cottagers relied on Longleat for employment; the older men were found odd jobs or granted an annuity. They expected, and usually received, timber, medical care and financial support during periods of hardship. Longleat had its own dispensary, administered by the housekeeper, and if an estate labourer was injured or fell ill his family was provided with a weekly food hamper in lieu of wages. In two months Jemima Dredge, a cottager with an unrecorded ailment, was given medicines, a cheese, grapes, beef tea, puddings, mutton, $\frac{1}{2}$ a pint of gin and $1\frac{1}{2}$ bottles of port.[14]

The wells, allotments and neatly-thatched cottages were visible symbols of a shared prosperity. And Alexander's generosity and the size of the staff offered proof of his influence and prestige. Longleat's wealth added to the status of all those who worked on the estate and gave them pride in their own achievement. Some carried it to an extreme. One tenant farmer bankrupted himself by overspending in imitation of the Thynnes. The Clerk of the Works prefixed a 'de' to his name and wrote a pamphlet on his own genealogy entitled *The Pedigree of the de Buckenhams.*

The domestic servants ensured that Alexander, Frances and their six children led lives of extreme luxury. But it was a life ruled by routine and at times must have seemed artificial and monotonous. Frances became so bored that she began going on daily drives through the park, gradually redesigning the roads and rides so that they took advantage of the changes in scenery. These excursions became a habit. And in old age she could be seen, whatever the weather, sitting upright in the back of her sociable (an open, four-seater carriage with a boxseat for the driver), wearing a low-cut dress with no sleeves and a handkerchief tucked into her bodice and being driven across the park. Throughout her marriage Longleat's administration was meticulously efficient. Her loose change was washed daily, her husband's bootlaces ironed before he dressed. The morning papers were toasted and ironed before being placed on the breakfast table. Alexander employed a courier whose sole functions were to make travel arrangements and accompany the family when they went abroad. The groom of the chambers lit the fires in the reception rooms, collected letters, delivered messages and kept the writing tables supplied with ink, pens and paper. The first footman looked after Frances. He would sit beside the coachman when she went out for her daily drive and run errands for her maid. Both the housekeeper and steward had their own maids and sitting-rooms and their privileges emphasized the rewards of country-house employment. Longleat's comfort, its restrained mood of leisure and plenty, isolated the house from the world beyond the estate boundary. By the end of the century the household had withdrawn into a tranquil backwater where the ripples of progress rarely ventured. Longleat's order and routine were evidence of stability in a changing world. It was this security, together with the social influence of the aristocracy, that allowed country-house life to continue after its political importance had vanished.

Nowhere were the traditions of the country house more obvious than below stairs. Longleat's servants created their own world, filling it with protocol and rituals that were exclusively theirs. James Barrie, Peter Pan's creator, wrote 'there will never be equality in the Servants' Hall' and nor was there. The servants evolved a class structure based on their own hierarchy that was rigid and complicated. The senior servants – the steward, housekeeper, chef, butler, valet, lady's maids and groom of the chambers – were as superior to the remainder of the staff as they were inferior to the Thynnes. They ate their evening meal in the steward's room and were entertained to tea by the housekeeper in her sitting-room. At lunchtime the under-servants entered the Servants' Hall and stood behind the long scrubbed benches until the senior servants had filed in in order of seniority. Once the daily joint had been carved and eaten it was carried out by the steward's room footman on a silver platter, followed by the senior servants who then withdrew to the steward's room for the remainder of the meal. The under-servants, now headed by the under-butler and head laundry maid, ate their pudding in their own sitting-rooms.

These formalities were adhered to when a shooting party or dance brought guests and their servants to the house. Visiting servants enjoyed the social precedence of their employers. A duke's butler accompanied the housekeeper into meals, a royal maid entered on the steward's arm. But a visiting servant, whatever his rank, was banished to the Servants' Hall if he neglected to wear evening dress.

Dances were held twice a week in the Servants' Hall to which bachelors employed on the estate were invited. Bothy boys, carpenters

and gamekeepers, dressed in freshly-blacked boots and corduroy jackets and trousers, trooped into the hall where they ate a cold meal prepared by the still-room maids and danced reels and quadrilles to a local pianist until 9.30 p.m. Every Christmas a Grand Servants' Ball was held in the Great Hall which the local tradesmen attended. A band played and the dancing was opened by Lord Bath and the housekeeper, Lady Bath and the steward.

A mixture of paternalism and tradition permeated the working day. Prayers took place in the chapel before breakfast. The family were always present and the servants entered the chapel in single file and in order of precedence. At five o'clock the housemaids exchanged their working clothes for black dresses, white caps and aprons and went round the house drawing curtains and filling wash-basins with hot water. Once the family had dressed for dinner the basins

were scrubbed and beds turned down.[15]

Longleat's kitchen staff led a very different life from the rest of the household. They ate all their meals in the kitchens and were excused morning prayers to prepare breakfast. In her memoir of life below stairs at Longleat, *Before the Sunset Fades*, the 6th Marchioness of Bath, now Daphne Fielding, described the work of the chef and six kitchen maids in the nineteenth and early-twentieth centuries:

> The French chef was A. Gaillard, a friend of the royal chef at Buckingham Palace. When the family were in London he would go to the Palace to lend a hand at any big dinner party; in return the Palace chef came to the house in Berkeley Square, where he prepared his own specialities, pedestals and statues of semolina to decorate the sweets. Charcoal was used for much of the cooking at Longleat, while the large joints were roasted on spits which were turned mechanically over an open fire.
>
> Every week three sheep of different species were butchered for the household, one Southdown, one Westmorland, and one Brittany, the last being used exclusively for small cutlets.
>
> Every morning the chef wrote out the menus on a broad slate and took them upstairs for the approval of Lady Bath. The battery of pots and pans was cleaned and polished with ale, soft soap and silver sand.[16]

Every morning a specially appointed gardener loaded a barrow with fresh fruit and vegetables and wheeled it the three-quarters-of-

The Grand Servants' Ball

a-mile to the kitchens. Another removed the horse droppings from the drive, whilst a third cut buttonhole carnations for the family and their guests. 'These "bouttonieres", wrote a visitor to Longleat, 'are not the dainty gems the swells wear, but three large carnations are required for each.'[17]

The kitchen gardens were dominated by the vinery, sixty yards long and complete with pillars, paths and arches. It was designed by the Clerk of the Works and built on the estate. The vinery was surrounded by hot-houses, in which melons, strawberries, peaches, even broad beans were grown, and their cropping season was carefully extended by the application of heat during the winter. Oranges were grown in tubs in the orangery. Prior to ripening they were placed on trolleys and taken into the house so that the family could pick the fruit from the trees.

The vegetable garden and greenhouses were maintained by twenty labourers and gardeners and two lads. The labourers tackled the digging and heavier manual work and Longleat's head-gardener once defined their intellectual capacity by stating that 'none of them do work requiring skill of any kind, for none of them are capable of doing skilled work of any kind.' His opinion of the two lads was equally low. 'Both of these boys would plant cabbages, but I have not directed them. It does require some skill to plant a cabbage properly.' The under-gardeners, known as 'bothy boys', tended to the hot-houses and did all the more delicate work. The two lads were apprentices. After blacking the head-gardener's boots, fetching the milk and stocking the greenhouse boilers, they spent their day weeding and hoeing.[18]

In the 1860s a fashionable landscape gardener called Markham Nesfield visited Longleat, leaving behind plans for additional shrubberies, rose walks and rustic steps leading down the side of the waterfall, but it seems unlikely that any of these schemes was carried out. Nesfield himself typified the pretentiousness of the Victorian attitude to gardening, once observing that the country-house park should only contain sheep and deer as cattle spoilt the view.

Soon after Nesfield's visit Alexander decided to improve Longleat's gardens. The work was directed by the head-gardener, William Taylor, and both the formal and landscaped gardens provided the necessary inspiration. He relied mainly on bedding plants and exotic shrubs and the gardens became flamboyant and ornate. 40,000 bedding plants were planted each year. The formal beds, brilliant with blues, yellows and scarlets and boasting all the swagger of the age, completely ignored the relationship between the house and the surrounding countryside – a relationship which had been an essential characteristic of both the seventeenth-century and landscaped garden. Large numbers of azaleas and rhododendrons were planted in the woods and the one-and-a-half miles of paths in the Pleasure Grounds were edged with bedding plants and laurel. During the summer months one of the seven flower gardeners fitted leather boots to the hooves of the garden staff cart horse, harnessed it to the mower and led it back and forth across the green ocean of turf that encircled the house.

Longleat's under-gardeners were paid 12/- a week. Holidays were few – two unpaid days to gather firewood, two paid days to plant and dig potatoes, half-days for the local flower show and Good Friday, full days at Christmas and Whitsun. Hours were long – in summer (March to November) 6 a.m. to 5.30 p.m. Winter work ended when it grew dark and Saturday work at 2 p.m.

The estate was administered by an agent and it seems that Alexander only took an interest in matters of policy. He became increasingly concerned at the cost of running the house and estate and wrote to Whitwell Elwin for advice, mentioning in his letter that 'each department swells and industry diminishes'. Elwin's reply, which has been preserved amongst its recipient's papers, contains a masterly attack on the professional agents employed by most landowners to control affairs and manage their estates:

Most agents are great robbers. Their influence is so immense in settling the prices you shall take, and the prices you shall give, who is to be employed and what is to be done that at every turn they have a vast power, which they use unsparingly, by putting money into their own pockets at the expense of their employers. They endeavour to make everything a profitable transaction to themselves, and the more numerous the transactions there are, the more numerous the items of profit. All they do is done extravagantly, and many things are done which ought to be let alone. They sell and let your goods cheap, and buy for you too dear, and accumulate superfluities to multiply percentages.[19]

After his marriage Alexander continued to travel abroad whenever possible. Frances accompanied him and the children were left in the care of their nurse. They usually sailed to Italy, occasionally breaking the voyage with halts in the Canary Islands and North Africa, and returning to England by train. Alexander's visits to Italy strengthened his passion for Italian design and in 1874 he decided to begin redecorating Longleat's State Rooms. The work took thirteen years and was supervised by an interior designer called J. D. Crace. The inspiration and ideas were Alexander's and Crace's task was to translate his employer's wishes into reality. The results are still visible. They lend the interior of the house an ostentation that conflicts with the restrained elegance of the external façade and it seems unlikely that Longleat's builder, John Thynne, would have shared his successor's enthusiasm for the rich brilliance of Italian design. The work completed the destruction of the Elizabethan interior, turning the house into the 'stately home' that greets the modern visitor.

The sixteenth-century Long Gallery was gutted and renamed the Saloon, an act of caprice which suggests that Alexander was determined to empty the room of any allusion to its origins. The walls were hung with Flemish tapestries depicting scenes in the life of Cyrus, King of Persia. The massive, hooded marble fireplace was copied from a similar one in the Doge's Palace, Venice, and the panelled ceiling was inspired by the Palazzo Massimo, Rome. The main body of the ceiling contains a series of cameo paintings of Greek myths intended to symbolize Power, Poetry and War. A panel in the window alcove reads 'John Alexander Thynne constructed afresh and decorated the panelled ceiling which thou seest.' The marquetry door-fittings and plasterwork frame for the panelling were made in Italy and a team of Italian craftsmen accompanied them to Longleat to install and complete the work.

The State Dining-Room was the next to be decorated. An ornamental ceiling was fixed into place, the floorboards in the room above were removed, and a series of oval and rectangular paintings from the School of Titian were lowered into the panels. The seventeenth-century Spanish leather tooled in Cordoba which hangs on the walls was given to Alexander by the Italian dealer who sold him the paintings. The Breakfast and Lower Dining-Rooms, the Red Library, Ante-Library and Drawing-Room were also redecorated. The heavily-gilded plasterwork and ornament-encrusted ceilings reveal a side of Alexander's character completely at variance with his austere public image. In what is now the Breakfast Room, then in use as a Billiards' Room, the gilded ceiling, copied from the Ducal Palace in Venice, frames a circular allegorical painting depicting 'Justice and Peace with the Lion of St Mark driving away discord.' The plaster details are an exact copy of those in the Doge's apartments. The intricacy of the work and the need for research provided Alexander with an occupation. He designed door handles and lock plates, chose upholstery and spent long hours placing the furniture and *objets d'art* in each of the completed rooms. It seems probable that he and Frances travelled out to Italy once a year: Frances to buy tapestries and paintings and Alexander to visit palaces, churches and libraries in search of further inspiration. On one of these visits Frances bought the Genoese velvet festal church hangings that now decorate the State Drawing-Room walls. When packed they were interlaced with gold thread, but on arrival at Longleat it was found that the thread had mysteriously been removed. The purchase of *The Rest on the Flight into Egypt* by Titian, which now hangs in the State Drawing-Room, may also date from this period.[20]

Shortly after the redecoration work started Benjamin Disraeli stayed at Longleat. During his visit he wrote a number of letters to two close friends, Lady Bradford and Lady Chesterfield, that provide an incisive portrait of the country-house way of life. The seventy-year-old statesmen was then Conservative Prime Minister and his host, according to the anonymous author of *The Foreign Resident*, was as 'unbending and narrow-minded a Tory as he is blue-blooded a peer.' Their politics apart the two men had few common interests and Disraeli's mood remained one of bored and amused detachment. A tall cupboard, containing a lavatory, had been specially built in the corridor outside his bedroom, but even this detailed attentiveness to his needs failed to curb his distaste for the country house. Disraeli was a realist. Perhaps he understood that by its insistence on independence and dedication to the most trivial of creature comforts the country house was in danger of becoming superfluous. In a letter to Lady Bradford he wrote 'If you find this a stupid letter it is the stationery. This paper, muddy ink, and pens which are made from geese on a common, entirely destroy any little genius I have.'[21] His first evening in the house he thought 'insipid and stupid and

John Thynne, 4th Marquess of Bath, in about 1870, by George Richmond.

The State Drawing Room.
The Red Library.

The Saloon.

The Lower Dining Room.

The Old Library by Richard Doyle in 1874. On the left are the 4th Marchioness and Canon Jackson.
The Great Hall in the nineteenth century by R. Pocock.

gloomy'.[22] The dinner dragged on interminably and the ladies' after-dinner chatter proved tedious and dull. 'The four ladies laugh together in chorus and almost unceasingly and when they retire at 11.30, and I wish, avoiding the smokers, to escape to my couch, I find them in the ante-chamber still laughing with their candle-sticks in their hands, which they will not light. At last they move off, but I find them again on the landing-place on the great staircase like a caravan halting, all talking at the same time and laughing in chorus.'[23]

Throughout the visit Frances was sitting for her portrait by a Lady Paget, 'whose matchless conversation, consisting of high art and court scandal, receives added lustre from her undulating figure, and the profusion of her cinque-cent jewels'.[24] But she found the time to drive Disraeli round the estate and show him Frome church and the view from Heaven's Gate. On another occasion Alexander took his guest on a tour of the State Rooms. But neither excursion could prevent Disraeli from becoming 'wearied to extinction and pro-foundly unhappy.'[25] Only Frances, who offered her services as secretary and was as gay and light-hearted as ever, relieved the boredom. Disraeli was not the only member of the house party to fall under her spell. He noticed Lord Malmesbury surreptitiously admiring her figure and Malmesbury eventually admitted that he thought 'Bath lucky to have such a friend to furnish his galleries.'[26]

When Disraeli paid a second, brief visit to Longleat in 1875 he and Frances renewed their friendship. Although, in a letter to Lady Chesterfield, he complained of Longleat's cold and stated how much he detested country houses, he compared Frances's good-humour to an invitation to the 'future life'.[27] After his departure he wrote her a characteristically flattering letter, still preserved among the family papers. 'How grieved I was to leave your enchanted roof last night without the honour or gratification of some conversation with yourself. I thought too as I made my farewell bow, you almost deigned to reproach me for what was my misfortune. I cannot bear being reproached by you. It is like being reproached by an angel.'[28]

In 1881 the Prince of Wales and Princess Alexandra stayed at Longleat for four days during the shooting season. Preparations began several weeks prior to their arrival. A manual fire engine was bought, the house was scrubbed and the larders and cellars filled to capacity. The State Room ceilings were washed with small beer by two carpenters who were made to wear carpet slippers by the housekeeper so as not to mark the floors. Alexander and his agent decided to present the prince with a loyal address signed by the tenantry. The response of the Somerset tenants was less than satisfactory and, in explanation, one of them wrote to their landlord: 'We shall not present so lordly an array of signatures as the Wiltshire tenantry, writing not being a strong point among us.'

The royal party arrived at Longleat by carriage on a dull December day. A bonfire had been lit in the park to welcome them and coloured lanterns were strung between the trees. Estate labourers carrying torches lined the drive. Alexander had planned two full days of shooting. Eight guns took part and the birds were roused by nearly a hundred beaters, each dressed in a mustard-yellow cape and armed with a stick. Small boys carried the shot. A marquee was erected in the woods and a two-course lunch was sent out in hay-boxes from the kitchens. On both days over 1000 pheasants were shot.

Before the Prince and Princess of Wales left Longleat a ball was held to which 600 other guests, including 'all the leading families in the county' were invited. Special trains linked Warminster with the remainder of Wiltshire. Full-size palm trees planted in tubs were placed in the State Rooms. After leaving their carriages and climbing the awning-covered steps that led into the house 'young ladies whispered "this is like fairy land", and even their elders were in an ecstasy of admiration.' The Prince of Wales, partnered by Frances in a gold-embroidered satin dress and wearing a diamond coronet, and Princess Alexandra on the arm of 'our Noble Host' stepped out on to the floor to begin the dancing. High above their heads eight chandeliers burned 1000 candles. In other rooms tables laden with food and drink awaited the attentions of the hungry or thirsty. There were woodcock, snipe and partridge, barons of cold beef, sucking-pig and hams in aspic, as well as carved coloured ices three foot high, champagne, hock, port and iced punch. Whilst the gentry danced and ate the coachmen huddled round a brazier in the stable yard and supped on kidneys and beer. Eventually they returned to their carriages and waited for the guests to walk out into the night.[29]

Two years later Alexander's eldest son, Thomas, reached the age of twenty-one and a second, equally lavish celebration was held in the house. The royal ball was evidence of the family's prestige, but Lord Weymouth's birthday celebrations gave Alexander the opportunity to present a potential landlord to his future tenants. The event was planned with military precision by Longleat's agent and tickets in a multitude of colours were sent to the 1000 people invited to attend. Four tons of beef and bread and 600 gallons of beer were given to the cottagers and heaps of laurel placed in the villages to encourage the decoration of the cottages. Bell-ringing, sports competitions and childrens' teas preceded the festivities. Tenants from outlying areas of the estate were lodged in tents erected in the park.

Apart from the presentation of gifts, the speeches, dancing and consumption of gargantuan amounts of food and drink, the agent hired a company of entertainers to amuse the guests. There was a Punch & Judy, mimics, clowns, performing dogs, a ventriloquist and slack-wire performer and a 'variety of Funny Little People (only 20 inches high) who will endeavour to amuse the audience.' For the less frivolous an operetta was staged in the house. In the evening James Pain, 'pyrotechnist to the Royal Yacht Squadron and Alexandra Palace', staged a firework display in the park. The set pieces included a representation of a naval bombardment 'depicting with realistic effect the interchange of shot and shell and the blowing up of the enemy's magazine.' Before the evening ended a forty-foot-high frame of Roman candles spelt out the words 'Long Life and Happiness to Lord Weymouth' and a flight of 500 rockets was sent up over Longleat's towers, forming a 'vast aerial bouquet' against the backcloth of a darkening sky. 'I can assure you', wrote Longleat's agent in a letter to his employer, 'that many looked upon the whole thing as a dream rather than a reality.'[30]

The indifference to expense and the sheer spectacle of both the royal visit and birthday celebrations confirmed Longleat's prosperity. An estate labourer, modestly treading in the steps of his fore-fathers and earning £30 a year quarrying, cutting reed, ditching and fencing, must have been awed by the Thynnes' wealth and behaviour. Alexander's income had never been higher and his influence and prestige were obvious. During the three centuries since Longleat had been built the Thynnes had expanded their interests, each generation adding to the amount of land and property that the family now owned. By 1880 they were established members of a ruling class in a nation whose dominion extended to every corner of the globe. The English aristocracy seemed immovable, as if they represented all that was most robust and pugnacious in the national character. But the firework display marked the summit of Longleat's fortunes. The gulf between the landed gentry and the country folk around them had grown so great that change had become inevitable. Dispensations of beef and beer were no longer a realistic substitute for higher wages and greater equality. In the last quarter of the nineteenth century the spread of democracy began to beat against the fabric of the country house and its way of life until finally the immense social changes of the twentieth century deluged through the breach.

Longleat's decline began with the collapse of British agriculture in the 1870s. Successive harvests failed. Imported grain, grown on the vast prairies of the United States and Canada, lowered English prices. Australia and New Zealand began exporting chilled meat. English oak was no longer needed to build battleships and the revenue from forestry fell. Longleat, like many other estates in Southern England, had never derived much benefit from the steel works and coal mines, the new factories and towns, that had been spawned by the industrial revolution. Its wealth depended on a landed income. Indeed, Longleat's geographical location in a farming area where the traditional rural values were less easily influenced by the urban north helped the Thynnes maintain their grip on the political institutions that supported them. Instead of adapting to change the gentry had taken refuge in the knowledge that 4000 squires owned more than half the land in England and Wales. As an increasing number of people left the land to seek their fortunes in the towns and abroad the economic importance of the countryside diminished. The rural labourer could not vote and enclosure had robbed him of a stake in the land. When agriculture collapsed few people were willing to rescue the landed interest.

A large proportion of Longleat's West Country estates lay on chalk downlands. The tenant farmers relied on an income from sheep and grain and when prices dropped many absconded or went bankrupt. Farms fell in hand and rents into arrear and Alexander was compelled to lower rents by about a quarter. Because he had spent his agricultural profits on celebration and the redecoration of the house he had no capital reserves on which to draw and he was forced to sell the 22,000-acre Irish estates to provide money for investment. His response to these setbacks was perhaps typical of the English landowner. Although he slightly reduced the number of labourers employed on the estate he refused to cut back on the garden staff and actually increased the amount spent on the shoot.[31] Instead of reinvigorating the farmland he allowed, in Kipling's phrase, 'the kept cock pheasant, master of many a shire' to roam through the woods that had once provided so much of Longleat's wealth.

Alexander's difficulties made him despondent and gloomy and his surviving correspondence reveals his concern at the growth of the middle classes, the reform of the franchise and changes in local government, all of which he thought posed a threat to Longleat's future. He and Frances began wintering abroad, in Italy, Egypt and Algeria. But these holidays could not prevent him worrying about the extravagance of his eldest son and the future of the estate. He was determined not to sell any more land and even discussed the possibility of closing up Longleat and living quietly in London. These anxieties proved a burden and, by the end of the 1880s, he had entered a period of depression and illness that punctuated much of his remaining life.

We know little about Alexander and Frances's relationship with their six children – 'Bath's little cubs' as Lord Randolph Churchill once called them.[32] But amongst the family papers stored in the Muniment Room is a diary kept by their second son, John, which casts a less than flattering light on the morals and behaviour of a young Victorian aristocrat on the brink of manhood. The diary was written between 1885 and 1887 and covers John's cadetship at Sandhurst and his entry as an officer into the 9th Lancers.

Soon after entering Sandhurst at the age of eighteen John became infatuated with a fellow cadet. He recorded the details in his diary. 'Oh Dundas, how I love you. You are supreme to me, both in morality and athletics. To be anything like a friend to you is an honour. Oh may God grant you be a friend to me. Oh God let us be in the same regiment. Let us live together, if necessary let us die together, good warm friends'[33] – a sentence which is as profound a string of Victorian sentiments as any that are included in the diary.

Dundas was invited to Longleat where the two men played rounders, tennis and cricket ('I scored 26 runs and was well clapped on coming into the tent'[34]). But it was an adolescent relationship and eventually drew to a close. Initially Dundas had been above reproach but the discovery that he, like John, had 'cribbed' the Sandhurst exam made him mortal. One evening when the two cadets had been drinking hock and consequently 'were rather jollier than usual' they began discussing women. John admitted in his diary that he had once been 'foolish enough to go with a woman. I hope my time for taking women is past. I believe it is as long as I remain good friends with Dundas. But I am afraid that I am so weak that if Dundas was a rake I should be too.'[35] Dundas *was* a rake and the discovery prompted John to redirect his romantic aspirations towards Lily Langtry and to begin mixing with the prostitutes that frequented the music-halls in London's East End.

John once described himself as a 'ripping harmless good-natured fellow',[36] but his parents thought him self-centred and vain; 'Mother says I think too much of myself. Father says so too. He says I talk only for effect.'[37] He was fond of practical jokes and delighted in recording their success in the pages of his diary. He would horrify guests at dinner by squinting and he once gave a female cousin, who was staying at Longleat, a pair of bloomers whose seat he had first removed; they were delivered on a silver tray by a footman.[38] An encounter with a London whore resulted in the mutual pouring of tea-slops over one-another. By the date of his commission into the Lancers he had decided that he liked 'having actresses and bar-maids.'[39] Visits to a purveyor of pornography and to the Alhambra music-hall, where he joked with the girls and renewed his acquaint-ance with the 'girl I had last term', are both mentioned in the diary.

John's philandering first reached the attention of his parents when Frances discovered that her son had taken to seducing barmaids in Frome, a small town four miles from Longleat where his elder brother was standing for parliament. He promised to reform and was sent to join his regiment in York. Shortly afterwards his horse galloped out of the barracks during an exercise and stumbled over some tram-lines, John was thrown from his saddle and killed. One of the final entries in his diary suggests that his years of debauchery were already drawing to a close. In listing the characteristics of the ideal bride he had decided that a woman with a 'sweet, gentle and lively nature' would make a better wife than one whose sole attribute was a 'magnificent figure.'[40]

In 1888 when County Councils were established and the aristocracy surrendered most of their traditional powers, Alexander was appointed first Chairman of Wiltshire County Council. He was also an Honorary Colonel in the Wiltshire Rifle Volunteers and a Trustee of the British Museum and National Portrait Gallery. None of these appointments interfered with his fondness for foreign travel and, in the autumn of 1895, he left Longleat for Algeria and Egypt, accompanied by his daughter Katherine (soon to marry Evelyn Baring, 1st Earl of Cromer, consul-general in Cairo and the man responsible for Egypt's modernization). Early in the new year he fell ill and he and Katherine decided to return slowly to Longleat. By the date of their arrival in Venice he was feverish and suffering from pneumonia.

Alexander was now sixty-five. During his life Longleat's fortunes had reached their summit and begun their decline. The reversals of the past few years had made him morose and unsociable. He had become 'prenaturally thin and singularly pedantic in his mannerisms.'[41] He had little faith in the ability of his eldest son, Thomas, to maintain Longleat and was pessimistic about the future of England and its empire. His shyness and love of privacy had prevented him from entering politics and, although he had written an influential pamphlet on the situation in the Balkans, his intellectual talents had largely been wasted. But his reserve hid a kind heart and even during the worst of the agricultural depression he had done his best to provide the local cottagers with full employment.

Alexander's hotel room in Venice looked out over the Grand Canal towards the Doge's Palace. Perhaps Katherine hoped that the city, the source of so much pleasure and inspiration during the years of redecoration, might encourage his recovery. But his condition deteriorated and in early April 1896 Frances and the children left London by train in an attempt to reach his bedside before he died. News that he had suffered a relapse was waiting for them when they changed trains in Milan on Easter Sunday. He died on the following day and his body was sent back to England for burial at Longbridge Deverill.[42]

9

THE FINAL YEARS, 1896-1946

'And what of the Stately houses of England? How many will survive the cruel and ruthless taxation? Why are we not allowed the right to live? Why should it be a crime that we have succeeded to places too large for present day requirements?'

Lady Newton, Epilogue to *Lyme Letters*, 1925.

Thomas Thynne, 5th Marquess of Bath, was thirty-four when he inherited Longleat and its estates. Despite the economic setbacks suffered by his father, Thomas could view the future with equanimity and optimism. His income had been reduced by the sale of the Irish estates but it was still sufficient to guarantee a life of leisure. His father had modernized Longleat, the gardens and woods had reached maturity, the stables boasted a choice of carriages and the house was administered with efficiency and ease. When Thomas inherited Longleat it seemed as much part of rural England as the villages and market towns that surrounded it. And yet, during the fifty years that he lived in the house, his way of life altered substantially. The introduction of death duties, two World Wars, the birth of the Labour Party, taxation and inflation turned the country house into an anachronism. Hopes of recovery rapidly diminished and many of the larger houses became a burden to their owners. Between 1890 and 1939 nearly 500 country houses were demolished, their estates broken up and sold. At times Thomas must have feared that Longleat might share a similar fate. The cost of heating and maintaining the house increased sharply during his occupation. After the 1st World War a lack of capital made any but the most minor repairs a virtual impossibility. Land prices never recovered from the agricultural depression of the 1870s and, by 1936, farm rents had reached their lowest point since 1800. Retrenchment became necessary if Longleat was to survive. Thomas economized wherever possible, selling land to preserve the house and nucleus of the estate. His efforts were only just successful. When he died in 1946 Longleat employed only one indoor servant and the house was occupied by a girls' school.

Thomas was born in 1862, the eldest of Alexander and Frances's six children. The only letter to have survived from his childhood suggests that his father's preoccupation with the redecoration of Longleat and long absences abroad forced Thomas to become independent and self-reliant. Their relationship was never close. The 4th Marquess mistrusted his son's reserve ('the evil he most has to combat') and Thomas's 'strange reluctance to open his mind'[1] made his father unwilling to involve him in the running of the estate. Thomas was educated at Eton and Oxford and he spent the summer vacations travelling alone through Austria and Germany. Shooting holidays in Scotland, visits to Henley and Lord's are also mentioned in the pocket accounts book he kept during this period of his life. After leaving Oxford he spent several months touring America and the accounts record the cost of a journey to Niagara and small losses at backgammon and poker. After returning to England he entered parliament as member for Frome.

In 1890 Thomas married the twenty-one-year-old Violet Mordaunt. It was an unexpected decision; their characters and backgrounds were very different and it seems likely that Thomas's engagement was disapproved of by the family. Thomas was quiet and shy and, even as a young man, displayed the dignity and poise suggested by the portrait of him which hangs in the house today. His childhood, spent in the security of Longleat, had been peaceful, comfortable and dull. He had led a conventional and uncomplicated life, but it was one to which his young bride was a stranger. Violet's own childhood had been overshadowed by a scandal over her paternity whose implications had a profound influence on her later life. Her mother, Harriet Moncreiffe, was only seventeen when in 1866 she married a close friend of the Prince of Wales, Sir Charles Mordaunt. After Violet's birth in 1869 Lady Mordaunt told her husband that he was not Violet's father and confessed that she had had a number of lovers and 'done wrong' with 'the Prince of Wales and others, often and in open day.'[2] In 1870 Sir Charles Mordaunt instituted divorce proceedings against his wife and, although he was not named as a co-respondent, the Prince of Wales was ordered to give evidence during the hearing. Letters and a valentine in the prince's hand-writing were found amongst Lady Mordaunt's papers and Sir Charles's servants swore that the prince had visited Lady Mordaunt regularly when her husband was out of the house. These disclosures shocked the nation. When the Prince of Wales appeared in court to deny that there had ever been any 'improper familiarity or criminal act' between him and Lady Mordaunt it was the first (and only) time any heir to the English throne has been compelled to answer such a question. The Mordaunt divorce was the first Victorian scandal to involve a member of the royal family. The rumours of the Prince of Wales' infidelity and the fact that Lady Mordaunt was suffering from a fever which rendered her temporarily insane when she first made her confession guaranteed public interest.[3] The popularity of the royal family fell sharply and an official enquiry was mounted to decide on Lady Mordaunt's mental condition. Sir Charles Mordaunt had to wait five years before he obtained a divorce, on the grounds that a Viscount Cole was probably Violet's father. But the truth remains unknown and the rumours and gossip that filled Violet's childhood had an un-doubted effect on her character. She believed strongly in the psyche and supernatural and was liable to vivid dreams which she once described as 'pictures in front of my eyes'. She hid her spiritualism beneath a calm and aristocratic competence, but the few of her private papers to have survived reveal a constant search for some faith to which she might anchor and find repose. Soon after her marriage she became a devout Christian Scientist and whilst still young suffered a succession of illnesses that turned her into a semi-invalid.

After moving into Longleat the 5th Marquess and his wife enjoyed the life of comfort and privilege that its ownership conferred. The game books record weekend shooting parties at which bags of over 2000 pheasants were common, the visitors' books the signatures of European royalty and fellow peers. Violet had menu cards engraved with her monogram and a violet. The menus were written in French and the seven-course dinners served to her guests offer proof of Longleat's hospitality and apparent wealth.

A change of master made little difference to the lives of Longleat's indoor servants. In 1902 the household numbered forty-three and consisted of the following:

1 House Steward
1 Butler
1 Under Butler
1 Groom of the Chambers
1 Valet
3 Footmen
1 Steward's Room Footman
2 Oddmen
2 Pantry Boys
1 Lamp Boy
1 Housekeeper
2 Lady's Maids
1 Nurse
1 Nursery Maid
8 Housemaids
2 Sewing Maids
2 Still Room Maids
6 Laundry Maids
1 Chef
2 Kitchen Maids
1 Scullery Maid
1 Vegetable Maid
1 Daily Woman

Violet redesigned the footmen's uniform but made few changes to Longleat's administration. Electricity was not installed in the house until 1928 and in winter the housemaids, whose annual wage was then £25, had to carry a candle and dustpan in one hand and sweep the darkened corridors with the other. Squeezed between the gun room and beer cellars was a basement lamp room in which oil and spare glasses for Longleat's 172 paraffin lamps were stored. Violet insisted that every bedroom be provided with eight candles and each one had to be trimmed or replaced when the rooms were dusted. But the early years of the twentieth century had little impact on the servants' traditional routine. The footmen still powdered their hair before waiting at table during a dinner party. During dinner the housemaids swept the sitting-room grate and rearranged the cushions. Every Christmas Violet gave each of them a length of material. On Christmas night, whatever the weather, they put on their thin chintz dresses and danced in the courtyard, whilst the family and their guests watched from the windows above.

Thomas's eldest son, John, was only ten months old when the family moved into Longleat. John had two elder sisters, Kathleen and Emma, and a third, Mary, was born in 1903. Two years later the delayed arrival of the local doctor by pony-trap meant that the birth of a brother, christened Henry Frederick, had to be supervised by a midwife.

Life for the children was monotonous and disciplined. They rose at seven o'clock and spent an hour practising piano scales in an unheated schoolroom. Breakfast was at eight and chapel at nine. The mornings were spent with their mother in her bedroom and at midday they went walking or riding. Their ponies were led by a 'tiger', a small boy whose only other duty was to sit on the carriage box when the family went out for a drive, his arms folded across his chest and wearing livery. After lunch in the Great Hall the children had a 'secret hour' during which they played amongst themselves, either in the house or garden. A bread-and-butter tea was eaten at four o'clock and they were in bed by seven.

Between May and July the family and seventeen servants stayed at their London house in Grosvenor Square. In the mews behind the house were stables and lodgings for the eleven horses and five coachmen needed when the family was in residence. The children attended a private day school in South Kensington and Thomas, who served briefly as Secretary of State for India in 1905, spent the afternoons in the House of Lords. Whilst Longleat was empty it was spring-cleaned, rooms were repainted and minor alterations completed. One summer the 200-year-old hand-bored alder wood drainage pipes that carried sewage away from the house were replaced.

Thomas's brother, Lord Alexander Thynne, and three sisters (the latter were known collectively as 'the aunts' by the children) were regular visitors to Longleat. The Muniment Room contains a letter written to Lord Alexander when he was in South Africa in 1902 advising him to 'come home and marry and raise up seed after your own kind, and make the race of Thynnes like the sand of the sea-shore, in multitude.'[4] The advice was ignored and although Lord Alexander returned to England and became an MP he remained a bachelor. He lived at Norton Hall, a vast and florid Gothic mansion near Northampton which had been left him by Beriah Botfield, a wealthy Midlands landowner. Botfield was an ostentatious but eccentric Victorian squire. Wishing to confirm his position in society he wrote a lengthy and occasionally inaccurate book called *Stemmata Botevilliana* which set out to prove that he and the Thynnes were related. After Lord Alexander was killed in action in 1918 his spinster sister, Beatrice, inherited Norton Hall. Although the house has since been demolished, its collection of Dutch paintings and 10,000 books are now housed at Longleat. Beatrice was the most eccentric of Thomas's sisters. She went to art school, was an atrocious gossip, and acted as a link between fashionable society and the world of Bloomsbury, headed by Lytton Strachey and Virginia Woolf, with whom she became friends. Virginia Woolf was fascinated by Beatrice and thought she possessed 'not only rank, beauty and easy, pleasant good manners but a kind of lazy pagan majesty, a natural grace.'[5] These qualities deserted Beatrice as she grew older. Her only evening dress resembled a sack and, whenever travelling, she wound khaki puttees round her legs which unwound as she walked. When she stayed at Longleat, a housemaid was ordered to look after her dog, to exercise it in the morning, wipe its feet and then lift it on to her bed. In 1912 she stayed with a Russian grand-duke at his summer house near St Petersburg. In the journal she kept during her visit she recorded her amusement at the activities of the 'drunk but jolly peasants' and her distaste for the 'painted ladies' in St Petersburg. She seems to have been particularly fascinated by violent death, for her journal contains detailed notes on several recent Russian murders.[6] Thomas's other sisters, Alice and Katherine, were both married. Alice could roll her eyes until only the whites were visible. She pouched her food like a squirrel and after meals delighted in slowly digesting the surplus food stored in her cheeks.

Violet's correspondence suggests that she was easily overawed by the innumerable Thynnes who flooded through Longleat. Cousins, great-uncles and nieces were all equally welcome. Violet lacked their family unity and kinship. She took refuge in her religion and wrote copious notes on the character of Christ and the meaning of the Lord's Prayer. Amongst her papers is an enigmatic letter that suggests her sense of isolation went far deeper than anyone realized. It was written to her by a friend with whom she had shared a railway compartment on a journey across France shortly before the start of the 1st World War. 'The situation is this, we have mutually fallen in love with each other. If I had been a man it would have been disastrous, but both being muddled women we are doing nobody any harm and ourselves I think a great deal of good, as we are able to give what the other lacks and help each-other to "play the game".'[7] The name of Violet's companion remains unknown, but there can be no doubt of the closeness of their relationship. Violet wanted her to visit Longleat, to be fussed over and share her 'most intimate thoughts'. We do not know when their friendship began or ended, or to what extent it compensated for Violet's loneliness at Longleat. She was a highly sensitive woman and her belief in second-sight and the psychic was fundamental to her attitude to life. Such qualities needed an outlet, for they were unsuited to the bustling, masculine and efficient world of the Edwardian country house.

Violet loved animals and started a Pets' Cemetery to the north of the house in which the family pets were (and still are) buried. Her love of animals was an additional barrier against loneliness; birds would eat off the palm of her hand and she could mesmerize the family pets. She believed implicitly in her dreams and regarded them as advance notice of future events. Early in 1891, when pregnant, she dreamt that she would give birth on Good Friday and be attended by a short, stout midwife. Her dream was ignored. The baby was not due until May and a tall, thin midwife had already been booked to assist at the birth. But Violet's premonition proved correct. Kathleen, her eldest daughter, was born prematurely on Good Friday and the delivery was attended by a plump relief midwife. On another occasion Violet dreamt she saw the 1st Marquess of Bath walking towards her wearing a wig and prune-coloured velvet coat. His portrait depicted him in a black coat but when the painting was cleaned the coat changed colour, becoming the shade of reddish-purple dreamed of by Violet.

In August 1914 the British Government declared war on Germany.

At first the outbreak of the 1st World War had little effect on the lives of the country gentry. They still dominated political and social life and enjoyed a near feudal control of the countryside. But as an increasing number of businessmen took up political appointments to aid the war effort, the political power of the landed aristocracy rapidly diminished. Increases in taxation undermined their social influence, and higher wages and the shortage of domestic staff affected their ability to maintain their homes. By 1918 the vast social upheaval caused by the war had made the final collapse of the country-house way of life almost inevitable.

First visible evidence of the war reached Longleat when a party of Belgian refugees were billeted in Horningsham. Their arrival prompted a small number of footmen, gardeners and gamekeepers to resign their posts and join the armed forces. Soon after, Thomas suggested that part of the house be turned into a military hospital. The government accepted his offer. Beds were placed in the Saloon, nurses moved into the Bachelor Rooms on the top floor, the 'Bath' bedroom became an operating theatre and the family turned one of the libraries into a sitting-room. Longleat remained a hospital until after the Armistice and many of the soldiers who convalesced in the house recorded their names in the visitors' book. Thomas paid a substantial portion of the hospital's running costs out of his income and his generosity during the war was rewarded when George V created him a Knight of the Garter.

Thomas's eldest son, John, Viscount Weymouth, was commissioned a 2nd Lieutenant in the Royal Scots Greys during the winter of 1914. By the following summer he was in barracks at York, eager to get to France and angry at the government's handling of the war. Life in camp was disagreeable. His batman was incompetent (he was later dismissed when found in bed with a 'strange woman') and his hut was unheated.[8] Weymouth's opinion of army life was not improved when he was ordered to exchange his non-regulation boots for a pair which gave him corns.[9] In October he surprised the family by arriving suddenly to spend his leave at Longleat; his sisters screamed and Violet fainted. Due to a shortage of cartridges the gamekeepers were using nets and traps to clear the woods of pheasant. Weymouth joined in, gaining useful practice with his service revolver. Shortly after returning to barracks his regiment was ordered to France. His last letter from York to Longleat mentions a young girl he thought might make his brother Henry, then ten years old, a future wife: 'You will notice that I am already mapping out Henry's career for him, poor wretch! I pity him if he follows my plan.'[10] His next letter, written from France just before Christmas, contains a request for six turkeys, a bath, basin, pipes and tobacco. He also wrote to a girl-friend asking her to send him 'China Town', 'Show me how to do the Foxtrot' and various other records for the battalion gramophone.

On Boxing Day Weymouth was told that his battalion would soon be going into action. He had already been on a brief tour of the front line and had written an excited letter home to say that he had seen 'three or four of our shells land plum in the enemy trenches. It was a grand sight. I have at last realized there is a war on.'[11] But his enthusiasm quickly palled. The mud, the shortage of shells and the reality of trench life made him wish that the war would end. He thought increasingly of Longleat and, after conscription was introduced early in 1916, wrote home to his mother to say that he could not imagine the house without any footmen or his father being looked after by a parlour maid. 'If that is going to be the case I am going to look after my own clothes when I come home. It would be awful being waited on by parlour maids at meals.'[12] In early January 1916 the 5th Cavalry Battalion, in which Weymouth was now serving, went into the front line at Hulluch, a small mining village on the northern sector of the Western Front. After a week in the trenches he wrote his last surviving letter to his parents. 'I am now at the trenches, or at least in the rest billets behind them, and go up again tomorrow (I hope for the last six days). I am afraid that I cannot raise any excitement (except that of funk) or enthusiasm over them.'[13] In early February he was again in the front line, sheltering in a dug-out from a three-day German bombardment. On the evening of the 12th he was ordered to fire a mine near the trench parapet. In the early hours of the 13th he was shot in the back of the head whilst standing exposed to enemy fire on the crater's rim. He never recovered consciousness and died within an hour. He was not yet twenty-one.

Amongst Violet's papers are nearly 100 letters of sympathy which she and her husband received after Weymouth's death was published in the casualty lists. George V wrote to record his sorrow at hearing of the 'sad incident to your fair young son'[14] and one of Weymouth's

A shooting party at Longleat during the visit by the Prince of Wales and
Princess Alexandra in 1881. The Prince of Wales is in the left foreground, the
4th Marquess on the right.
Longleat Fire Brigade in 1881.

Violet Mordaunt, 5th Marchioness of Bath, in about 1900.
Thomas Thynne, 5th Marquess of Bath, in the 1880s.

Longleat from the South.

Henry Thynne, 6th Marquess of Bath, in 1971 by Graham Sutherland.

brother-officers tried to console Violet by insisting that 'to be killed in action is a glorious honour, a magnificent fate.' But most of the letters came from family friends and, with their reference to dead husbands, sons and brothers, they emphasize with tragic clarity the losses suffered by the aristocracy in the 1st World War. The sons of the landed gentry had been born into a strong military tradition and, as junior officers, they had been trained to disregard their own safety. In 1916 officer casualties were proportionally six times higher than those of other ranks. One of the letters preserved at Longleat was written by a fellow-officer who had served with Weymouth in France. 'I hardly know how to write to you. I was talking to him about half-an-hour before, and he was so well and full of life. He came down to my dug-out earlier in the night and had some tea with me, and a nice talk about you and home, and I don't think anyone could have had fewer cares or seemed more at peace with everyone and everything than he did. I passed him on the way up the trench from one of my guns to the other, sitting smoking a cigarette, and just had a word or two with him about midnight, and at three o'clock when I came back the same way someone told me he had been killed.'[15]

Weymouth was buried in the British Military Cemetery at Vermelles and his cap badge and tunic buttons were returned to the family. On the night he died Violet dreamt she saw him lying in a dug-out with his head propped on a pile of blankets. She was describing the scene to the family at breakfast when news of his death reached them by telegram. Her dream proved accurate. She later discovered that after being shot Weymouth had been carried into a dug-out and placed on a pile of blankets. The dream gave her a feeling of shared suffering. The thought that she had been with her son when he went 'onward and upward' comforted her and she was able to tell a friend that although she missed him she was 'proud of his life and the manner in which he died.'[16]

Weymouth's death meant that his brother Henry succeeded to his title and became heir to Longleat. Even today Henry Thynne, 6th Marquess of Bath, can recall standing outside Longleat in 1916, looking up at the house and saying to himself in fear, 'How can I look after you? I'll never be able to do it.'

The 1st World War ended in November 1918. Three generations

of Thynnes died during the war. Thomas's mother, his eldest son and his brother Lord Alexander, who as a Lieutenant-Colonel in the Wiltshire Regiment had been killed in action seven weeks before the Armistice. Longleat faced an uncertain future. Although agricultural land had increased in value during the war the rents had remained almost static. The agricultural wage had trebled to 46/- a week, food and coal prices had risen and women, on whom Longleat depended for the nucleus of its domestic staff, had gained the vote. Weymouth's death meant that a percentage of the estate's value would have to be paid in death duties. Longleat was no longer needed as a military hospital and it had to be turned back into a family home. The cost of maintaining the house was obviously going to be far greater than in 1914. But the real impact of the war on the structure of English society was unknown and few people understood how the changes it had created might affect the future. Many of the country gentry regarded the war as an interruption and, now it was won, were determined to try and recapture the spirit and mood of pre-war England.

Life in the early 1920s was aggravated by unemployment. Between 1914 and 1918 400,000 female servants had left domestic service to aid the war effort. Many had been widowed. They were willing to exchange the uncertainties of peace for the security of below-stairs life in a country house. The ease with which the traditional routines were re-established lulled the country gentry into a false sense of security. Even the present Marquess, who was only a teenager at the time, could see no reason why the way of life enjoyed by his ancestors could not last indefinitely. To maintain Longleat Thomas needed capital and, between 1919 and 1921, he raised £350,000 by selling 8600 acres of the estate. Many other landowners also sold land and it has been estimated that in the four years prior to 1921 a quarter of England changed hands. As estates were broken up and sold and tenants became owner-occupiers, the sense of community fostered by the country house began to fade. The number of people dependent on the local gentry for their incomes declined and the character of rural England gradually changed.

In 1923 Longleat employed over twenty indoor servants. The arrival of the motor-car made the groom and coachmen redundant and the eventual installation of electricity made the housemaid's life much easier. But life in the Servants' Hall continued as before. The footmen were still issued with the silk stockings, white gloves, patent-leather shoes and cockade hats of their traditional livery. Much of the protocol and pomp that had once regulated life at Longleat was abandoned, but its hey-day was still celebrated at balls and formal dinners.

Before the war Thomas had been appointed Chairman of Wiltshire County Council (he held the post for nearly forty years) and in 1922 he was created Lord Lieutenant of Somerset. A year later the Prince of Wales (later Edward VIII) stayed at Longleat when touring the West Country. The room in which he slept remains unchanged to the present day. The writing materials laid out on the desk, the half-tester bed and hand-painted Chinese brocade which covers the walls make it as evocative of Longleat's past as any other room in the house. After leaving Longleat the prince wrote to Violet and his letter has been preserved amongst the small folio of letters sent to the Thynnes by members of the royal family. 'I am only sorry I was out all day and saw so little of your lovely place. I only hope you are none the worse for having sat up so long in the evenings, and also that Lord Bath is not too tired after those long and strenuous days with me.'[17]

Violet's health grew worse after the war. She spent much of the time on a chaise-longue or in a wheelchair but occasionally visited the cottagers, travelling to their homes in a basket-work trap pulled by a Dartmoor pony. Her death in 1928 accentuated Thomas's shyness and reserve. He took the need for economy very seriously and refused to replace his clothes or allow his shoes to be resoled. Dressed in a battered felt hat and threadbare overcoat and accompanied by his Great Dane *Stephen*, he would walk round the park and gardens. Two of his daughters were married, Kathleen to Oliver Stanley and Emma to the Marquess of Northampton, and he was content to remain quietly at Longleat.

In 1926 Thomas's surviving son, Henry, Lord Weymouth, reached the age of twenty-one. To celebrate the occasion a pontoon bridge was built over Half-Mile Pond and 1000 guests were entertained to lunch, tea and a fireworks display. Henry had broken his nose at school, but his lean face and square jaw were characteristic of the Thynnes. His closest friend was a seventy-year-old gamekeeper called Dick Futcher who countered his shyness by encouraging him to meet and mix with people of a different background to his own. Futcher 'talked broad Wiltshire, sang bawdy songs and drank unbelievable quantities of beer' and the two men often toured the countryside on a motorbike visiting local inns.[18]

Henry had been educated at Harrow and Oxford. By his own admission he was lazy at school and read agriculture at university because it allowed him to own a motor-car. At Oxford he soon established a wide circle of extrovert and eccentric friends, amongst whom were Evelyn Waugh, Harold Acton, Robert Byron and Brian Howard (described by Waugh as mad, bad and dangerous to know'), and together they formed part of a fashionable group known to gossip columnists and the public as the Bright Young People (or Things). The Bright Young People were a creation of the Twenties. They danced the Charleston and Black Bottom, mixed exotic cocktails and attended the fancy-dress parties given by Laura Corrigan, widow of an American steel millionaire who gave away jewellery and gold sock-suspenders to her guests. Life for the Bright Young People was an endless party – 'Masked parties, Savage parties . . . Greek parties . . . almost naked parties in St John's Wood, parties in flats and studios and houses and ships and hotels and nightclubs, in windmills and swimming baths', said Evelyn Waugh in *Vile Bodies*. At Wembley Fun Fair they abandoned the boats which took them through River Caves decorated with scenes from Dante's *Inferno* and splashed through the water playing ukuleles. When a game of 'follow my leader' led them through Selfridges' Oxford Street store they enraged customers and shop assistants by climbing over the counters. When friends stayed with Henry at Longleat they met every evening in the Bachelor Rooms at the top of the house and secretly mixed cocktails. If Thomas approached, a dog-fight was started between Henry's Sealyham and a friend's mongrel and the drinks were then hidden in the confusion.[19]

This period of Henry's life has been described by his first wife, now Daphne Fielding, in her volume of autobiography *Mercury Presides*. Daphne, herself a Bright Young Thing, was the only daughter of Lord Vivian and she had met Henry when he was at Harrow. By 1926 they had decided to marry. Thomas was strongly opposed to the idea and wrote to Lord Vivian to say that 'Henry was too young to think of marriage and needed a very steady wife'. To this Lord

Vivian 'bombastically replied that he disapproved of Henry and thought he would be a very unsuitable husband for his daughter, to whom he intended making this thoroughly clear.'[20] But family opposition was no deterrent and the young couple made plans for a secret wedding. The banns were read in St Paul's, Knightsbridge, and both Henry and Daphne used their middle names to avoid the chance of publicity. The two charwomen cleaning the church were the only witnesses at the wedding ceremony. Shortly afterwards Thomas, who had no idea that his son was now married, persuaded him to go to America, perhaps hoping that Daphne's absence might end their affair. After working on a Texas cattle ranch, Henry sailed through the Panama Canal and down the west side of South America. He returned to England determined to announce his marriage and with the offer of a job in the Bolivian oil-fields. By then all family opposition to their marriage had crumbled, but rather than reveal that they were already man and wife they decided to plan a second wedding. They were married again in 1927; Daphne's wedding dress was designed by Norman Hartnell, then fresh from Cambridge, and the wedding photographs were taken with a 'box' Brownie by a young and unknown photographer called Cecil Beaton. A year later, and undoubtedly with some reservations as to his son's capacity for hard work, Thomas handed over the administration of the Longleat estate to Henry.

Over the next ten years Henry's affection for Longleat developed into a determination to preserve the house and estate when they became his. He had spent a year learning the rudiments of estate management but now, at home at Longleat, he came face to face with the countless problems that plagued country landowners between the wars. The farms, cottages and roads had been badly neglected and major improvements were needed if the estate was to be made profitable. A shortage of capital and higher wages made the employment of a large outdoor staff impossible. The days of thirty gardeners were finally over and Longleat had to adapt if it was to survive. Henry decided to expand the forestry programme and new plantations were established. His knowledge of forestry is now considerable and even today, in his seventies, he still helps with the thinning and planning of a planting policy. Another of his improvements involved the gardens. These had been added to and altered by every successive marchioness, irrespective of proportion or planning. Although many of the flower beds had been planted with vegetables during the war and since grassed over, there were still large areas that needed to be cleared. The bedding plants and formal garden were no longer practical and Henry hoped to lower the maintenance costs of the park and gardens by simplifying their design. Longleat's azaleas and rhododendrons were well known and it was decided to supplement these with other rarer shrubs. In 1929, with the help of the garden-designer Russell Page, he began cutting back the eighty-year-old undergrowth of rhododendrons that had 'rolled on through the woods like a heavy sea and formed thickets fifteen foot high or more.'[21] Once the woods had been cleared they were gradually replanted with shrubs and trees. Today, nearly fifty years later, these shrubs have reached maturity and provide a superb setting for the woods that surround the house.

In 1929 Henry entered politics to please his father, becoming Conservative candidate for Frome. He spent the next two years making speeches and opening bazaars, neither of which he much enjoyed, and in 1931 was elected to the House of Commons. He regarded the House as a waste of his time and hated being an MP. 'I appreciate that it can be very interesting if you're inclined that way. I had to live in London and leave the estate behind, and when I came down for the weekend I had to make still more speeches. I held office for four years and then I'm afraid I resigned.'[22] During those years he made only one speech in parliament. He chose tea as his subject and spoke, briefly, to a noisy and uninterested House of Commons.

Soon after their marriage the Weymouths moved into an elegant Georgian house close to Longleat. To supplement her income Daphne began writing newspaper and magazine articles and through them they became friends with Lord Beaverbrook. They spent their summers abroad, boar-hunting in France or cruising in the Mediterranean. In 1934 they bicycled to Austria to visit Daphne's mother and two years later accompanied Beaverbrook on a cruise through the West Indies, Thomas allowed them two weekend house parties a year at Longleat. The first in June and the second during the shooting season when they entertained their guests to a picnic lunch in the 'big glass vine-house, sitting on chairs placed over the hot pipes under a canopy of leaves and clusters of grapes'.[23] The birth of a daughter, Caroline, was followed in 1929 by the birth of a son who died young. Between 1932 and 1937 three more sons were born and the eldest, Alexander, is the present Viscount Weymouth and heir to the estate.

In September 1939 war returned to Europe. After returning early from a bicycling holiday in Denmark Henry joined his regiment, the Royal Wiltshire Yeomanry, and soon left for Palestine. He was wounded in 1942 during the Battle of El Alamein and after convalescing became British Liaison Officer to the American 19th Corps. Known affectionately as 'Hank the Yank', he was still serving with them when they landed on the Normandy beaches four days after D-Day. After the American entry into the war a large American military hospital was built in the grounds at Longleat and Daphne began working there as a telephone operator and hospital librarian.

In May 1939 Thomas offered to lend Longleat to the Royal School for Officers of the Army, a girls' public school near Bath whose buildings had been requisitioned by the Admiralty. His offer was accepted and on 8 September, five days after the declaration of war, a party of cleaners arrived at Longleat to begin storing the furniture and preparing the house for occupation by the Royal School. The housekeeper refused to allow them into the house. Even the butler failed to make her see reason and, after an hour's argument, Thomas was forced to intervene. She was led away in tears. For more than thirty years Longleat's management had been her responsibility. The war and 300 girls were to end the domestic traditions that had been part of Longleat's way of life since the building of the house. In 1939, when the indoor servants were dismissed and the Royal School took up residence, Longleat's household numbered fourteen and consisted of the following:

1 Housekeeper
1 Cook
1 Butler
3 Laundry Maids
3 Housemaids
1 Pantry Lad
2 Motor Men
2 Odd-job Men

Once Longleat's furniture had been stored in the stables and chapel eighty lorry-loads of school furniture were dumped on the front steps and the house, whose electricity was then provided by its own generator, was connected to the national grid. The girls returned to school in late September and on their first evening at Longleat were all struck 'by the incongruity of their familiar school furniture, looking small, shabby and lost against the long fringed curtains and delicate Chinese wallpapers: black iron bedsteads and green slop pails standing on polished oak boards with painted cherubs looking down upon them'.[24] Their dormitories were scattered through the house. There were beds in the Saloon, attics and corridors. For the next eight years the girls of the Royal School were to hang their gym slips in a cupboard that had once belonged to Marie Antoinette.

Thomas retained only four ground-floor rooms for his own use and his cooking was done in the still-room by the housekeeper. But whatever the inconvenience or discomfort of his new life he found the change refreshing. In a letter to the school's headmistress he wrote, 'I am quite honest that I am enjoying every moment. It is twenty-five years since I had children running about the house; I have enjoyed my life even when alone, but I never realized how lonely I have been, and I love hearing the children all over the place – in fact I keep my door open on purpose'.[25] He gradually became part of the school. The girls always gave him a slice of their birthday-cakes and a row of empty plates could always be found in his rooms.

Thomas led a quiet, simple life throughout the six years of the 2nd World War. His children were all married and petrol rationing made travel difficult. Fred Chapman, the head-gardener, was a regular visitor to the house. After finishing work and changing into his best clothes he would return to Longleat once every two weeks and cut Thomas's hair. Queen Mary, then living at Badminton, was another visitor and two of her letters to Thomas have been preserved. The first includes a suggestion that the caves at Cheddar, owned by the Thynnes since 1908, might be useful for the storage of oil, and the second, written in the summer of 1940 after the fall of France, expresses her concern at Thomas's health. 'I beg you to take care and rest. At our age the air-raid warnings are not pleasant, besides the many shocks we have to bear.'[26] In 1942 Thomas celebrated his eightieth birthday. The schoolgirls had hoarded their rations to make him a birthday-cake and as a present put on a pageant of Longleat's history in the Orangery.

Thomas died in 1946. His cedar coffin lay in state for two days in the Great Hall and he was then buried in Longbridge Deverill. The girls of the Royal School lined Longleat's steps as he left his home.

SAVING LONGLEAT

*'People put me down as a bit mad, but the situation is
simply that I love this place so much that – although I'm
basically shy – I force myself to do things to attract people
to Longleat and so make money to preserve it.'*[1]

Henry Thynne, 6th Marquess of Bath, 1966.

Henry Thynne, 6th Marquess of Bath, was forty-one in 1946. No
longer the Bright Young Thing of the 1920s, but an ex-Member of
Parliament and a retired major, he became owner of one of the largest
country houses in England on the death of his father. As well as
inheriting Longleat and its 16,000-acre estate, he faced a £700,000
bill for death duties. A year later the Royal School returned to Bath
and he had to decide what was to be done with his inheritance.
Although Henry Bath's early years had been cushioned by comfort
and affluence he was hard-working, down-to-earth and obstinate.
His father's death posed immense problems but he was determined
to keep Longleat in his possession. He quickly realized that if Longleat
was to survive the uncertainties of post-war Britain he would have
to deny himself the life of ease enjoyed by so many of his ancestors.
His first priority was to tidy up the house after its eight-year occupation by the Royal School. But what was to be done after that?
Longleat was his, but was he to move in and make it his home?

In 1947 Longleat had been standing for nearly 400 years. For most
of those years it had been looked after and promptly repaired by
skilled craftsmen whose standards of work ensured its upkeep. The
servants were vital to Longleat's maintenance. A well-trained housemaid and house carpenter were more important to its conservation
than any number of chefs, butlers and footmen. And in 1947 a large
domestic household was a thing of the past. The roof was in need
of repair, two chimneys were in danger of collapsing and the activities

of the death-watch beetle had weakened many of the timbers that held the house together. Only part of the damage was visible, for Longleat's façade disguised its true condition. The state of the internal walls, ceilings and floors was largely unknown. The cost of renovation was certain to be high. The economic depression of the 1920s and 1930s had hindered improvements to the estate, the farms needed reorganization and the American hospital and an RAF depot occupied part of the grounds. Amongst the first tasks tackled by Henry after his father's death was the replanting of 1500 acres of woodland that had been requisitioned and felled during the war; 250 German prisoners-of-war were employed to help with the work.

Longleat's preservation depended on the acquisition of capital and an increased income. After selling 5400 acres of land to help pay the death duties, Henry realized that he could not afford to maintain Longleat out of his private income. Longleat and its gardens cost £30,000 a year to run and the Baths and their four children did not require a home with 118 rooms. Longleat's future seemed bleak. All over England country houses were being shuttered and closed. Many were demolished, several became institutions and the owners of numerous smaller houses struggled on as best they could. Henry searched for an alternative that would guarantee Longleat's survival and keep it in the hands of the Thynnes. In the spring of 1948 he decided to restore the house to its pre-war condition and then open it to the public as a commercial enterprise. It was an imaginative decision, but a gamble, and once news of his intentions reached the Press he was nicknamed the 'mad Marquess'. Today, with the advantage of hindsight, his solution may seem obvious, but in the late 1940s many regarded it as foolhardy and impetuous. Petrol rationing was still in force, there were restrictions on materials and labour, and repair grants lay in the future. Although the Cheddar Caves – some fifteen miles from Longleat – continued to attract a large number of visitors, no country house in private ownership had yet opened to the public on a regular commercial basis. But Longleat's condition was grave and when, in 1948, two of Henry's sisters opened the house for one day in aid of charity the response gave him the confidence to press on with his plans.

The task of making the house ready for its public opening began immediately. The roof lead was lifted and timbers repaired. The 5th Marquess's ground-floor bedroom was converted into a small

souvenir shop. The furniture was brought back into the house from
the stables; much of it was seriously dilapidated and many of the
curtains, carpets and tapestries had been attacked by moth. Carpenters,
picture-restorers and French-polishers set to work and a group of
nuns from Bristol mended the tapestries. Local women, many of
whom had served as housemaids before the war, returned as cleaners
and gradually floors were scrubbed and polished, curtains hung and
walls and ceilings washed. There were moments when Henry re-
gretted his decision to open Longleat to the public. Much more
needed to be done than he had first anticipated. Costs were high and
his resources limited. But there was no going back. With the advice
of his elder sisters, who remembered Longleat's original interior
from their childhood, the furniture was moved into position and
the family plate and silver laid out in the three dining-rooms to be
opened to the public. The 4th Marchioness had kept many of her
dresses and these, along with parasols, hats, coronation robes and
other family clothes, were taken out of storage and put on display.
The 200-year-old State Coach was repainted in the Thynne livery
and placed at the foot of the Grand Staircase. Henry decided to
commission a short history of the house and family and, after
Evelyn Waugh had rejected a suggestion that he be its author on the
grounds that he could never write the history of 'such a black Protestant family as the Thynnes',[2] Daphne researched and wrote
Longleat in three weeks. Part of the west-wing basement was converted into a café, drives were tarred and every pond and lake on
the estate with the exception of Shearwater was dredged. To
encourage visitors to walk round the gardens they had to be redesigned. Once again Russell Page helped with the work. Hedges
were trimmed, paths widened, flowering cherry trees planted in the
Orangery garden and a large formal rose garden was laid out and
planted to the east of the house. Henry was anxious not to spoil
Longleat's character and the house and gardens were made as evocative of their past as their new purpose allowed.

Longleat, 'The Treasure House of the West' and England's first
privately-owned stately home to admit the public on a regular
basis, opened its doors in April 1949. Apart from a few National
Trust houses Longleat had no rivals, and the publicity that accompanied its opening was immense. In an England of ration coupons
and austerity, where the Premier Earl of England, the 21st Earl of

Shrewsbury, had been forced to set up a roadside vegetable barrow outside his family seat in order to earn a living,[3] Longleat's opening combined a nostalgia for vanished splendour with sound commercial enterprise. Henry stood on the front steps to welcome the first arrivals. Members of the family acted as guides and his seventeen-year-old heir, Alexander, administered the car park. By the end of the year over 135,000 people had paid 2/6d each to visit the house and a new tourist industry had been born.

Henry's success at attracting visitors to Longleat persuaded many other stately-home owners to, in his words, 'jump on the band-wagon'. As an increasing number of houses opened their doors it became possible to assess the importance of their contents. Although every county in England had its share of country houses their architecture and decoration had largely been ignored. The extent and value of their art collections was unknown and many people regarded them as symbols of an outmoded way of life. Having lost their economic and political influence, survival now depended on the willingness of the public to visit them and help pay for their upkeep. Longleat's example proved that this was possible and what began as an attempt at 'refloating one's fortunes on a flood of half-crowns, motor coach parties and "set teas"'[4] has since developed into a major industry. In recent years interest in the country house has extended to the gardens, their traditional self-sufficiency, and to even the below-stairs life led by the servants.

Since 1949 the country house has played a prominent role in the growth of tourism. The resourcefulness and resilience of owners has given the country house a national reputation and they are now recognized as an important contribution to England's heritage. Within fifteen years of Longleat's opening 600 other houses had followed suit. In 1973 forty-three million people visited places of historic interest. Due partly to a greater fascination with the past, higher standards of education and increased mobility, these figures owe much to Henry Bath's imaginative solution to the problems that faced Longleat in 1947.

Henry's concern for Longleat absorbed all his energies in the years after the house first opened. Five years' separation from Daphne during the war had affected their marriage and in 1953 they were divorced. They both remarried in the same year, Daphne to Xan

Fielding, whom she had first met on a photographic expedition to Crete soon after the war, and Henry to Virginia Tennant. The present 6th Marchioness of Bath was born Virginia Parsons, daughter of *The Daily Mail*'s drama critic and Viola Tree, the actress and writer. Her grandfather was the famous Edwardian actor-manager, Sir Herbert Beerbohm Tree, and the wit, caricaturist and writer, Max Beerbohm, was an uncle. Since their marriage the Baths have lived in a converted mill four miles from Longleat. In 1958 they had a daughter, Silvy Cerne.

Once Longleat was open and the house producing an income Henry was able to continue with the restoration work and make improvements to the estate. Between 1947 and 1957 over £300,000 was spent on reconstructing farm buildings and, as tenancies fell in, reapportioning the land into more economic units. Henry admits that he gains little pleasure from owning rented land, but the tenanted farms provide employment for families that have traditionally depended on Longleat for their livelihood. In 1950 the three-quarter-mile avenue of elms that ran between the house and the South Lodge were felled. Many were diseased and dangerous and they have since been replaced with a double line of flowering tulip trees. During the 1950s the huts belonging to the American hospital were demolished, the concrete roads were broken up and all the land requisitioned during the war reabsorbed into the estate.

Longleat's restoration is a continuing process. The damage caused by the death-watch beetle has proved immensely costly and over £80,000 has so far been spent on repairs and insecticide treatment. Two carpenters are employed inside the house and they have replaced many of the beams and joists; some were so rotten that a small number of steel girders have had to be inserted to help strengthen the walls. In the Old Library on the top floor the work of mending the tapestries and rebinding the books still goes on. Each page of the rarer books has to be individually treated against attack by a paper-eating moth, and hidden costs such as these, of which few people are aware, absorb all the income from visitors to the house. Although the furniture has been restored and paintings cleaned there is still much to be done. Longleat is open to the public on all but Christmas Day and, with over 250,000 visitors a year passing through its doors, regular maintenance work is vital to its upkeep. Guides, cleaners and caterers are all employed in the house. There is a librarian, a publicity officer and an administrator, and Longleat's staff now equals the number of servants employed by the 4th Marquess in the nineteenth century. Henry has said that 'every penny spent in the house goes back into the house' and Longleat's contents are probably in better condition today than at any other time in their history. Although some of the restoration work has been supported by grants, the visitors' income has allowed improvements that otherwise would have been impossible. This is true of other country houses, and it has meant that one of the outstanding features of the British tourist industry has been paid for without substantial aid from public funds.

Henry has used part of Longleat's income to add to its five libraries. He has built up a collection of first editions of children's books which is housed in the Old Library and his Churchill Collection, probably the finest in private ownership, has recently been exhibited in the house. The Churchill Collection began in the 1940s with the purchase of *The Malakaland Field Force* for £3 and has since expanded to include postage stamps, cigars, Churchill's clothes and racing colours, his paintings, a motor-car and 'anything I could lay my hands on'. To provide contrast Henry Bath has also bought many of Adolf Hitler's personal belongings, amongst which are fifty-nine uninspired architectural water-colours painted by Hitler. He is now building up an Edward VIII Collection and has already acquired a red pillar-box stamped with Edward's monogram and the royal coat-of-arms.

During the early 1960s Longleat's annual attendance figures began to remain steady. Rivalry between stately-home owners had become fiercely competitive and the house, gardens and deer park were no longer an adequate attraction. Increased leisure time had widened the social background of the visitors and many were dissatisfied with a brief tour of the house. Without adding to its facilities, Longleat's popularity seemed certain to decline. In 1964 Jimmy Chipperfield, an animal trainer and member of a well-known English circus family, approached Henry and suggested that part of the estate be turned into a Safari Park and stocked with lions in the hope that it might persuade visitors to spend an entire day in the grounds. At first Henry did not understand. 'I thought he meant a zoo! I asked him where he wanted to put all the cages and he said "I don't want any cages. The lions will go free and the visitors will be caged in their cars". I was horrified. I had to get up and pour myself a drink.'⁵ Once his initial astonishment had abated Henry realized that a Safari Park might increase Longleat's attendance figures. He and Jimmy Chipperfield decided to go ahead with the idea, Henry paying for the roads and fences and Jimmy Chipperfield for the purchase of fifty lions and their upkeep until the park was ready to open. Early in 1965 a cautious letter was sent to the local authority requesting permission to erect a fence to 'restrict the movement of certain animals.' Permission was given, but when the identity of the 'certain animals' was revealed there was an immediate public outcry. *The Times* attacked the entire project, declaring in a leader that 'cattle, sheep and deer ought to be good enough for a Wiltshireman.'⁶ Henry has since explained the reasons for the hostility. 'Nobody realized that Jimmy Chipperfield, an expert on wildlife, was going to run it and be solely responsible for it. They all thought the 'mad Marquess' was going to have lions rampaging about the countryside. There was very nearly a public enquiry.'⁷

Whilst Henry placated local opposition and supervised the completion of the reserve, Jimmy Chipperfield purchased the lions. Ten of the animals used in the filming of *Born Free* were bought for £10 each, but the others, which came from a variety of unlikely places, amongst them Jerusalem Biblical Zoo, Spain and Denmark, were more expensive. The reserve opened in April 1966. It was the first Safari Park of its kind in Europe and, although tickets were £1 per car, all the initial expenses were recovered by the end of the year.⁸ Since then other animals, including cheetahs, elephants, giraffes and rhinoceros, have joined the lions and the Safari Park has established itself as a familiar attraction, both at Longleat and at an increasing number of other country houses. Over the past ten years a Pets' Corner, restaurant, and collection of Dolls' Houses have all been opened. Monkeys now occupy an island on Half-Mile Pond and sea-lions swim in its waters. Recently the Victorian Kitchens have been restored and a Kitchen Shop opened. Although some of these secondary attractions detract from Longleat's beauty they have widened its appeal and provided a firmer financial base from which to face a still uncertain future.

Longleat's survival is due almost entirely to Henry Bath's flair for showmanship and his willingness to take risks. Born at a time when Longleat's future seemed assured, he has adjusted to its changing needs with remarkable equanimity. Quiet and shy by nature, and happiest when dealing with the forestry problems on the 4500 acres of the estate now devoted to trees, he has forced himself to seek publicity in order to preserve his family home. His portrait, painted in 1971 by Graham Sutherland against a background of parkland and oak trees, captures his individuality. He is now over seventy years old but is still actively involved in running Longleat. He employs an administrator but admits that he is 'like a man who buys a dog but does all the barking himself – it's rather one of my faults. I like to know everything that's going on and when I don't I get rather cross.'⁹ His liking for a pinch of snuff, his occasional outspokenness, his affection for red-and-white spotted ties and above all his good-humour and frankness, disguise his regret at having had to open Longleat to the public. But necessity demanded it and, by encouraging the maximum number of visitors, he has become one of England's best-known peers. He has turned Longleat into a household word.

Longleat's future will be determined by Henry Bath's eldest son, Alexander, Viscount Weymouth. Painter, musician, writer, politician, by his own definition a 'failed preacher',¹⁰ Alexander's way of life has been consistently individualistic and often eccentric. He was educated at Eton and served two years' National Service in the Lifeguards, but from an early age was determined to become a painter. His best-known work remains the redecoration of Longleat's west wing – where he now lives – with a series of giant murals. He began the work in 1964 at the age of thirty-two, using household paints and sawdust. From the start his family were bitterly opposed to his plans and only finally gave way when they realized the ease with which his 'dilettante dabblings' could be removed. To Alexander the bare walls of the west wing seemed the best place on which to express the philosophy he had developed at art school in Paris, at Oxford University, and during the eight years he had lived in seclusion at Longleat. The work offered a creative challenge. 'Here was I, a young man who had been trained to emerge as a painter; and here were these walls, demanding to be painted.'¹¹

Alexander began the murals by painting ten panels depicting the Ages of Man for his drawing-room. He painted alone and the work took two years. Each panel is twelve foot high and four foot wide and the Age of Adolescence, with its snails and puppies and its teenagers trying to catch the moon with butterfly nets, is typical of their content. The decoration of the west wing continued throughout the 1960s and a group of young assistants were employed to help with some of the intermediary stages. By 1969 the Paranoia Murals, the Ages of History panels, the Picture Murals, which incorporate most of his earlier canvases, and a series of abstract paintings had all been completed.

Alexander's most notorious contribution to Longleat's redecoration was the Kama Sutra bedroom. The room contains a four-poster bed reputedly slept in by George III when he visited the house, and the walls feature, in the words of their creator, 'thirty-three aphrodisiac apples, containing a variety of sexual performances from a multiracial cast . . . suspended from huge phallic trees.'[12] Henry Bath remains unconvinced both by the style and content of his son's work. 'I wouldn't like to live with them. I'm an old square. Not that pornography worries me, I just don't like modern art.'

Alexander regards himself as a 'polyp working on his own little section of the coral reef' and the personal quality of his work is in marked contrast with the formality of the State Rooms in the east wing. The extent of the murals is formidable. All the walls and corridors on the ground floor of the west wing have now been decorated and Alexander has already turned his attention to the floor above. Whatever their merit the murals are a unique achievement and Alexander hopes that he has contributed something original and valid to Longleat without infringing its unity.

Alexander's appearance and disregard for convention have always attracted curiosity and opinion. Although he went through a form of self-styled anti-marriage in 1966 his wish to father large numbers of children has yet to come true. In 1969 he married Anna Gael Gyarmathy, a Hungarian actress then living in Paris. They have two children, a daughter and son, who live at Longleat and are looked after by a nanny. Anna still lives in Paris and she and Alexander only spend three months of the year together. Such an arrangement may be unorthodox but their marriage has survived and Henry Bath has called Anna 'the only woman who could accommodate' his son's eccentricity.

Since his marriage and the completion of the first stage of the murals Alexander has devoted part of his time to writing. In 1972 his first novel, *The Carry-Cot*, was published. Autobiographical, nightmarish and at times violent, it nevertheless sums up its author's attitudes to the aristocracy, the family and marriage. Alexander has recently published a second novel, a science fiction story called *The King is Dead*.

All Alexander's activities are inextricably bound up with one another and he has always refused to accept any distinction between his creative work and his role as Lord Weymouth, heir to Longleat. In 1974 he stood for parliament as a Wessex Regionalist. His involvement with regional politics still continues and the flag of Wessex now flies over Longleat. Although Alexander is as unpredictable as ever, he is now in his mid-forties and has been forced to consider Longleat's future. The attitudes of father and son could not be more different. Whereas Henry is devoted to keeping Longleat in the possession of the Thynnes, Alexander would welcome state ownership. To prevent the dispersal of the contents and the break-up of the estate, he believes that houses like Longleat should be bought by the state and then administered by a group of regional public ownership corporations. The resident family would be given security of tenure and all decisions made jointly. The estate is now his responsibility and he has already begun thinking of ways to add to Longleat's attractions. A maze has been planted to the north of the house and he would like to link Shearwater, the Safari Park and house by cable-car. Like the State of Wessex, the cable-cars may never become a reality, but both are typical examples of Alexander's belief that a radical and imaginative approach to long-term problems is needed if Longleat is to survive.

Despite his son's optimism Henry remains pessimistic about Longleat's future. Increasing maintenance costs and the possibility of additional taxation being introduced threaten his ambition to keep Longleat in the ownership of the Thynnes. Longleat's popularity will surely allow it to survive as a private enterprise for longer than most country houses, but if the number of visitors declines it will become impossible to maintain the house in its present condition. The alternatives are few. The house could be temporarily closed down, handed over to the National Trust, or sold. To the 6th Marquess of Bath, the twelfth Thynne to own Longleat, any one of them would be a tragedy. The house has belonged to the Thynnes for more than 400 years. A Thynne still lives in it today, and that continuity is essential if Longleat is not to become a museum – a relic of the vanished way of life it so superbly evokes. In *Facts and Legends*, a small book of notes compiled by Henry Bath when Longleat first opened to the public, he wrote 'To Longleat, therefore I dedicate these notes until such time as the ownership passes away from the family of Thynne. After that – what the heck!'

ABBREVIATIONS

L.P.   The Correspondence, Papers, Court Papers, etc, of the Thynne Family.

R.O.B.   The Records of the Building of Longleat.

W.C.R.O.   Wiltshire County Records Office, Longleat Estate Papers. (These papers are in the process of being returned to Longleat for storage in the new Muniment Room, but, as yet, have not been recatalogued.).

D.N.B.   The Dictionary of National Biography.

Girouard   Mark Girouard, The Development of Longleat House between 1546 and 1572. The Archaeological Journal Vol. CXVI (1959).

Jackson   Canon J. E. Jackson The History of Longleat (Devizes 1868).

S.B.   Beriah Botfield, Stemmata Botevilliana, Memorials of the Families of De Boteville, Thynne and Botfield (1858).

S.T.   Cobbett's Complete Collection of State Trials Vol. IX, pp. 1–126, ed. Howell (1811).

Vizetelly   Henry Vizetelly, Count Konigsmark and Tom of Ten Thousand (1881).

REFERENCES

Chapter 1

1 R.O.B. Vol. I, f440.
2 L.P. Correspondence of John Thynne, Letters to John Thynne junior, Vol. I, 1578.
3 R.O.B. Vol. I, f3, 7. Jackson, 5.
4 L.P. Book 64.
5 Will Darell's Knavery. R.O.B. Vol. III, f208.
6 For the Thynne/Dodd Correspondence see R.O.B. Vol. I, ff195–341.
7 R.O.B. Vol. I, f208.
8 R.O.B. Vol. I, f135. 21.6.1547.
9 R.O.B. Vol. I, ff165–166.
10 R.O.B. Vol. I, f24.
11 For Thynne's attention to detail and appetite for writing letters see R.O.B. Vol. I, ff25–35.
12 R.O.B. Vol. I, f59.
13 R.O.B. Vol. I, f371.
14 Sir Richard Colt Hoare, History of Modern Wiltshire (1824), Heytesbury Hundred, 63.
15 R.O.B. Vol. III, f207.
16 R.O.B. Vol. I, f66.
17 R.O.B. Vol. I, f72.
18 Will Darell's Knavery. R.O.B. Vol. III, f207.
19 Calendar of State Papers, Foreign. i, 45.
20 For Thynne's evasion of questions by the Council see Manu-

scripts of the Marquess of Bath, Vol. IV, The Seymour Papers (1968), 25.11.1549.
21 R.O.B. Vol. I, f377.
22 R.O.B. Vol. I, f383.
23 R.O.B. Vol. I, f440.
24 R.O.B. Vol. I, f387.
25 R.O.B. Vol. I.
26 L.P. Correspondence of Sir John Thynne, Vol. I, f2.
27 ibid., f9.
28 This letter comes from a separate collection of Seymour Papers at Longleat and was printed by Canon J. E. Jackson in an Appendix to Wulfhall and the Seymours (Devizes 1875), p. 45.
29 R.O.B. Vol. II, f117.
30 For Spicer's work at Longleat see Girouard, pp. 207–216.
31 R.O.B. Vol. I, f29.
32 R.O.B. Vol. I, f21.
33 R.O.B. Vol. II, September 1555.
34 L.P. Vol. VII, f116 & 121.
35 L.P. Book 107.
36 L.P. Book 63.
37 R.O.B. Vol. II, f159.
38 ibid., f195.
39 Thomas Fuller, A History of the Worthies of England, ed. Nichols (1811) Vol. 2, 462.
40 R.O.B. Vol. III, f67.

41 R.O.B. Vol. II, f221.

42 L.P. Book 146, f69.

43 For a draft of the letter see R.O.B. Vol. III, f80; for the letter itself *The Seymour Papers*, Vol. IV, 31 October 1579.

44 Pynson's *Book of Cookery* (1500).

45 For Lovell's letter of introduction see L.P. Vol. III, f61.

46 Albert E. Baynton, *Horningsham Chapel* (1952).

46bR.O.B. Vol. III, f195.

47 ibid., f198.

48 Letters of Francis Thynne, L.P. Vol. XL, f83.

49 L.P. Vol. IV, f35.

50 ibid., f50.

51 L.P. Book 155, f155.

52 L.P. Book 154, 2.9.1574.

53 Jackson, 17.

54 Will Darell's Knavery. R.O.B. Vol. III, f203.

55 L.P. Vol. II, f219.

56 ibid., f207.

57 L.P. Book 161, f13.

58 For events at Longleat after Thynne's death see L.P. Vol. LII, f98.

Chapter 2

1 L.P. Vol. VIII, f2.

2 L.P. Vol. V, f173.

3 L.P. Vol. VI, f227.

4 For Joan's letters to her husband see L.P. Vol. V, ff1–14.

5 For all this see L.P. Household Accounts, Books 162–172, L.P. Vol. LVII, Kitchen Accounts 1581–1603

6 L.P. Vol. VII, f39.

7 L.P. Vol. VI, f48.

8 ibid., f80.

9 ibid., f302.

10 L.P. Vol. LIV, f15.

11 For all this see L.P. Vol. VIII, f59, 60–63.

12 ibid., opp f7.

13 ibid., f2.

14 ibid., f1.

15 ibid., f9.

16 ibid., f2.

17 ibid., f6.

18 ibid., 4.8.1612.

19 L.P. Vol. VII, f90.

20 L.P. Vol. VIII, f43.

21 For events at Longleat after Sir Thomas Thynne's death and the Long Suit that followed see L.P. Vol. LIX, f2, 4, 12, Vol. LXII, f1, Box XXXVIII–XLIV.

22 For life at Longleat prior to the Civil War see L.P. Vol. IX, Vol. LXVI Household and Stock Accounts, Books 35–52, Books 125, 131, 173.

23 L.P. Box XV, f240, 241, Box XVI, f201.

24 L.P. Vol. LXXXVII, ff58–60.

25 L.P. Vol. LXII.

26 For all this see Mary Boyle, *Biographical Catalogue of the Portraits at Longleat* (1881), 89–90.

27 John Aubrey, *Brief Lives* (1976), 347.

28 Mary Boyle, *Catalogue of Portraits at Longleat*, 91.

29 John Aubrey, *Miscellanies* (1696), quoted in *S.B.* No. 113, cccli.

30 L.P. Box XVI.

31 ibid., ff30–31.

32 L.P. Book 174, f55.

33 ibid., f61b, Vol. X, f47, 232, 234. (Aubrey records that Glanville was a well-known Wiltshire eccentric. Later in his career he was to write a book on

witches and witchcraft.)

34 Arthur Bryant, *King Charles II* (1933), 166.

35 Bishop Seth Ward. L.P. Vol. X, f178.

36 For Wren's work at Longleat see L.P. Vol. X, f213, Vol. XX, f28, Vol. XXX, f103.

37 L.P. Vol. X, f206.

Chapter 3

1 D.N.B. Thomas Thynne (1648–1682).

2 L.P. Vol. XI, f121–130.

3 L.P. Vol. X, 15 July 1669.

4 For events at the wedding see L.P. Vol. XI, ff108–119; Vizetelly, 52–55, 123.

5 S.B. No. 116, ccclxxxiv. *The Romance of the Peerage.*

6 Vizetelly, 27–30.

7 S.B. No. 116, ccclxxxiv. Quoted from Countess d'Aulnoi, *Travels*, 74.

8 Vizetelly, 31–32.

9 For all this see Vizetelly, 80–87.

10 S.B. cccxxiv. *The Confession of George Boroski, the Polonian* (1682).

11 ibid., cccxxv.

12 S.B. cccxx. *The Last Confession, Prayers and Meditations of Lieutenant John Stern* (1682).

13 For Reresby's account of events after the murder see *The Memoirs of Sir John Reresby* (1735) pp. 135–144. For the murder see Narcissus Luttrell, *A Brief Historic Relation of State Affairs* (1857) Vol. I, 164.

14 'A hew and cry after Blood', Vizetelly, 71.

15 Vizetelly, 49.

16 S.B. No. 106, cccxiv. Broadsides Amongst Miscellaneous Sheets 1651–1716 in British Museum.

17 S.T., 59.

18 For all this see Luttrell Vol. I, 166–167.

19 S.B. cccxix.

20 S.B. cccxxx. Gilbert Burnet and Anthony Horneck, *An Account of the Deportment of Captain Vratz, Lieutenant Stern and George Borosky, the Murderers of Thomas Thynne Esq.; both in the prison and at their execution* (1682).

21 *The Diary of John Evelyn*, ed. Bray (1862), Vol. II, 174.

22 For an additional account of the trial see Luttrell, Vol. I, 167–168.

23 S.T., 61.

24 ibid., 73.

25 S.B., cccxxxi.

26 S.B., cccxli.

27 S.B., cccxxiii.

28 S.B., clxxv. Quoted from Reresby's *Memoirs.*

29 Evelyn's *Diary*, ed. Bray, Vol. II, 174.

30 Vizetelly, 119.

31 Evelyn's *Diary*, ed. Bray, Vol. II, 174.

32 Vizetelly, 126.

Chapter 4

1 L.P. Vol. XVI.

2 ibid.

3 D.N.B.

4 Pepys met Thomas before he sailed and found him a 'pretty gentleman'. See *Pepys Diary*, ed. Latham and Mathews (1972), Vol. VII, 27 September 1666.

5 L.P. Vol. XIII, f214.

6 Letters of John Fell, Bishop of Oxford, to 1st Viscount Weymouth. L.P. Vol. XII.

7 L.P. Vol. XXXIII, 1 November 1673.

8 ibid., 9 February 1675.

9 L.P. Vol. XI, f101.

10 L.P. Vol. XIII, f279.

11 ibid., f275.

12 ibid., f82.

13 Lady Mary Thynne's letters to her son. L.P. Vol. XXXI.

14 The Correspondence of Thomas Allen. L.P. Vol. XXII.

15 L.P. Book 85.

16 L.P. Vol. XXXIV, f99.

17 L.P. Vol. XII, f39.

18 L.P. Vol. XVIII.

19 L.P. Vol. XXXIII. 27 January 1682.

20 L.P. Vol. XI, f90.

21 L.P. Vol. XIII, f42, 45. See also f58 for Thomas's suspicion that his wife encouraged the gardener's attentions.

22 L.P. Vol. XII, 19 April 1684.

23 L.P. Book 85.

24 L.P. Vol. XIII, f101.

25 ibid., f103.

26 L.P. Vol. XII, f168.

27 L.P. Vol. XIII, f105.

28 L.P. Vol. XII, f185.

29 ibid., f168.

30 ibid., f187.

31 ibid., f188.

32 ibid., f189.

33 ibid., f192.

34 L.P. Vol. XXIX, f8.

35 L.P. Vol. XII, f59.

36 For all this see Charles Chevenix Trench, *The Western Rising* (1969).

37 For all this see Lady Mary Thynne's letters to her son, L.P. Vol. XXXI.

38 L.P. Vol. XIII, f106.

39 ibid., f110.

40 ibid., f118.

41 ibid., f54.

42 For all this see Christina Hoyle, *English Home-Life* 1500–1800 (1947), 143, 144.

43 L.P. Vol. XIII, f66.

44 L.P. Vol. XII.

45 For all this see L.P. Book 85, Vol. LXVIII, f92.

46 L.P. Vol. XXIX.

47 L.P. Vol. XII, 27 November 1687.

48 L.P. Vol. XXIX.

49 L.P. Vol. XIV, 18 January 1686.

50 L.P. Vol. XX, f295.

51 L.P. Vol. XIV, 2 January 1687.

52 ibid., 7 January 1687.

53 L.P. Vol. XIV.

54 L.P. Vol. XII.

55 For all this see L.P. Vol. XIV, f325.

56 Lady Mary Thynne's letters to her son. L.P. Vol. XXXI.

57 L.P. Book 189.

58 L.P. Vol. XIV.

59 For all this see L.P. Vol. XI, ff99–111.

60 L.P. Vol. XIII, f158.

61 L.P. Vol. XIV.

62 L.P. Rack E. Cage 6, Parcel 5.

63 L.P. Vol. XXXV.

64 L.P. Vol. XIII, f205.

65 Jackson, 30.

66 *D.N.B.*

67 ibid.

68 L.P. Vol. XIX, f18.

69 L.P. Vol. XXVII, f52.

70 L.P. Vol. XIV, f283.

71 L.P. Vol. XXII, f245.

72 Longleat Papers, The Viscount Weymouth Grammar School,

Carrickmacross, 1711–1956.

73 ibid.

74 L.P. Vol. XXXIII, 22 January 1673.

75 L.P. Vol. XXII, f162.

76 Narcissus Luttrell, *A Brief Historic Relation of State Affairs* (1857) Vol. V, 491.

77 The Longleat Papers of George Harbin, Vol. LXXVII, f129.

78 L.P. Vol. XIV, f299.

79 L.P. Vol. XXIV, 26 April 1710.

Chapter 5

1 L.P. Rack E, Cage 11, Parcel 11, Miscellaneous Papers of Thomas, 2nd Viscount Weymouth.

2 For Lady Mary's character see Mrs Delany, *A Memoir*, ed. Paston (1900), 26.

3 L.P. Rack E, Cage 11, Parcel 2.

4 L.P. Vol. LXXIX, ff140–154.

5 *D.N.B.*

6 L.P. Rack E, Cage 11, Parcel 2.

7 ibid.

8 ibid.

9 Mrs Delany, *A Memoir*, 75.

10 L.P. Rack E, Cage 11, Parcel 11.

11 L.P. Box 84.

12 L.P. Rack E, Cage 11, Parcel 11.

13 ibid.

14 L.P. Rack E, Cage 11, Parcel 4, Petitions.

15 Mary Delany, *Autobiography and Correspondence*, ed. Llanover (1861), Vol. I, 411. For her attempts to arrange Thomas's marriage see pp. 297–299.

16 Mrs Delany, *A Memoir*, 75–76.

17 ibid., 80.

18 Sarah Churchill, Duchess of Marlborough, *Letters of a Grandmother* 1732–1735, ed. Scott Thomson (1943), 29 June 1733.

19 Mrs Delany, *A Memoir*, 80.

20 L.P. Vol. LVXXVII.

21 Mary Delany, *Autobiography and Correspondence*, Vol. I, 424.

22 ibid., 425.

23 L.P. Rack E, Cage 11, Parcels 3 & 4.

24 Mary Delany, *Autobiography and Correspondence*, Vol. I, 453.

25 ibid., 454.

26 For a full account of Louisa's final illness see Mary Delany, *Autobiography and Correspondence* Vol. I, letters to Mrs Ann Granville between 24 December 1736 and 4 January 1737.

27 ibid., 584.

28 ibid., Vol. II, 361.

29 L.P. Rack E, Cage 11, Parcel 9.

30 ibid., Parcel 7.

31 ibid., Parcel 9.

Chapter 6

1 L.P. Rack E, Cage 7, Parcel 7.

2 Mary Delany, *Autobiography and Correspondence*, ed. Llanover (1861), Vol. 11, 361.

3 *D.N.B.*

4 Richard Addison, *The Spectator*, No. 414, 25 June 1712.

5 L.P. Box XXX, f289, 290.

6 Ralph Dutton, *The English Garden* (1937), 89.

7 Horace Walpole. Quoted in Russell Page, *The Education of a Gardener* (1962).

8 Mary Delany, *Autobiography and Correspondence*, Vol. II, 611.

9 Quoted in Edward Hyams, *Capability Brown and Humphrey*

Repton (1971).

10 Mary Delany, *Autobiography and Correspondence*, Vol. II, 547.

11 *The Correspondence of Emily, Duchess of Leinster and Lady Caroline Fox, Lady Holland 1731–1814* (1949).

12 Mary Delany, *Autobiography and Correspondence*, Vol. II, 547.

13 For all this see L.P. Rack E, Cage 7, Parcel 7.

14 Horace Walpole, *Memoirs of the Reign of George III*, ed. Le Marchant, Vol. IV, 241.

15 *The Diary of Mrs Lybbe Powys*, ed. Climenson (1899). Quoted in *The English Garden*, 92.

16 Edith Sitwell, *English Eccentrics* (1971), 41–42.

17 Walpole, *Memoirs of George III*, Vol. II, 176.

18 ibid., Vol. IV, 241.

19 See *The Letters of Horace Walpole*, ed. Toynbee (1904) Vol. VI, 246.

20 Walpole, *Memoirs of George III*, Vol. II, 177.

21 ibid., Vol. IV, 237.

22 *Town and Country Magazine* 1771, Vol. III, Issue 28, 65. See also *Notes & Queries* (1905) Vol. IV, 242.

23 Herbert Croft, *The Abbey of Kilkhampton* (1780), 11.

24 For details of the ownership of the estate see Mary Delany, *Autobiography and Correspondence*, Vol. I, 359–360.

25 L.P. Rack E, Cage 7, Parcel K, f3.

26 ibid.

27 ibid., f13.

28 ibid.

29 ibid.

30 *Letters of George III*, ed. Dobree, 133.

31 *D.N.B.*

32 *The Morning Herald*, 6 August 1782.

33 L.P. Rack E, Cage 7, Parcel 5.

34 For details of the forestry at Longleat see L.P. Vol. LXXVII.

35 L.P. Rack E, Cage 7, Parcel 5.

36 ibid.

37 ibid., Parcel 8.

38 *The Diary of Fanny Burney*, ed. Gibb (1940), 260–261.

39 *D.N.B.*

40 For details of the visit of George III to Longleat see *S.B.* No. 118, cccxcix–cccciii.

41 *The Diary of Fanny Burney*, 261.

Chapter 7

1 L.P. Rack E, Cage 8, Parcel 15. Written 28.1.1828.

2 L.P. Accounts 1796.

3 L.P. Rack E, Cage 7, Parcel 5. Correspondence of Thomas Davis.

4 For details of Wyatville's work at Longleat see L.P. Rack E, Cage 8, Parcel 7.

5 Humphrey Repton, *Designs for Longleat* (1804).

6 ibid.

7 ibid.

8 ibid.

9 L.P. Box 32.

10 Humphrey Repton, *Fragments on the Theory and Practise of Landscape Gardening* (1816).

11 For all matters connected to Webb's murder see W.C.R.O., Longleat Estate Papers, Box 2.

12 L.P. Rack E, Cage 8, Parcel 5 and Papers of 2nd Marquess of

Bath, Selected Accounts.

13 William Cobbett, *Rural Rides*. Quoted in H. J. Massingham, *Wisdom of the Fields* (1945).

14 Isabella, 3rd Marchioness of Bath, *Domestic Economy* (1829), quoted from Cobbett's *Cottage Economy* (1821).

15 L.P. Large parcel at back of Rack E, Cage 13. Letter dated 30.7.1820.

16 L.P. Rack E, Cage 13, Court Case Papers, Bath v Weymouth 1827.

17 ibid., Letter to Lord Grenville 13.5.1820.

18 ibid., Correspondence between 2nd Marquess of Bath and Lord Weymouth, 1820–1832.

19 ibid., Court Case Papers, 1820–1832.

20 L.P. Rack E, Cage 8, Parcel 15.

21 ibid.,

22 L.P. Rack E, Cage 13, Large Parcel, The Affairs of Ld. Edward Thynne.

23 ibid., Parcel 14.

24 ibid., Parcel 5.

25 ibid., letter dated 2.14.1837.

26 ibid., Parcel 1, Naval Appointments and Good Conduct Certificates of the 3rd Marquess of Bath.

27 L.P. Rack E, Cage 13, Parcel 15.

28 ibid.

Chapter 8

1 *The Letters and Private Papers of W. M. Thackeray*, ed. Ray (1946), Vol. III, 102.

2 *Society in London* (1885), 85.

3 *The Times*, 21.4.1896.

4 L.P. The Minority Papers 1837–
1851, Rack E, Cage 14, Parcel 1.

5 L.P. Correspondence between 4th Marquess of Bath and Whitwell Evans, Government Box, No. 13.

6 L.P. Rack E, Cage 9, Parcel 1.

7 ibid.

8 L.P. Correspondence between 4th Marquess of Bath and Whitwell Evans, Government Box, No. 13.

9 L.P. Rack E, Cage 9, Parcel 1. 16.9.1861.

10 *The Letters of Disraeli to Lady Bradford and Lady Chesterfield*, ed. Zetland (1929), Vol. I, 133.

11 W.C.R.O. Longleat Estate Papers, Box 35.

12 For all the details, letters and newspaper reports mentioned here see the 4th Marquess's Government Box, No. 38.

13 L.P. Rack E, Cage 9, Parcel 1.

14 L.P. Dispensary Books, 1883–1886.

15 For a full account of the work of the servants at Longleat in the late nineteenth century see The Marchioness of Bath, *Before the Sunset Fades* (1957).

16 ibid., 10.

17 A. Farquharson, *The Parks and Gardens at Longleat* (1882).

18 For the work of the gardeners see W.C.R.O. Longleat Estate Papers, Box 2.

19 L.P. Correspondence between 4th Marquess of Bath and Whitwell Evans, Government Box, No. 13.

20 For details of Crace's work at Longleat see L.P. Rack E, Cage 9, Parcel 6.

21 *The Letters of Disraeli to Lady*

Bradford and Lady Chesterfield, ed. Zetland (1929), Vol. I, 130.
22 ibid., 133.
23 ibid.
24 ibid.
25 ibid., 131.
26 ibid., 134.
27 ibid., 308. L.P. Letters from the Royal Family and others, 1875.
28 L.P. Letters from Royal Family and others, 1875.
29 For all this see W.C.R.O. Longleat Estate Papers, Box 1.
30 For all this see ibid., Box 33.
31 For a detailed examination of the effects of the agricultural depression on Longleat see F. M. L. Thompson, *English Landed Society in the Nineteenth Century* (1963).
32 Quoted in L.P. Letters of 4th Marquess of Bath to J. Trevor White 1886–1888.
33 L.P. *The Diary of John Thynne,* at back of Cage 9, 15 April 1885.
34 ibid., 12 August 1885.
35 ibid., 2 August 1885.
36 ibid. 17 April 1885.
37 ibid., 2 February 1886.
38 ibid., 8 July 1886.
39 ibid., 23 January 1887.
40 ibid., April 1887.
41 W.C.R.O. Longleat Estate Papers, Box 117.
42 For details of the 4th Marquess's final illness see ibid.

Chapter 9

1 L.P. Letters of 4th Marquess of Bath to J. Trevor White 1886–1888.
2 *The Times,* 19 February 1870.
3 For the fullest account of the Mordaunt divorce see Virginia Cowles, *Edward VII and his Circle* (1956).
4 L.P. Letters from Hugh Shaw-Steward to Lord Alexander Thynne, 1902–1904.
5 Quentin Bell, *Virginia Woolf* (1972), Vol. II, 81.
6 For all this see L.P. Lady Beatrice Thynne's Visit to Russia, 1912.
7 L.P. The Correspondence of Lady Bath.
8 L.P. The Correspondence of the 5th Marquess of Bath, 1887–1919. For Lord Weymouth's correspondence between 1914 and 1916 see the Correspondence of the 5th Marquess (Rack E, Cage 10) and the Correspondence of Lady Bath.
9 L.P. The Correspondence of Lady Bath, 1 June 1915.
10 ibid., 4 October 1915.
11 ibid., 3 December 1915.
12 ibid., 27 December 1915.
13 ibid., 29 January 1916.
14 L.P. Letters from the Royal Family and others.
15 L.P. The Correspondence of Lady Bath, J. M. Moncreiffe's letter, February 1916.
16 ibid., 29 November 1916.
17 L.P. Letters from the Royal Family and others, 21 July 1923.
18 Daphne Fielding, *Mercury Presides* (1954), 125.
19 For all this see *Mercury Presides,* 107–109.
20 ibid., 115–116.
21 Russell Page, *The Education of a Gardener* (1962), 26.
22 *The Wessex Magazine,* 1974,

No. 5, 11.

23 *Mercury Presides*, 152–153.

24 Honor Osborne & Peggy Manisty, *The Royal School for Officers
of the Army* 1966, 146.

25 ibid., 147–148.

26 L.P. Letters from the Royal
Family and others, 5 July 1940.

Chapter 10

1 Mary Chipperfield, *Lions on the
Lawn* (1971), 69.

2 Daphne Fielding, *Mercury Presides* (1954), 214.

3 Quot. Harry Hopkins, *The*

New Look (1963), 182.

4 ibid.

5 *The Wessex Magazine* (1974)
No. 5, 13.

6 *The Times*, 2.9.1965.

7 *The Wessex Magazine* (1974)
No. 5, 13.

8 For the full story of the lion
reserve see Mary Chipperfield,
Lions on the Lawn (1971).

9 *The Wessex Magazine* (1974)
No. 5, 14.

10 Alexander Thynne, *Lord Weymouth's Murals*.

11 ibid.

12 ibid.

BIBLIOGRAPHY

Airs, Malcolm *The Making of the English Country House, 1500–1640* (1975).

Ashley, Maurice *England in the Seventeenth Century* (1952).

Aubrey, John *'Brief Lives', Chiefly of Contemporaries, set down by John Aubrey, between the years 1669 & 1696.*

Bath, Daphne (6th Marchioness) *Longleat* (1949).

Before the Sunset Fades (1957).

Manuscripts of the Marquess of Bath *The Seymour Papers* (1968).

Bath, Isabella (3rd Marchioness) *Domestic Economy* (1829).

Benton, Albert E. *Horningsham Chapel* (1952).

Bindoff, S. T. *Tudor England* (1950).

Botfield, Beriah *Stemmata Botevilliana, Memorials of the Families of De Boteville, Thynne and Botfield* (1858).

Boyle, Mary *A Biographical Catalogue of the Portraits at Longleat* (1881).

Bryant, Arthur *English Saga* (1940).

Protestant Island (1966).

Burgon, J. W. *The Life and Times of Sir Thomas Gresham* (1831).

Burney, Fanny *The Diary of Fanny Burney* ed. Gibb (1940).

Chevenix Trench, Charles *The Western Rising* (1969).

Chipperfield, Mary *Lions on the Lawn* (1971).

Cobbett's Complete Collection of State Trials, Vol. IX, ed. Howell (1811)

Cook, Olive *The English Country House* (1974).

Cornforth, John *Country Houses in Britain – can they survive?* (1974).

Cowles, Virginia *Edward VII and His Circle* (1956).

Delany, Mary *The Autobiography & Correspondence of Mrs Granville, Mary Delany* ed. Llanover (1861).

The Dictionary of National Biography.

Disraeli, Benjamin *The Letters of Disraeli to Lady Bradford and Lady Chesterfield* ed. Zetland (1929).

Dutton, Ralph *The English Country House* (1935).

The English Garden (1937).

Evelyn, John *The Diary of John Evelyn* ed. Bray (1862).

Farquharson, A. *The Parks and Gardens at Longleat* (1882).

Feeney, Patrick J. *Longleat* (A guide for visitors to the house).

Bibliography

Fielding, Daphne (see also under Daphne Bath, 6th Marchioness) *Mercury Presides* (1954).

Girouard, Mark The Development of Longleat House between 1546 and 1572, *The Archaeological Journal* Vol. CXVI (1959).
Robert Smythson and the Architecture of the Elizabethan Era (1966).

Hoare, Sir Richard Colt *The History of Modern Wiltshire* (Heytesbury Hundred), (1824).

Hoyle, Christina *English Home Life, 1500–1800* (1947).

Hyams, Edward *The English Garden* (1964).
Capability Brown and Humphrey Repton (1971).

Jackson, Canon J. E. *The History of Longleat* (1868).

Luttrell, Narcissus *A Brief Historic Relation of State Affairs* (1857).

Marwick, Arthur *The Deluge, British Society and the First World War* (1965).

Norman, Diana *Stately Ghosts of England* (1963).

Osborne, Honor & Manisty, Peggy *The Royal School for Officers of the Army* (1966).

Page, Russell *The Education of a Gardener* (1962).

Palmer, A. *Movable Feasts* (1952).

Plumb, J. H. *England in the Eighteenth Century* (1950).

Plumptre, Dean *The Life of Ken* (1888).

Pollard, A. F. *England under the Protector Somerset* (1900).

Reresby, Sir John *The Memoirs of Sir John Reresby* (1735).

Repton, Humphrey *Designs for Longleat* (1804).

Roberts, Harry *English Gardens* (1946).

Sackville-West, Vita *English Country Houses* (1946).

Stroud, Dorothy *Capability Brown* (1950).
Repton (1962).

Summerson, John *Architecture in Britain, 1530–1830* (4th edition 1963).

Taylor, A. J. P. *The First World War* (1963).

Thompson, F. M. L. *English Landed Society in the Nineteenth Century* (1963).

Thomson, David *England in the Nineteenth Century* (1950).

Thynne, Alexander *Lord Weymouth's Murals* (A guide for visitors).
The Carry-Cot (1972).
A Regionalist Manifesto (1975).

Trevelyan, G. M. *English Social History* (1944).

Vizetelly, Henry *Count Konigsmark and Tom of Ten Thousand* (1881).

Walpole, Horace *Memoirs of the Reign of George III* ed. Marchant (1845).

INDEX

Compiled by Lornie Leete-Hodge